State Building in Boom Times

State Building in Boom Times

Commodities and Coalitions in Latin America and Africa

RYAN SAYLOR

OXFORD
UNIVERSITY PRESS

OXFORD
UNIVERSITY PRESS

Oxford University Press is a department of the University of Oxford.
It furthers the University's objective of excellence in research, scholarship, and education by publishing worldwide.

Oxford New York
Auckland Cape Town Dar es Salaam Hong Kong Karachi
Kuala Lumpur Madrid Melbourne Mexico City Nairobi
New Delhi Shanghai Taipei Toronto

With offices in
Argentina Austria Brazil Chile Czech Republic France Greece
Guatemala Hungary Italy Japan Poland Portugal Singapore
South Korea Switzerland Thailand Turkey Ukraine Vietnam

Published in the United States of America by
Oxford University Press
198 Madison Avenue, New York, NY 10016

Cataloging-in-Publication data is on file with the Library of Congress

9780199364954

9 8 7 6 5 4 3 2 1

Printed in the United States of America on acid-free paper

CONTENTS

ACKNOWLEDGMENTS

The publication of this book is the culmination of a long and rewarding process, during which I have accrued numerous debts to people who have helped shape and improve the manuscript. I owe thanks to Dave McBride at Oxford University Press for his interest in this project from when I first sent him a prospectus and his help guiding it and me to this delightful end. I am especially grateful for his efforts to seek out constructive reviewers. I thank Oxford's anonymous reviewers for their time, insights, and suggestions. Their efforts made this book considerably better.

Elements of this book have appeared elsewhere, and I thank the publishers of the following journals for permission to reprint aspects of those works herein. I would also like to acknowledge my appreciation of these journals' editors and anonymous reviewers, who indirectly contributed to the improvement of the book manuscript. Portions of chapter 5 were published as "Probing the Historical Sources of the Mauritian Miracle: Sugar Exporters and State Building in Colonial Mauritius," *Review of African Political Economy* 39(133) (September 2012): 465–478, reprinted with the permission of its publisher, Taylor & Francis Ltd. My discussion of the politics of credit accessibility in Chile, Argentina, Colombia, and Nigeria is the subject of "Commodity Booms, Coalitional Politics, and Government Intervention in Credit Markets," *Review of International Political Economy* 21(3) (forthcoming, June 2014), also reprinted with permission from Taylor & Francis Ltd. My conceptualization and measurement of the concept of state capacity is informed by and draws upon "Concepts, Measures, and Measuring Well: An Alternative Outlook," *Sociological Methods & Research* 42(3) (August 2013): 354–391, published by Sage Publications. An early version of the book's theoretical argument and Chilean case study was the subject of "Sources of State Capacity in Latin America: Commodity Booms and State Building Motives in Chile," *Theory and Society* 41(3)

(May 2012): 301–324, reprinted with permission from Springer Science + Business Media.

This book germinated at the University of Virginia as a dissertation under the direction of David Waldner, Gerard Alexander, and Herman Schwartz. Each of them has provided me intellectual inspiration, probing yet constructive criticism, and valuable professional advice over the years.

Andrew Brooks kindly and enthusiastically volunteered as my research assistant during his undergraduate years at the University of Tulsa. I was also fortunate to receive unexpected assistance from Sandra Angulo and Constanza Medina at the Biblioteca Nacional de Colombia; they generously located some primary sources for me while I was writing chapter 6.

Many people were generous with their time and insight and assessed the manuscript at various points of development. I deeply appreciate the feedback I received from Richard Allen, Catherine Boone, Chris Darnton, Boniface Dulani, Yaprak Gürsoy, Jeremy Kuzmarov, Sean McEnroe, Joel Migdal, Bill Storey, Rachel Vanderhill, Hassan Wahab, and Hiroyuki Yamamoto. They helped make the book better than it otherwise would have been. My colleagues at the University of Tulsa were kind enough to review a draft of the manuscript; Jeff Hockett read the manuscript with an especially detailed editorial eye, for which I am grateful. Ariel Ahram, Hillel Soifer, and Nick Wheeler deserve special recognition. I turned to them repeatedly for their sage advice and am thankful for their assistance.

I would like to thank my family and friends for their support and encouragement: Mom, Dad, Brady, Yuka, Lincoln, Janet, Jeremy, Doug, John, Carol, Jenny, Kate, Scott, Grace, Alexis, Lyle, Dave, Mike, and Dan. But, by far, I owe my largest debt of gratitude to my wife, Tara. She tirelessly discussed ideas, read drafts of the book, and pressed me to clarify my meaning, even and especially when I thought it clear enough. Along the way, we shared the profound joy and amazement of raising our children, Evelyn and William. Evelyn tells me that she too is writing a book, though its subject is vague and always changing. (William presently thinks that books are things one tries to eat.) I hope that, if Evelyn does write one someday, she will be as fortunate as I have been to have such a superb partner and wonderful children. I dedicate this book to the three of them.

R.S.

CHAPTER 1

The Multiple Motives behind State Building in the Developing World

The Revenue Imperative and State Building in the Developing World

People live in astoundingly different conditions throughout the world. Citizens in the United States and Western Europe have come to expect that they will live in the context of unprecedented material wealth, abundant public goods, and accountable democratic governments. Billions of people around the world have no such expectations. Instead, their lives are carried out precariously, often in grinding poverty. Public goods are scarce, as many troubled communities must drink contaminated water, commute on broken infrastructure, and hunt for educational opportunities. Too often their governments are capricious and despotic. Understanding why some countries are rich and democratic, while others are poor and authoritarian, is among the most important topics pondered by academic researchers, policymakers, and concerned citizens alike.

The past generation of social scientists has resoundingly declared that state capacity figures centrally in elucidating these differences. Governments that preside over a capable state apparatus can ensure the rule of law, which is necessary for well-functioning democratic regimes. Without properly enforced legal protections, governments may simply encase the procedural trappings of democracy, rather than upholding substantive forms of accountability between rulers and citizens.[1] The existence of state capacity likewise facilitates the provision of public goods and thereby enhances public well-being.[2] And perhaps most important, substantial state capacity is now regarded as a prerequisite

[1] Bratton and Chang (2006).

[2] Ziblatt (2008).

for transformative economic development.[3] Without state capacity, governments cannot provide the dense web of regulation needed to create transparency, lower transaction costs, and establish conditions conducive to long-term investment.[4] This finding has profoundly influenced policymakers. The World Bank and International Monetary Fund, once champions of strict neoliberal conditionality and steadfast critics of government involvement in the economy, now underscore the role of "good governance" and well-functioning state institutions in economic development. This about-face fundamentally reverses their understanding of the state's role in the economy. State capacity is now widely accepted as a pivotal concept to understand the developmental differences observed throughout the world.

Yet, if the past generation of scholarship has pinpointed beneficial effects of state capacity, the origins of it are less well understood. State capacity refers to the ability of government officials "to actually penetrate civil society, and to implement logistically political decisions throughout the realm."[5] One finds the boldest examples of robust state capacity in advanced industrial European countries. Although there are many opinions on the precise sources of state capacity in Europe, a conventional wisdom holds that the seventeenth and eighteenth centuries were when modern states, replete with permanent standing bureaucracies, became commonplace across the continent. European states were becoming viable national entities, which controlled their borders, taxed their citizens, and provided public goods like law and order. At the heart of these state building projects stood rulers who were deeply preoccupied with obtaining revenue to fight wars, which were endemic and increasingly expensive. This revenue imperative propelled rulers to establish and invigorate the standing bureaucracies that we today associate with the modern state.[6]

One is hard-pressed, however, to find many such impressive state building accomplishments throughout the non-European world. A number of scholars have adopted, with impressive results, Charles Tilly's bellicist logic that "war made the state" to explain why many developing societies have failed to replicate the state building of many European countries. Less war in the non-European world begot weaker states in general. These researchers also point out that even when non-European states would go to war, they could usually fund their war-making with foreign aid or loans. Consequently, state building

[3] Evans (1995).

[4] North (1989).

[5] Mann (1984: 189). Mann's definition is for "infrastructural power," which scholars more commonly call state capacity. I discuss conceptualizations of state capacity further in chapter 2.

[6] See especially Tilly (1975, 1992).

outside of Europe has arguably been stunted because of a tepid revenue imperative.[7] In fact, some scholars maintain that the state building exemplars outside of Europe, such as the United States and certain East Asian countries, have fared well precisely because they have confronted a weightier revenue imperative.[8]

In recent years, the idea that the revenue imperative enormously influences a country's political development has also been harnessed by scholars of the "resource curse." They maintain that export commodities that generate rents, like minerals and oil, dissuade state building because they provide revenue windfalls. Rulers can satisfy their revenue imperative without building a penetrating taxing apparatus, with negative implications for state capacity overall. Agricultural commodities are considered more auspicious for state building, since they arguably force the creation of greater extractive capability.[9] Even so, all commodity exports can be taxed easily at ports, if not at the point of production. Such easy revenue enables flimsy state building among primary commodity exporters in general, particularly compared to their resource-scarce counterparts.[10] Overall, many developing countries are apparently locked in a dually disadvantageous position: they are not subject to the bellicist pressures that impelled state building in early modern Europe, and their lucrative exportable resources obviate the need to enhance the state's extractive prowess.

But, as these scholars would readily acknowledge, "state capacity" is about much more than extractive capabilities. The notion of state capacity also includes the establishment of law and order, the provision of various other public goods, and the existence of well-functioning government institutions—and not simply for tax collection or war-making. However, prominent theories suggest that the widespread lack of bellicist pressures and the prevalence of natural resource wealth in the non-European world ought to yield lethargic state building in general. Yet one nonetheless finds "extreme variation" among states outside of Europe.[11] These states "are not generic. They vary dramatically in their internal structures and relations to society."[12] This lack of correspondence between theory and evidence is not merely because bellicist approaches and the resource curse literature examine a constricted portion of the concept of state capacity, though this tendency contributes to it. More fundamentally, theories predicated on the revenue imperative presume a "top-down" logic of

[7] Centeno (2002) and Herbst (2000).

[8] Pollack (2009) and Stubbs (1999), respectively.

[9] Karl (1997: 46); Dunning (2008: 45–52); Ross (2001a; 2012); and Shafer (1994: 35–36).

[10] Cf. Doner, Ritchie, and Slater (2005).

[11] Slater (2010: 3).

[12] Evans (1995: 11).

state building whereby rulers build states in response to revenue needs. This outlook needs to be coupled with greater attention to the societal pressures that elicit state building from the "bottom-up," in order to arrive at a fuller appreciation of the determinants of state capacity in the developing world.

Alternative State Building Motives

This book surveys certain bottom-up state building projects that are not readily explained by rulers' pursuit of revenue. In particular, it examines how good economic times can impel social actors to press for new public goods and stronger institutions, as well as the circumstances under which governments are inclined to fulfill these requests. As a point of departure, I recognize that the less hostile security environment facing more recent state builders has altered the sources of state capacity in the non-European world. The enveloping bellicist pressures of early modern Europe could very well spawn public goods provision and stronger institutions, especially for the purpose of taxation. But, as many scholars trenchantly demonstrate, geopolitical conditions in the non-European world have not triggered such comprehensive state building. One must therefore investigate motives other than the revenue imperative in order to account for the many ways in which states get built, given the rich variation in outcomes throughout the developing world.

If the revenue imperative offers a "supply-side" state building logic, this book explores two motives which form part of the "demand-side" for state building. The first motive is the desire to maximize private profit. Economic actors regularly think that new public goods can help them achieve their economic goals and lobby the state for their provision. Governments are often uniquely situated to supply public goods, and public goods provision can be a major impetus to the growth of state capacity. The initial provision of a public good typically demands that states generate new power, and the ongoing maintenance of them usually requires states to do things they previously had not. For instance, when states supply transportation infrastructure, they first must develop the technical expertise to build roads or railroads, and then they must maintain them, both through physical upkeep and the ongoing regulatory oversight of the transportation network. The provision of new public goods is not a fleeting stimulus to state capacity, in other words, but instead usually augments government capabilities over the long term.

Many scholars illustrate how expanding trade in Europe positively contributed to the emergence of proto-states, particularly as rulers began to provide public goods. Hendrik Spruyt, perhaps better than anyone else, demonstrates how merchants' pursuit of profit led to the appearance of nascent states in

Medieval Europe, as merchants pressed rulers for public goods such as secure trade route.[13] New institutional economists, such as Douglass North, likewise place public goods—in his case, property rights—at the center of European economic development and the rise of modern states.[14] Scholars of the developing world, especially staples and dependency theorists, similarly recognize that private actors' economic pursuits can redound benefits to the state, even if they have traditionally highlighted the reasons why developing states have been unable to fully benefit from trade.[15] States are thus not only instigators of economic growth and development, but can handsomely benefit from facilitating social actors' economic pursuits as well.

A second state building impetus analyzed herein stems from social actors' desire to secure distributional political advantage. Institutions possess distributive implications, as scores of researchers have detailed, and social actors usually try to ensconce their political advantages through them. Changing economic circumstances are one of the many times when relative power may shift among social actors and potentially cause institutional change. Good economic times, for instance, may propel rising economic actors to try to recalibrate institutional frameworks to their liking. When rising actors are excluded from political power, they can pose a threat to existing power holders and compel them to fortify institutions to frustrate their competitors' ascent, particularly if power holders believe their basic interests to be in jeopardy. The ensuing institutional change can profoundly augment state capacity, especially as central states come to exert greater influence over local affairs.

Yet jockeying between the "ins" and "outs" is a perennial feature of politics, and most developing countries possess institutions with middling capabilities at best. For as inviting as institution building may be, it is also fraught with costs and uncertainty. Social actors are reluctant to strengthen institutions unless they believe a failure to do so would risk catastrophe. For example, an alternative to the bellic model of European state formation holds that feudal landed elites and an ascendant bourgeoisie sparred for years without much remarkable institution building. But when the bourgeoisie appeared ready to seize the upper hand—and thereby imperil the prevailing system of nonallodial property rights, the cornerstone of landed elites' power—feudal barons banded together to form a state.[16] Dan Slater similarly details how, in more recent times, postwar governments in Southeast Asia regularly confronted challenges to their power but built authoritarian leviathans solely

[13] Spruyt (1994).

[14] North (1981) and North and Thomas (1973).

[15] On staples theory, see especially Hirschman (1977) and Watkins (1963). Two seminal statements on dependency theory are Cardoso and Faletto (1979) and dos Santos (1970).

[16] Hechter and Brustein (1980).

when threats to them were endemic and deemed unmanageable.[17] The desire to obtain and maintain distributional political advantage is an enduring feature of politics, but it induces substantial institutional change only under uncommon circumstances. Overall, the pursuits of profit and distributional political advantage can motivate state building projects—undertakings for which theories built on the revenue imperative regularly cannot provide a good accounting.

Boom Times and State Building in Coalitional Perspective

This book explores how these demand-side motives have influenced state building in the non-European world. Although the arguments made herein could conceivably be applied to various circumstances, I emphasize how the pursuits of profit and distributional political advantage have affected state building during good economic times. First, boom times transmit clear incentives for economic actors to expand production. Their euphoria may be tempered, however, by hitherto unrecognized barriers to expansion. Economic actors often conclude that new public goods can allay these obstacles, and, when provided, new public goods promote the growth of state capacity. Second, good economic times do not uniformly enrich all sectors of an economy and thus entail a shift in the relative distribution of economic power. I describe in the following chapter how shifting economic power sometimes creates an elemental threat to ruling coalition members, who will subsequently embark on momentous projects of institutional strengthening to ensconce their power. In general, good economic times should regularly activate and intensify the demand-side state building motives identified above.

In particular, I illustrate these arguments by analyzing the first major international commodity booms in six countries. Commodity booms have been and, for many countries in the developing world, remain important economic events. They are a salient type of good economic times. However it may seem counterintuitive to point to commodity booms as harbingers of state building, given the solidifying belief that a "curse" plagues commodity-exporting countries. As I note above, resource wealth provides easy tax revenue. And since scholars regularly maintain that taxation is fundamental to a state's capacity,[18] resource wealth arguably yields feeble institutions and weak state capacity overall.[19] Resource booms generate substantial revenue windfalls, which are

[17] Slater (2010).

[18] For instance, scholars commonly use measures of taxation as proxies for state capacity overall (e.g., Barnett 1992: 42–47; Skocpol 1985: 16–17; Slater 2010: 35; Thies 2005, 2007).

[19] Karl (1997: 46), Sala-i-Martin and Subramanian (2003), and Shafer (1994: 35–36).

tempting to plunder or use as political patronage. Many scholars accordingly expect that resource-rich countries will have bureaucracies characterized by rent-seeking and corruption,[20] unless institutional safeguards to temper such corrosive behavior exist when resource wealth is discovered.[21] This expectation is best known with respect to fuel and mineral exporting countries, but some researchers have found that countries with spatially concentrated plantation crops, as well as cocoa and coffee, suffer institutional debility as well.[22] In varying degrees, the conventional wisdom on the resource curse maintains that resource wealth, because of its fiscal implications, augurs low levels of state capacity.

Yet some of the countries examined in this book impressively strengthened their state capacity during resource booms, and for reasons unconnected to the revenue imperative. Instead, bottom-up, demand-side motives propelled their state building projects. Commodity booms in Chile and Argentina, for example, fundamentally altered politics by enriching economic competitors to the ruling political coalition. These ascendant actors constituted an exigent, diametrical threat to existing power holders, who embarked on ambitious projects of institution building in order to deflect elemental challenges to their economic and political power. Some countries also enlarged their state capacity as a byproduct of public goods provision, which confounds the prevalent expectation that rent-seeking, rather than beneficial government intervention, will flourish during resource booms. Although my case studies feature a diversity of public goods being sought, exporters repeatedly asked their governments to provide new transportation infrastructure and facilitate credit accessibility to help them maximize profit from export opportunities. These routes to new state capacity ultimately hinged on coalitional politics, as "export-oriented" coalitions consistently implemented policies that contributed to the growth of state capacity, whereas coalitions that excluded exporters did not initiate state building projects.

Coalitional politics was the pivotal reason why some of the six countries surveyed in this book seemed to succumb to the pathologies of the resource curse, while others bucked this noteworthy trend. Three of my case studies—Colombia, Ghana, and Nigeria—lend credence to the idea that a curse plagues resource-rich countries, as their commodity booms produced economic and

[20] Karl (1997: 60) and Leite and Weidmann (1999). See also Ross (2001b) on the "rent seizing" that can accompany resource booms.

[21] Karl (1997: 213–220); Mehlum, Moene, and Torvik (2006); Robinson, Torvik, and Verdier (2006); and Smith (2007).

[22] Isham et al. (2005).

political chaos. But, in each country, I show how these "cursed" developments were politically contingent: they transpired because ruling political coalitions excluded exporters and were inclined to prey upon resource wealth. In three other countries—Chile, Argentina, and Mauritius—exporters held similar preferences for public goods, and because they were part of the ruling coalition, their governments assisted their economic and political goals. Coalitional politics was the crucial mediating factor accounting for which states benefitted from commodity booms, and which ones did not.[23]

Perhaps the most provocative contention of this book is that the state building pathologies associated with natural resource wealth are as much, if not more, a function of coalitional politics than the fiscal properties of export commodities. Chile and Mauritius are commonly lauded as exceptions to the resource curse, since both have historically depended on commodity exports but feature capable states. The arguments I present in the next chapter suggest that they only seem peculiar because existing scholarship has not devoted enough attention to how coalitional politics mediates the contingent state building possibilities encapsulated within resource booms. My findings complement studies that point to robust and effective government institutions as one means to avoid the resource curse. This book argues that, even when weak institutions prevail, export-oriented coalitions can not only help countries avoid the resource curse, but can help them turn resource wealth into a blessing. I conclude the book by considering how my arguments and case studies recast our understanding of the pitfalls that have been associated with natural resource wealth.

Commodity Booms and State Building in Latin America and Africa

I employ comparative historical analysis to investigate the coalitional basis of the state building divergences of six countries: Chile (1848–1883), Argentina (1852–1886), Mauritius (1825–1895), Colombia (1880–1905), Ghana (1945–1966), and Nigeria (1945–1966). I selected these cases because they display variation in my independent and dependent variables—political coalitions and state capacity—as I discuss further in the following chapter. Although these countries exhibit manifest differences, this disparateness helps highlight what they shared, particularly a dependence on primary commodity

[23] Doner, Ritchie, and Slater (2005); Slater (2010); Spruyt (1994); and Waldner (1999) similarly emphasize the importance of coalitional politics to state building.

exporting and exporters who wanted governmental support of their economic and political endeavors. These cases were also characterized by weak institutions and low state capacity at the time of their first major commodity booms, which helps to eliminate a potential reason for why some of them contravened the expectations found in the resource curse literature. Ultimately, I view these case studies as explorations into the viability of a coalitional approach to explain variation in state formation amid boom times in developing societies.

These cases coincided with the two largest and longest upward secular trends in commodity prices historically. The nineteenth-century cases were set in the midst of an extraordinary and prolonged global commodity boom, triggered by falling transport costs, Europe's industrial revolution, and worldwide trade liberalization. The twentieth-century cases occurred in similar circumstances, as commodity prices were booming due to postwar European reconstruction, the Korean War, and further trade liberalization.[24] The external stimuli experienced in my case studies typified many countries around the world in these eras.

As I detail in the coming chapters, exporters developed remarkably similar public goods preferences in response to commodity booms in these six countries, despite the various cultural, religious, geographic, and temporal differences between them. Countries in which export-oriented actors led ruling coalitions (Chile, Argentina, and Mauritius) embarked on significant projects to provide new public goods to assist export production, and these activities stimulated a growth in state capacity. Governments in countries in which exporters were politically marginalized (Colombia, Ghana, and Nigeria) spurned such requests, and state capacity stagnated. Resource booms also substantially destabilized domestic politics in five cases (all but Mauritius) by enriching exporters who were excluded from political power. Each situation held the theoretical potential for institution building, as ruling coalition members might have conceivably ensconced their existing advantages within fortified institutions. But only when political confrontation featured export-oriented actors both within and outside the ruling coalition (Chile and Argentina) did power holders perceive that they confronted a diametrical threat and embark on institutional strengthening. When actors without export-oriented interests led ruling coalitions, they concluded that they faced a serious political challenge but not an elemental threat; they therefore employed simpler, non-institutional solutions to foil rising exporters. In the end, these six cases exhibit striking consistency in the ways in which ruling coalitions

[24] Williamson (2012).

responded to the contingent state building opportunities accompanying resource booms.

In Chile (1848–1883), booms in wheat and copper stimulated impressive state building. Chile's new export opportunities triggered public goods seeking by export-oriented actors, who sought railroads to alleviate transportation bottlenecks and joint stock banking to improve credit accessibility. But not all exporters were part of the ruling political coalition, as Chile featured a situation of "dual enrichment" (which I explicate in the following chapter). Consequently, the state provided railroads and overhauled its credit market institutions in ways that distributively empowered landed elites near Santiago, who led the ruling coalition. Copper producers from the desert north and yeomen wheat farmers from the southern periphery, who were politically marginalized, were ignored by the government and aggrieved by public policy. These marginalized exporters responded by initiating two civil wars during the 1850s. Ruling coalition members found the threat deeply troubling, for they not only fleeced these marginalized exporters to fund their side-payments, but feared that being displaced from power would prevent them from participating in the wheat boom. The ruling coalition therefore strengthened state institutions, especially at the municipal level, to contain their opponents. These state building efforts included the pacification of the country's southern frontier, where budding wheat production was creating a yeomanry that threatened elite hegemony. These efforts collectively led to a substantial growth in Chilean state capacity.

Argentina's (1852–1886) wool boom produced similar gains in state capacity. As in Chile, ranchers in Buenos Aires province, who dominated the country's politics, successfully pressed the state for new public goods. Railroads, institutions to improve credit accessibility, and territorial pacification to open up new ranchlands all contributed to a growth in state capacity. Meanwhile, the government largely refused to assist credit accessibility in the country's other littoral provinces, where sheep ranching was blossoming under the control of ranchers at odds with *porteños* in Buenos Aires. Early in the boom era, Buenos Aires' ranchlands became saturated with sheep, and wool production began moving northward into the other littoral provinces, which were then part of the Argentine Confederation, a political entity independent from Buenos Aires. Even after the Buenos Aires government subjugated the Argentine Confederation in 1861, and re-forged "Argentina," *porteño* ranchers believed that upstart ranchers in former Confederation territory were conspiring to undermine wool production in Buenos Aires. Ruling coalition members felt the threat posed by these economic and political competitors was so severe that they embarked on institution building to derail their ascent. By the 1880s, these powerful *porteño* pastoralists had solidified Buenos Aires' hegemony over the rest of the country, in part because they had persistently extended institutional power into the hinterland. The result was an impressive expansion of Argentine state capacity.

Mauritius' (1825–1895) sugar boom serves as a final illustration of commodity booms' positive state building potential. Mauritius was dominated politically by a narrow stratum of export-oriented sugar elites, similar to ruling coalitions in Chile and Argentina. Sugar planters continually pressed the state for public goods throughout the nineteenth century, including for coercive labor "regulation," new transportation infrastructure, credit accessibility, and research and development initiatives. Public goods provision encouraged a remarkable growth of state capacity. But, unlike Chile and Argentina, Mauritius' sugar boom enriched only export-oriented actors within the ruling coalition; there was no analogous group of politically marginalized exporters who also benefitted from boom times. Consequently, the state exerted little institutional power outside of the capital city, Port Louis, because ruling coalition members did not face a noteworthy threat and had no motivation to build robust institutions. State capacity in Mauritius therefore grew but not to the degree observed in Chile and Argentina. Nevertheless, Mauritian state capacity was qualitatively different at the end of its first major commodity boom than in the three countries where export-oriented actors were fully excluded from political power.

Colombia's (1880–1905) first major commodity boom, in coffee, occurred during *la Regeneración*, an era when export-oriented actors were politically marginalized. The boom impelled exporters to seek improved transportation infrastructure and supportive banking and monetary policies, as in the other case studies. But the leaders of *la Regeneración* did not have direct stakes in exporting and did not represent the coffee heartland, so state policy barely aided coffee production. Railroads were built in piecemeal fashion and away from coffee zones, for example. The era was punctuated by multiple civil conflicts, including the catastrophic War of the Thousand Days (1899–1902). Yet rising exporters and civil war did not provoke subsequent institution building. Unlike in Chile and Argentina, Colombia's ruling coalition members were not themselves export oriented and thus regarded rising exporters as a serious challenge but not an exigent and diametrical threat. They felt institution building was unnecessary because their opponents, although exacting, did not endanger their basic interests. In sum, the coalitional difference between Colombia and the three aforementioned cases meant that Colombian state capacity did not grow during the country's first major commodity boom.

Ghana's (1945–1966) cocoa boom mimicked the Colombian experience in key respects. Cocoa producers in Asante, Ghana's cocoa heartland, found themselves progressively marginalized after the Second World War, as the colonial British government (until 1957) substituted its alliance with tribal chiefs for a coalition with the leaders of a burgeoning urban nationalist movement. The marginalization of cocoa producers was a mainstay of Ghanaian politics, especially with the ascent of Kwame Nkrumah, who led the decolonization push. When cocoa producers sought new public goods to promote exports, the government ignored them and chose instead to capture cocoa earnings through a marketing board and divert them as patronage to urbanites. Asante chiefs subsequently built alliances with leaders from other cocoa-producing communities and forged a violent opposition movement, known as the National Liberation Movement. Nkrumah paid the movement little heed for months, despite a deteriorating situation in Asante, because the movement did not jeopardize his fundamental interests. He eventually assailed the opposition with carrots and sticks but did not fortify institutions. Ghana remained a weak state, much like the outcome in Colombia a half-century earlier.

The final case study, of Nigeria's (1945–1966) postwar agricultural commodity booms in cocoa, groundnuts, and palm oil, indicates that evidence of a resource curse predates the rise of oil production in Africa's most populous state. Nigeria's agricultural booms led export producers to develop public goods preferences that were indistinguishable from those in Chile. Variance in coalitional politics is what differentiated Nigeria from Chile. Exporters were politically marginalized in Nigeria and did not receive new state-supplied transportation infrastructure or improved credit accessibility, which forestalled a pathway to new state capacity. A ruling coalition led by nationalist politicians, who lacked direct stakes in exporting, instead preyed upon resource wealth, much like in Ghana. Nigeria's export producers could do little to oppose these antagonistic policies, as they were segmented geographically and by export commodity. Exporters could not mount a serious challenge to power holders, and state institutions remained weak. I further discuss in the case study that ethnic diversity had little to do with these outcomes, contrary to a prevalent understanding of Nigerian politics. (I discuss rival hypotheses in each case study chapter, as well as at the end of chapter 2.) Overall, coalitional politics played the decisive role in Nigeria's unfortunate outcomes, just as it did in the other cases in which export-oriented actors were politically marginalized.

Despite this basic conclusion, I want to caution the reader against infusing my findings with any righteousness on the part of exporters. Although commodity booms in Chile, Argentina, and Mauritius spawned impressive state building, export-oriented actors in each country narrowly pursued their self-interest in ways that harmed vulnerable communities. Chile's ruling landed elites pressured the state to violently dispossess yeomen farmers of their land in frontier areas because they feared socioeconomic change, to say nothing of the devastation they wrought on the Araucanian Indians, who today remain marginalized in Chilean society. Argentine ranchers used their state to subjugate gauchos and "pacify" the country's Indian tribes, with little concern for either group's well-being. And sugar planters in Mauritius used the state to harshly repress the laboring classes under conditions that have been compared to slavery, in the hopes of keeping them economically and politically supine. State building was nasty and brutish in these countries. Moreover, ruling coalitions in Chile and Argentina substantially enhanced their institutional control due to their commodity booms, but these institutions were not necessarily normatively better or more efficacious at solving social problems or enhancing well-being;[25] they merely signified that centralized power holders had heightened their control of peripheral affairs. One thus finds something of a developmental paradox in Chile, Argentina, and Mauritius.

The goal of this book is not to identify an ideal pathway to new state capacity but rather to explore how boom times and coalitional politics affected state building in six countries. I aim to complement existing studies that emphasize rulers' top-down pursuit of revenue as the instigator of state formation. I highlight certain bottom-up motives that are underappreciated in the extant literature—specifically how the pursuit of profit can lead to public goods provision and how the quest for distributive political advantage can trigger institutional strengthening. I describe more fully in the following chapter how these routes to new state capacity pivot on coalitional politics. The chapter explicates why, contrary to the conventional wisdom, resource booms are not necessarily moments for despair, even in countries reliant on rent-generating commodities like oil or minerals. Rather, the effects of natural resource wealth are contingent and hinge on coalitional politics.

[25] A considerable literature illustrates how decentralized, polycentric arrangements often function more effectively and justly than centralized forms of rule (e.g., Ostrom 1999; Wunsch and Olowu 1990).

CHAPTER 2

Boom Times, Coalitional Politics, and State Building

Top-down theories of state formation feature the self-interested ruler as the driving force behind state building. This book examines how self-interested social actors can prompt a growth in state capacity from the bottom-up. Sometimes social actors are unintentionally beneficent, as their narrow pursuit of economic goals leads them to demand new public goods from the state that can trigger an expansion of state capacity. Other times, social actors ruthlessly pursue their own political aggrandizement, which can result in fortified institutions—not unlike how rulers in early modern Europe gave birth to the modern state. Indeed, like the archetypical ruler, whose economic and political pursuits play the central role in many accounts of European state formation, I focus on how social actors in the developing world can engender substantial state building as a means to achieve their economic and political goals.

State Capacity, Public Goods, and Institutions: The Conceptual Terrain

STATE CAPACITY

The study of state capacity is daunting, because the notion of state capacity encompasses an enormous range of government activities, from taxation and institution building to census taking and mail delivery. I begin this chapter with a definitional section in which I conceptualize state capacity, the book's overarching dependent variable. I later present my theoretical argument, case selection rationale, measurement scheme, and stance on leading rival hypotheses. Together, these elements constitute an investigation into how the provision of public goods and stronger institutions (two terms that I also define in this section) can stimulate the growth of state capacity. State capacity refers to the ability of state managers to penetrate society by extracting resources, exercising coercion, and deploying authority via political alliances, the military, or an administrative apparatus. In its essence, state capacity means what Michael Mann terms infrastructural power: "the capacity of the state to actually penetrate civil society, and to implement logistically political decisions throughout the realm."[1] Political scientists and sociologists tend to refer to such capabilities as state capacity, not infrastructural power, so I follow that tendency herein. They have also settled on a relatively stable understanding of what state capacity means, as depicted in table 2.1. There is consensus that state capacity includes the ability to penetrate society to deploy authority, especially for revenue extraction and other regulative functions. The control of territory and the use of coercive force to that end are also central to the notion of state capacity, given that the use of force is the "*means* peculiar" to the state.[2]

The predominant trend in the study of state capacity has been to examine how it originates from extractive (or taxing) activities, as I note in chapter 1.

Table 2.1 **Conceptualizations of State Capacity**

The State	***Barnett*** **(1992: 41–49)**	***Grindle*** **(1996: 3–8)**	***Huber*** **(1995)**	***Mann*** **(1984)**	***Migdal*** **(1988: 4–5)**	***Skocpol*** **(1985: 16–17)**	***Slater*** **(2010: 3–4)**	***Smith*** **(2007: 52–55)**
Controls territory			X	X		X	X	
Possesses preponderant coercive force	X	X	X	X		X	X	
Extracts revenue	X	X	X	X	X	X	X	X
Penetrates society via alliances, military, or institutions	X	X	X	X	X	X	X	X
Regulates social relationships	X	X	X	X	X		X	X
Directs (some) economic production	X					X		

[1] Mann (1984: 189). See also Soifer (2008).

[2] Weber (1972: 55, emphasis in original).

Most scholars regard revenue extraction as the sine qua non of the state and therefore fundamental to what it means to possess state capacity. The belief that extractive capacity can tell scholars much about state capacity in general stems from landmark studies of European state formation.[3] In early modern Europe's bellic crucible, rulers' quest for revenue forced them to gain control over territory, disarm competing militarized groups, encourage economic growth, and build standing institutions. In other words, the pursuit of revenue had spillover effects to state capacity broadly understood. However, in the non-European world, the absence of pressing geopolitical concerns has enabled rulers to satiate their revenue needs without such transformative state building projects. Consequently, when scholars apply theories predicated on the revenue imperative to the developing world, they may ably account for a dearth of state capacity, where it exists; but bellicist theories tell one less about how state capacity develops in a relatively pacific environment, like that found historically throughout much of the non-European world.

This book provides insights into the development of aspects of state capacity that are not integrally connected to revenue extraction. Specifically, it looks to how social actors have generated bottom-up pressures for the provision of new public goods and stronger institutions, which are closely linked to the dimensions of state capacity other than "extracts revenue" noted in table 2.1. Such developments include the establishment of territorial control and preponderant coercive power, the invigoration of penetrative capacity, and the elaboration of the state's regulative functions. This book probes facets of state capacity that will normally be unaccounted for by revenue-based theories of state building and thereby complements bellicist studies that account for the paucity of extractive capacity throughout the non-European world. Below I define what I mean by public goods and institution building, before describing the conditions that induce such state building projects in the chapter's next section.

PUBLIC GOODS

The term "public goods" covers an expansive class of goods that can be provided by the state or private actors. I use this general term throughout the book because it covers the various types of public goods sought in the cases under investigation. "Pure" public goods, such as clean air or national defense, are the best known type of public goods. These goods are characterized by non-excludability (people cannot be excluded from their consumption) and

[3] Above all, studies by Charles Tilly (1975; 1992).

non-rivalrousness (individual consumption of the good does not diminish its benefits for others). They render benefits to people who were not directly charged for their provision, and these benefits are known as positive externalities.[4]

Positive externalities are found in a wide range of goods, not just pure public goods. There are "impure" public goods, which fall in-between pure public goods and private goods. One type of impure public good is a local public good, such as regional transportation infrastructure. Its benefits accrue unevenly and to the benefit of some areas, so a local public good does not qualify as a pure public good, even though it renders positive externalities. "Club goods" are another type of impure public goods. These are goods that are non-rivalrous but feature an exclusion mechanism regulating their consumption. For example, people pay membership fees to use a country club, but one's round of golf does not use up the golf course for others.[5] Impure public goods are characterized by positive externalities and are distinct from private goods, even if the benefits of impure public goods sometimes accrue to the advantage of certain social actors.

The actors profiled in the book's case studies sought a variety of public goods in response to boom times. They commonly wanted three public goods that, when provided, promoted the growth of state capacity. The first public good was territorial pacification, the process through which state officials eliminate "rival claimants to the national territory."[6] The notion of territorial pacification was implied in Weber's writings on the state, which he defined as "a compulsory organization with a territorial basis" whose "claim . . . to monopolize the use of force is as essential to it as its character of compulsory jurisdiction and of continuous operation."[7] In Chile, for example, pacification followed the subjugation of the Araucanian Indians in the southern frontier, while in Argentina the process involved the pacification of regional *caudillos* as well as Indian tribes. Territorial pacification signals a state's control over territory and its possession of preponderant coercive force—and thus marks the accomplishment of a significant state building task. Territorial pacification qualifies as a pure public good because its benefits are non-excludable and non-rivalrous.[8]

[4] Cornes and Sandler (1996).

[5] Although club goods are subject to congestion or crowding, which can encroach on their non-rivalrousness (Cornes and Sandler 1996: 272–277).

[6] Centeno (2002: 108–109).

[7] Weber (1972: 56).

[8] Although, of course, those groups that are neutralized during the process of territorial pacification would not consider it to be a benefit.

Social actors repeatedly sought two other public goods that were impure in nature. They solicited for improved transportation infrastructure, which qualified as an impure local public good when new railroads or roads were part of an integrated network. Such logistical infrastructure reduced transportation costs and therefore rendered positive externalities. Where fairly integrated transportation infrastructure developed, states augmented their penetrative capacity as well, because new infrastructure resources facilitated the deployment of state agents into the hinterland.[9] New bureaucratization also tended to accompany new infrastructure and expanded state regulative oversight of society. But in other cases, the development of transportation infrastructure was comparatively incoherent: road-building contracts were allocated as private goods, the resulting roadways were disjointed, transportation costs remained high, and no positive externalities developed. Such happenings did not mark a growth in state capacity, since a segmented infrastructure poorly assisted the deployment of state agents.

State assistance with credit accessibility was another impure public good that social actors sought in the case studies. I detail how exporters pursued policies to promote credit accessibility, though the content of the policies varied, from the establishment of joint stock banking and facilitation of long-term mortgage lending to a reform of land registration laws and changes in monetary policy. Governments in Chile, Argentina, and Mauritius promoted credit accessibility by assisting capital accumulation, reducing information costs, and creating risk-bearing institutions—innovations that had broad, positive economic ramifications in Europe centuries earlier.[10] These efforts reduced transaction costs and created positive externalities. Facilitating credit accessibility inclined the development of state capacity, and not simply due to attendant bureaucratization. Once Chile authorized the Banco Nacional de Chile, for instance, the private bank acted as the state's banker and facilitated state building similar to (but on a scale less than) the Bank of England during England's formative state building era.[11] Such financial establishments often helped underwrite transportation infrastructure and various other public works, too.[12] In short, the provision of public goods redounded benefits to the state. Lastly, public goods have additional favorable but diffuse effects on state capacity because they enhance collective well-being and thereby heighten acquiescence to a state's rule.[13] Overall, the provision of new public goods normally signifies a growth of state capacity.

[9] Herbst (2000: 84–87, 159–170).

[10] North (1990: 125).

[11] Carruthers (1996).

[12] See Ardant (1975: 219–220).

[13] Mann (1986: 143–155).

INSTITUTIONS

A country's prevailing institutional framework is central to whether it possesses penetrative power in particular and state capacity in general. "Institutions," as elusive as the notion may be, are commonly defined (following Douglass North) as "the rules of the game in a society or . . . the humanly devised constraints that shape human interaction."[14] North's conception of institutions, though often associated with rational choice analyses, can encompass both formal and informal institutions.[15] This expansive notion is valuable, as formal institutional changes do not necessarily yield new state capacity (even if they are intended to) and some of the institutional strengthening analyzed in this book involved non-codified developments in informal practice.

One way that students of state capacity differentiate among institutions is by considering the extent to which central government officials have displaced societal notables from local administration and implanted state agents in their place. This process is known as the movement from mediated to unmediated institutions. Mediated forms of rule refer to situations in which autonomous elites carry out government directives at the local level. Alternatively, unmediated institutions describe arrangements whereby state agents supplant local notables as the key administrative force at the local level. Scholars of state building generally believe that unmediated institutions mark higher levels of state capacity because they enhance the likelihood that centralized rulers can implement their decrees,[16] even if unmediated institutions may ultimately be less adept at solving social problems than decentralized, polycentric arrangements.[17]

Historically, most governments have exerted their authority through mediated institutions. Michael Mann, in his sweeping history of social power, notes that rulers have typically employed one of two strategies of mediated rule. First, they have ruled indirectly through local elites. This low-cost strategy was (and, for many contemporary rulers, remains) appealing because of its simplicity. But it is problematic because of the obvious limitations to ensuring that a ruler's decrees are implemented. After all, a reliance on local

[14] North (1990: 1). Mahoney (2010: 14) similarly defines institutions as "rules or generalizable procedures that provide a guide for behavior and that promote predictable patterns of interaction."

[15] E.g., Firmin-Sellers (1996: 11) and Mahoney (2010: 14–15).

[16] Waldner (1999: 19–24). These institutional frameworks should be thought of as ideal types, as "states range along a continuum, and no states occupy the extremes of fully mediated or fully unmediated rule" (p. 19).

[17] E.g., Ostrom (1999); Scott (1998); and Wunsch and Olowu (1990).

notables couples rulers with potential competitors who retain authority over local communities, which they may possibly mobilize against the dictates of a central ruler.[18] Many Latin American governments have existed historically in close association with landed elites; states gained valuable ruling partners but often found themselves unable to displace entrenched powerbrokers when they wanted to establish more unmediated forms of rule.[19] In Africa, the reliance on tribal chiefs as the de facto agents of European rule created similar obstacles to the exercise of colonial state power.[20] Both examples illustrate how indirect rule through local elites epitomizes a mediated state.

Some rulers have tried to rule directly through military officers, in the hopes of having their dictates more reliably implemented at the local level. But, like indirect rule through local notables, trying to rule directly through the military is wrought with problems, given the temptation for military leaders to act as autonomous local leaders.[21] Rulers tried to govern through military officers more commonly during Europe's pre-modern militaristic empires than in the modern era. Modern European colonial powers tended to rule indirectly through local elites in Latin America, Africa, and elsewhere. Sometimes colonizing powers deliberately created their allied caste of local notables, as did Spain in much of Latin America.[22] Other times, European powers aligned themselves with indigenous elites, as they did throughout colonial Africa. Consequently, countries in the non-European world generally inherited from their colonial overlords mediated institutions that utilized local notables for administration.[23]

Unmediated institutions differ fundamentally from mediated institutions. An unmediated institution, in its purest form, exists when a central ruler removes local elites from administrative roles and replaces them with individuals employed by the state. Such administration raises the likelihood that a ruler's decrees will be implemented, since a bureaucrat's main source of well-being comes from his administrative position, whereas a local notable's welfare derives principally from landed wealth or whatever else designated him as

[18] Mann (1986: 143). Weber (1972: 1058) notes, in a discussion such situations, that local notables seek "to cut off the direct relationship between ruler and common subjects and to direct both exclusively to the local office incumbent for their respective claims—for taxes and military services, on the one hand, and for legal protection on the other."

[19] Hagopian (1996).

[20] Phillips (1989).

[21] Mann (1986: 143–146).

[22] Góngora (1974) and Lynch (1992b).

[23] The exception may be Japanese colonial rule and its comparatively penetrative colonial bureaucracies (Kohli 1994, 2004).

a notable in the first place.[24] The movement toward unmediated institutions is therefore contentious, for it entails curtailing the relative power of local powerbrokers while expanding the state's local administrative oversight. It marks a basic shift in power relations as central rulers encroach on local autonomy. The process of building unmediated institutions usually also involves "changes in systems of taxation, justice, public works, and much more."[25] I remain agnostic as to whether unmediated institutions are normatively desirable, as various scholars have noted how attempts to elaborate central institutional control have been abysmal.[26] I am simply interested in the local intrusion of the central state's tentacles, for better or worse.

This book examines the movement toward unmediated institutions with respect to local governance. In particular, I examine changes in how states dealt with local government functions such as mayoral appointments, municipal fiscal affairs, the holding of elections, and judicial administration. (I discuss my measures of institutional characteristics later in the chapter.) Central states tilt the balance of administrative power toward themselves as they wrestle control of some of these functions away from local notables, even if they do not fully implant state employees at the local level.[27] Among my case studies, Chile made great strides to exert state authority in localities during the nineteenth century, whereas Colombian localities remained parochial and largely insulated from central state dictates. States substantially augment their control over local affairs as they move toward unmediated institutions, which signify new state capacity, just as the provision of public goods marks a growth in state capacity. The chapter's next section describes how good economic times can lead to new public goods, stronger institutions, and more state capacity in general.

A Coalitional Approach to State Building: The Theoretical Argument

Throughout the non-European world, there is great variance in the prevalence of public goods, the strength of institutions, and state capacity. This book helps to account for such variation by showing how coalitional politics affects how countries respond to the contingent state building possibilities encapsulated within resource booms. More generally, though, this book is about

[24] Cf. Weber (1972: 223–226, 973–975).
[25] Tilly (1992: 109).
[26] E.g., Scott (1998).
[27] Cf. Smith (2007: 54).

how social actors jockey for power during good economic times. In the first subsection, I depict a simplified world, in which "economic actors" and "political elites" pursue what I call their generative and distributional goals. Their variant social bases inform what their goals are, how they build political coalitions to pursue them, and how much coalitional flexibility they have in doing so. I then discuss how the coalitional jockeying between these groups affects whether good economic times will translate into the provision of new public goods, stronger institutions, and the growth of state capacity. Finally, in the third subsection, I relax some of my simplifying assumptions to better elucidate how resource booms have historically influenced state building in the developing world.

ECONOMIC ACTORS, POLITICAL ELITES, AND THEIR COALITION-BUILDING INCLINATIONS

This book isolates how certain bottom-up social pressures can lead to the growth of state capacity. As such, this book is centrally concerned with social power. There are two basic types of social power, which Michael Mann terms collective and distributive power. They deeply influence social actors. Collective power refers to power that is generated through cooperation. It is non-zero-sum, meaning that all members of a group can benefit by working together and creating new power, even if the newly created power is spread unevenly within the group and/or subsequently used at the expense of a third party.[28] As a non-zero-sum form of power, collective power is about making something together, not taking something from someone else. I accordingly refer to a social actor's desire to get collective power as its generative aim.

Distributive power, by contrast, is a zero-sum form of power whereby one actor gains power at the expense of another. If collective power is about making something through cooperation, then distributive power is about taking something through exploitation. Distributive power is characteristic of all settled human societies that feature some degree of institutionalization and social stratification.[29] For instance, many early human settlements (as opposed to nomadic hunter-gatherer groups) took root in river valleys, which facilitated settled agriculture. Such settlements reaped astounding gains in collective power, especially when they practiced irrigated agriculture. But with these gains came a division of labor, dwindling exit options, and "social cages." Those who found themselves with relative advantages tried to preserve

[28] Mann (1986: 6) and Parsons (1960: 220–221).

[29] Mann (1986: 6–7) and Parsons (1960: 219–220).

them, while those who were disadvantaged desired to ameliorate their weakness. The quest for distributive power has since been a fundamental feature of sociopolitical relations.[30] I refer to this generic pursuit as a social actor's distributional aim. Below I argue that a social actor's ultimate source of power—whether from the economic or political realm—informs how they define their generative and distributional goals, as well as how they try to achieve them.

A basic way that social actors pursue their goals is by forming political coalitions. Coalitions are groups of social actors that support a leader and tend to receive benefits for doing so in return. A "leader" can be thought of as the preponderant force or senior member within a coalition.[31] Leaders initiate and manage coalition-building efforts by offering side-payments to attract followers. Side-payments are "compensatory measures aimed at facilitating agreement between actors . . . by roughly balancing inequities arising from cooperation."[32] Many things can function as side-payments, from actual or quasi-pecuniary payments to promises about future policy, threats, or even culturally rooted charismatic appeals.[33] Coalition leaders may use side-payments that are narrowly political (e.g., the promise of an exclusionary regime) or sociocultural (e.g., appeals to religion, ethnicity, or ideology). But, in the end, coalition leaders almost always employ side-payments that provide followers tangible, material benefits.[34]

I expect that coalition leaders prefer material side-payments to political or sociocultural ones for a few reasons. First, leaders who build winning coalitions capture the reins of government and thus control policymaking. The state is an unparalleled mechanism to distribute "carrots" to followers, which should dispose ruling coalitions to utilize material side-payments to exploit this advantage. Second, access to the state also provides coercive power, or the "sticks," to repress opponents and maintain a narrowly political side-payment, like an exclusionary regime. But repression is costly, and the resources expended to suppress opponents may be more efficiently deployed to cultivate supporters with material side-payments.[35] Finally, sociocultural side-payments are fairly ethereal, which inclines coalition leaders to supplement them with tangible benefits once in power, as I discuss below. I anticipate that material side-payments will constitute the crux of a leader's coalition-building strategy, even if one employs a hodgepodge of side-payments overall.

[30] Mann (1986: 73–78).

[31] E.g., Riker (1962: 10–12); Slater (2010: 15); and Waldner (1999: 34–35).

[32] Friman (1993: 390).

[33] Riker (1962: 103–114).

[34] See Waldner (1999: 35).

[35] Put idiomatically, "one catches more flies with honey than with vinegar." See Acemoglu and Robinson (2006: 220); Dunning (2008); and Slater (2009: 208).

Leaders' social background informs how they try to build political coalitions. I segregate coalitions into two analytic types based on a coalition leader's ultimate origin of power. Doing so highlights how coalition leaders' social background can vary fundamentally. To preview, I describe how "economic actors" derive power from control of economic resources and regard political power as a means to achieve their economic ends. I juxtapose them with "political elites," who lack noteworthy economic power and instead derive their well-being from their ability to cultivate a political following. Political elites thus regard political power as an end, not a means to an end.[36] I contend that this elemental difference profoundly affects these actors' state building inclinations. For now, I consider a simplified world in which economic actors and political elites not only designate a coalition's leader but also describe its membership. I proceed as if coalitions led by economic actors are only populated by economic actors, and vice versa. Coalitional membership is rarely so homogeneous in actuality, of course, and later in the chapter, I relax this restrictive assumption. Meanwhile, the analytic clarity afforded by simplifying what is admittedly a complex world helps lay bare how economic actors and political elites strive to gain and maintain power.

Economic Actors

Economic actors, such as landowners and merchants, derive power from control over "economic production, distribution, exchange, and consumption." Economic actors enhance their collective power by pursuing profit and creating new wealth through the production and exchange of goods. Sometimes, economic actors need to cooperate with the state in order to generate collective power, for reasons I discuss below. Economic activities may not be purely consensual, and their outputs may be unevenly distributed (hence, class distinctions). But over time, population growth, technological innovations, and natural resource exploitation have led to a massive growth in collective power in the economic realm.[37] Overall, economic actors' generative aim is to maximize their economic wealth and power.

Economic actors also seek to gain and maintain distributional political advantage as a means to further their economic goals. Economic actors desire to hold a distributive advantage vis-à-vis other social actors because it helps them obtain their preferred public policies. Economic actors might seek a wide range of government policies to help them generate collective power, including the provision of new public goods. So too might they want to set tax

[36] The distinction between "economic actors" and "political elites" is inspired by Michael Mann's typology of power (1986: 24–27), as well as by Bates (2008).

[37] Mann (1986: 24–25, 520, quote from 24; 1993: 2–3, 7–8, 12–14).

policy. Since economic actors' power is ultimately rooted in economic assets, they naturally would like to secure favorable tax rates to limit the economic surplus that is captured by the state. Indeed, many scholars trenchantly demonstrate how fights over redistributive taxation are fundamental to politics.[38] Economic actors surmise they can best achieve their desired policy results—and, thus, advance their economic goals—by possessing a political advantage relative to other social actors.

Economic actors' basis of social power also affects the types of side-payments they prefer to use when building a coalition. Unsurprisingly, social actors want to avoid harming the elemental basis of their power when devising side-payments. Economic actors are therefore drawn to political and/or sociocultural side-payments, rather than material side-payments. But because material side-payments tend to be efficacious, economic actors will probably employ some of them to build and maintain a coalition. They will strive to ensure that these side-payments do not infringe on their economic interests and instead tap segments of the economy that are inconsequential or, at worst, peripheral to their economic goals. Overall, economic elites' generative aim—to enhance their economic power—thoroughly informs their political behavior.

Political Elites

There are other social actors who derive power not from economic assets but rather from their ability to cultivate a following. These actors are "political elites," including intellectuals, military commanders, and leaders of ethnic groups, religious communities, ideological circles, or nationalist movements. Political elites—sometimes referred to as political entrepreneurs—are distinctive because they do not principally derive power from the economic realm. Their power is ultimately ideological or symbolic in nature.[39] Such extra-economic power can be formidable, particularly as triggers of collective mobilization.[40] Yet symbolic power is "predominantly diffused"[41] and relatively ineffectual as a durable side-payment. Political elites therefore usually have difficulty augmenting their collective power in the longer term through symbolic or ideological appeals alone.[42] They will consequently seek

[38] E.g., Acemoglu and Robinson (2006); Boix (2003); and Dunning (2008).

[39] Mann (1986: 22–24, 1993: 35–42).

[40] Slater (2009: 208–209, 214–224) shows how "communal elites" in Southeast Asia have harnessed symbolic power to mobilize supporters and profoundly influenced the region's politics.

[41] Mann (1993: 6–7).

[42] See Snyder (2006). Mann (2006: 348) notes that "even the most visionary ideologies are not born immanent and transcendent. They become so after complex social processes involving coalition-building."

out material resources to build and fortify a coalition, and the state apparatus is an ideal medium through which to acquire and allocate such resources. Indeed, even if one pursues power for her own enrichment, she nonetheless needs a coalitional basis of support and must nurture her supporters with side-payments.[43] And since people respond well to tangible side-payments, political elites' desire to generate collective power is bound together with efforts to acquire influence over how resources are distributed via the state apparatus.

Like economic actors, political elites want to gain and maintain distributional political advantage vis-à-vis other social actors. But, unlike economic actors, political elites typically consider attaining political advantage to be an end in and of itself, whereas economic actors regard political power as a means to advance their economic goals. This differential posture stems from the role that the state plays in helping political elites generate collective power. To political elites, the state is vital to help them solidify and nurture a coalition; it is by capturing the state that political elites can enhance their collective power. By comparison, economic actors rely much less on the state to generate collective power, even if they do request state assistance to achieve their economic goals from time to time.

Political elites, because of their extra-economic basis of power, are comparatively unencumbered when it comes to devising side-payments. They do not have economic interests to protect and can therefore use a wider range of material side-payments. In other words, political elites possess relative flexibility in coalition building. Political elites may tap segments of the economy where producers face sizable collective action barriers and will likely remain incapacitated. Or, they might alter their side-payment mix depending on which sector is experiencing growth. Political elites may calculate that the enrichment being enjoyed in one economic sector might allay hostility toward policies that tax growing wealth. Economic actors have less flexibility in coalition building. Later I argue that political elites' flexibility in crafting side-payments makes them less likely to initiate state building projects during boom times.

I conclude this subsection by describing an abstract situation that makes clearer how these actors' sources of power and side-payment preferences affect coalition building. Consider a simplified scenario with three actors: two

[43] Bates (2008: 34–40) refers to this situation as the "incumbent's dilemma." Recent studies (e.g., Brownlee 2007; Levitsky and Way 2010) illustrate how authoritarian rulers rely on coalitions to maintain their power, in contrast to earlier research that often depicted dictators as detached from their underlying societies. As Bueno de Mesquita et al. (2003: 28) put it: "Make no mistake about it, no leader rules alone."

economic actors (A and B) and a group of political elites. Each actor desires to be the coalition leader and plans to build their coalition with some material side-payments, given their efficaciousness. If political elites are the coalition leader, they have considerable flexibility in coalition building because they can tap sectors A and/or B for side-payments. Their side-payment strategy can be fluid and responsive to changing circumstances. Such flexibility is unavailable to economic actors A and B, according to this heuristic. Economic actor A has but one source for material side-payments: economic sector B. And vice versa. Economic actors A and B would consequently find themselves in an intractable situation when one of them leads the ruling political coalition, as one economic actor is necessarily the fiscal target of the other (see table 2.2).

Although this heuristic is merely suggestive, it reflects a good portion of the political dynamics in the book's case studies. In most cases, there were usually two consequential economic actors. Sometimes, they were rival export sectors, or rivals within a single export sector. Other times, a dominant export sector targeted a diffuse economic actor (e.g., consumers) to fund its side-payments. Groups of political elites also played important roles in some countries, especially when they led ruling coalitions. In sum, the distinguishing features summarized in table 2.2 affected how social actors jockeyed for power in the case studies. What is more, in the next section I describe how differences in social actors' generative aim and relative flexibility in coalition-building affect whether good economic times yield state building via the provision of new public goods and institutional strengthening.

POLITICS AND STATE BUILDING AMID GOOD ECONOMIC TIMES

Economic change can have profound political ramifications, and the politics of "hard times," in particular, has garnered noteworthy attention from political

Table 2.2 **Overview of Social Actors**

Elements	*Economic Actor A (B)*	*Political Elites*
Source of power	Economic	Extra-economic
Generative aim (collective power)	Economic power	Political power
Distributional aim (distributive power)	Maintain relative political advantage	
Target for material side-payments	Economic sector B (A)	Economic sector A and/or B

scientists.[44] Yet—in contrast to the view that "good times slake the propensity to contest and challenge"[45]—I find political contention as social actors pursue their generative and distributional goals amid times of economic expansion. These struggles have potential state building implications. First, good economic times can reveal barriers to economic expansion and prompt economic actors to seek new public goods. Second, good economic times usually shift the relative distribution of economic power, which may upset the balance of political power and create contingent opportunities for institutional change. Whether either situation results in state building hinges on a country's constellation of coalitional politics.

Public Goods Seeking

Good economic times have straightforward implications for economic actors: they want to maximize their wealth and profit from new economic opportunities. But often they cannot because their pursuits reveal obstacles that did not constrain prior levels of economic activity. Economic actors regularly conclude that state-supplied public goods can assuage such barriers. In Medieval Europe, for instance, precarious trade routes and the lack of standardized weights and measures gave rise to merchant preferences for public goods in order to reduce transaction costs.[46] Public authorities are often uniquely situated to provide public goods. Certain legal, fiscal, and institutional frameworks can be provided only by government. Other times, the government is the only entity with sufficient capital or coercive resources to supply a collective good. Finally, and perhaps most important, governments can subsidize or fully cover the costs economic actors would otherwise incur to fund public goods. Such actions can spread the cost of new public goods among all actors, even if new (impure) public goods asymmetrically benefit certain actors.[47]

I expect the composition of ruling political coalitions to dictate government posture toward public goods requests. To continue with the earlier heuristic, assume that economic actor A is the main beneficiary of good economic times and wants new public goods. If economic actor A leads the ruling coalition, it will impel the state to provide them. I expect an opposite policy response from coalitions led by political elites or economic actor B. In these situations, providing public goods to economic actor A would direct scarce resources away

[44] Especially Gourevitch (1986) and Smith (2007).

[45] Gourevitch (1986: 9).

[46] See North and Thomas (1973: 29–30, 65, 91–156) and Spruyt (1994).

[47] This logic is essentially a mirror image of Bueno de Mesquita et al.'s (2003) reasoning for why rulers prefer to use public resources to distribute narrow, as opposed to broad, goods to supporters when possible.

from ruling coalition members and toward a political outsider. Not only would the coalition leader be assisting its opponent's generative aim but the coalition leader may very well imperil its own distributional goal, insofar as economic actor A can translate new collective power into distributive power.

However, one might expect a coalition leader to be inclined to provide public goods regardless of who asks for them, since public goods assist economic growth and thereby create wealth capturable for side-payments. In other words, when political elites or economic actor B lead the ruling coalition, they might calculate that their anticipated gain in distributive power would outweigh the benefit that economic actor A would accrue in collective power. Two other reasons to expect a general tendency toward public goods provision are that many scholars depict the state as relatively autonomous in policymaking and intent on maximizing its revenue.[48] States would be predisposed to provide public goods, according to this logic, given that public goods facilitate the creation of taxable wealth. Yet I find that states are normally beholden to their underlying ruling coalitions, and the distributive implications of potential public goods overwhelm any generic inclination to provide them. "Rulers" may therefore behave in seemingly paradoxical ways that impoverish their economy and polity, because of the interests of their coalitional constituents. My view is supported directly by my case studies and buttressed indirectly by a sizable literature on the dearth of public goods throughout the developing world, which suggests there is no functional logic behind public goods provision.[49] In sum, although good economic times often give rise to preferences for new public goods, coalitional politics accounts for why those desires may go unfulfilled.

Institution Building

Social actors' distributional aim can also lead to institution building during good economic times, though outcomes likewise hinge on coalitional politics. The basic reason why economic change might induce institutional change is because institutions possess distributional implications.[50] They are not neutral arbiters of politics. And since good economic times usually alter relative economic power, those experiencing growth in their collective economic

[48] Levi (1988).

[49] Alesina, Baqir, and Easterly (1999); Baldwin and Huber (2010); Habyarimana et al. (2007); and Lake and Baum (2001). On the distributive facets of public goods provision, see Kramon and Posner (2013) and Lieberman and McClendon (2013).

[50] The distributional potential of institutions is well recognized by historical institutionalists (Mahoney and Thelen 2010: 7–9; Steinmo, Thelen, and Longstreth 1992), rational choice institutionalists (Knight 1992; Tsebelis 1990: 104–115), and even sociological institutionalists (Stinchcombe 1987).

power want to translate these gains into distributive political power. The potential resulting contention can provoke the movement toward unmediated institutions, depending on how those experiencing economic enrichment are situated vis-à-vis the ruling coalition. Recall that mediated rule prevails when societal notables serve as the government's de facto administrators at the local level, whereas unmediated institutions exist when notables have been replaced by administrative agents who are directly beholden to the state. I argue that good economic times will yield such consequential institutional change only when they enrich actors who constitute a diametrical threat to existing power holders. Ruling coalition members in such situations will conclude that institution building is imperative because the costs of inaction are potentially catastrophic.

In contrast to the positive inducements that motivate public goods seeking, I emphasize how threats—negative inducements for action—spur projects of momentous institutional change. Threat refers to the costs that a group (or coalition) expects to incur if it acts or fails to act.[51] The shifts in relative economic power that commonly accompany good economic times can create perceived threats from inaction, particularly the fear "that existing benefits will be taken away or new harms inflicted" due to a failure to act.[52] Yet only some circumstances elicit threats sufficiently exigent to prompt the movement toward unmediated institutions. Consider again a situation in which economic sector A is the primary beneficiary of good economic times. When economic actor A leads the ruling political coalition, I anticipate little institutional change because existing institutions are probably tailored to its liking.[53] Since good economic times are fortifying existing power holders, institutional strengthening would be superfluous because coalitional outsiders are growing relatively weaker.

Now, consider some institutional implications when economic actor A is politically marginalized. One scenario is when political elites lead the ruling coalition. In this situation, economic actor A will strive to translate its rising economic power into greater political influence. This development poses a political challenge to political elites and possibly imperils their side-payment strategy. Political elites might therefore find institution building enticing

[51] Goldstone and Tilly (2001: 183). In the social movements literature, "threat" is juxtaposed to "opportunity," or positive inducements for action. See especially Goldstone and Tilly (2001: 182–183) and also Almeida (2003); Meyer and Minkoff (2004); Tarrow (1998: 76–77); and Tilly (1978: 133–136). My argument on institution building draws inspiration from Slater (2010: 47–50), for whom the notion of threat is important as well.

[52] Almeida (2003: 347).

[53] On the reasonableness of this assumption, see Knight (1992: 126–139); Mahoney (2010: 14–17); and Mahoney and Thelen (2010: 7–9).

because it could ensconce their current advantages and avert their ejection from power.[54] But institution building is riddled with uncertainty.[55] It is also costly, requiring scarce resources that could otherwise be consumed as side-payments. These costs extend into the future, as institutions need ongoing maintenance, lest they be co-opted by local notables opposed to the ruling coalition.[56] Political elites can likely avoid the costly and uncertain process of institution building by amending their side-payment strategy (i.e., by targeting economic actor B) and/or employing non-institutional tactics (e.g., short-term repression) to foil their political rivals. Ultimately, political elites are unlikely to perceive economic actor A as a diametrical threat because the two actors derive their social power from different sources (see table 2.2). Hence, political elites will conclude that institution building is unnecessary because, although economic actor A is a political menace, it is not an existential threat as well.

Economic actor B, by contrast, will perceive economic actor A to be an elemental threat and consequently strengthen institutions to ensconce its power. According to my heuristic, economic actor B targets sector A for material side-payments and knows that, if it is displaced as the coalition leader, it will be targeted to fund actor A's side-payments. The situation is intractable. Yet this threat goes beyond a redistribution of wealth—though, as studies of regime dynamics demonstrate, the targets of such redistributive policies often regard them as categorically intolerable.[57] Actor B will likely interpret the threat posed by actor A as impinging upon its future economic prospects, too. States and markets are actively embedded, and economic actors regularly need government assistance to maximize their economic power.[58] Coalitional exclusion therefore suggests a future inability to maximize economic power, and the fear of future losses is a particularly salient form of threat, prospect theorists argue.[59] Economic actor B will perceive that it faces a diametrical, exigent, and potentially catastrophic threat and therefore initiate the movement toward unmediated institutions to preserve its current distributional political advantage.

Overall, the conditions under which good economic times lead to stronger institutions are restricted and hinge on coalitional politics, as does the process of public goods provision (see table 2.3). The simplifying assumptions made

[54] This logic is expressed formally by Acemoglu, Egorov, and Sonin (2008) and Acemoglu and Robinson (2008) and illustrated empirically by Hechter and Brustein (1980) and Slater (2010).

[55] Knight (1992: 44–47). See also Hechter and Brustein (1980) and Reno (1997).

[56] Mann (1986: 165–167).

[57] E.g., Acemoglu and Robinson (2006); Boix (2003); and Dunning (2008).

[58] E.g., Evans (1995); Gerschenkron (1962); and Weiss and Hobson (1995).

[59] See Tarrow (1998: 86).

Table 2.3 **How Coalition Leaders Respond to Boom Times in Economic Sector A**

Coalition Led by	*Provide New Public Goods?*	*Institution Building?*
Economic actor A	**Yes**[a]	No
Economic actor B	No	**Yes**
Political elites	No	No

Note: Bold text and shading designate expectations for a growth in state capacity.
[a] Impure public goods provided to the distributive benefit of ruling coalition members.

thus far help to lay bare what I believe to be the core coalitional logic underpinning state building during good economic times. But these abstractions miss important historical nuance and wrongly imply that public goods provision and institution building are mutually exclusive. In fact, some comparatively successful state builders in the developing world have provided public goods and built unmediated institutions. I relax some of my simplifying assumptions in the following subsection and situate the foregoing arguments in the context of international commodity booms, which have been a particularly important type of good economic times for developing countries historically.

INTERNATIONAL COMMODITY BOOMS, COALITIONAL POLITICS, AND STATE BUILDING

Commodity Booms

The politics surrounding exporting has profoundly influenced state building for many developing countries. This actuality served as a cornerstone of dependency theory in the 1970s but was overshadowed during ensuing decades of "statist" scholarship. Today, the subject of exporting and politics is experiencing a renaissance, due in part to studies of the resource curse. This book contributes to this burgeoning literature by examining how international commodity booms have affected state building historically. I focus narrowly herein on commodity booms that result from rising prices in global markets ("international commodity booms"), instead of booms caused by a rapid expansion of production amid stagnant world prices.[60] Focusing on international commodity booms limits my analysis to exogenous shocks to a country. Booms engendered by rapid production increases, rather than rising prices, are spurred by endogenous developments within a given country and may therefore be qualitatively different from exogenous price booms. Lastly, although

[60] Ross (2001b: 10).

commodity prices exhibit cyclical tendencies, the generalized causes and duration of price booms and slumps are not well understood. Commodity booms are rightfully characterized as exogenous shocks.[61]

Commodity booms have been important historically for countries outside of Europe. Most of these countries were incorporated into the world economy via colonialism, which (at least initially) rendered them dependent on primary commodity exports for economic vitality.[62] Hence, countries in the non-European world should have been sensitive to changes in international markets, giving commodity booms the potential to reverberate strongly throughout them.[63] Another reason to analyze the political effects of booms is because commodity exports can be taxed easily as they move through ports and are tempting targets to fund side-payments. The temptation to raid export sectors is particularly robust amid boom times. Indeed, the availability of easy revenue figures centrally in the belief that natural resource wealth dissuades state building because it satiates a ruler's revenue imperative.[64]

There is no widely accepted, specific definition of what constitutes an international commodity boom. Cashin, McDermott, and Scott offer an influential definition and conceptualize a commodity boom as a general and sometimes precipitous rise in international commodity prices, compared to prices for manufactured products. But unlike Cashin, McDermott, and Scott, who conduct shorter term analysis, I analyze longer term secular trends associated with commodity price increases. (They find that the average commodity price cycle was about 5.6 years between 1957 and 1999.)[65] I emphasize secular trends because state building is a long-term process.[66] Highlighting secular trends, rather than individual trade cycles, better aligns developments in the international economy with their associated state building.

[61] Cashin, McDermott, and Scott (2002) and Deaton (1999: 28–33). On commodity price uncertainty, see Dehn (2000).

[62] Valenzuela and Valenzuela (1978). Recent scholarship indicates that commodity specialization and its accompanying price volatility have been central to growth throughout the "periphery" historically (Blattman, Hwang, and Williamson 2007).

[63] The focus on hard economic times as instigators of noteworthy political contestation and change stems in part from the belief that such times are uncommon and constitute critical junctures (e.g., Gourevitch 1986). Yet in contemporary primary commodity markets, at least, booms—not slumps—are relatively uncommon (Cashin, McDermott, and Scott 2002), suggesting that boom times may be more destabilizing than hard times to the economic and political status quo.

[64] E.g., Doner, Ritchie, and Slater (2005) and Smith (2007: 54).

[65] Cashin, McDermott, and Scott (2002).

[66] Dunning (2008) similarly analyzes secular trends in his analysis of natural resource wealth and regime dynamics.

The case studies analyzed herein coincided with the two largest upward secular trends in commodity prices since 1800. The first boom occurred during the long nineteenth century, from 1800 to 1914 or so. Falling transport costs, Europe's industrial revolution, and trade liberalization (notably with independence in Latin America) stimulated growth in commodity exports to Western Europe. Ronald Rogowski characterizes the period after 1840 in particular as hitherto "recorded history's swiftest and most comprehensive expansion of international commerce." Countries in the global periphery, including Latin America and Mauritius, enjoyed an upward trend in their terms of trade throughout the century. Following a secular bust during the interwar period, a second major trade boom began at the end of the Second World War and continues today. European reconstruction, the Korean War, and further liberalization facilitated trade growth which "eclipsed" the nineteenth-century boom. The early years of this boom were particularly auspicious for commodity producers in Africa and elsewhere, though since the 1980s commodity prices have experienced a secular decline even as global trade has remained robust.[67] The booms experienced in each case study were part of general changes in the international economy.

How an international commodity boom came to affect political development in each case study ultimately hinged on coalitional politics. I take the type of political coalition present in each country at the time of its commodity boom as a given initial condition. The book's explanatory strength is little compromised by this starting point, as there does not seem to be any factor systematically responsible for variation in coalition types in the six cases under investigation. Prevailing coalitions were forged largely by case-specific factors, and I identify the historical developments that yielded a particular coalition in each case study chapter. The rise of coalitions led by political elites in Nigeria and Ghana, for instance, stemmed from various developments, including the depletion of colonial resources, urbanization, and growing trade unionism during the Second World War. Similarly, Colombia's coalition type shifted occasionally during the nineteenth century. From 1850 to 1880, economic actors with tenuous links to export markets ruled Colombia but were displaced by a coalition of political elites before the country experienced its coffee boom in 1887. Regardless of how a particular political coalition came into being, once commodity booms struck, coalitions led by political elites and those led by export-oriented actors behaved contrastingly toward policy questions with state building implications.

[67] Williamson (2012). Quotes from Rogowski (1989: 21, 88).

Theoretical Relaxations

To better and more realistically appreciate how commodity booms have affected state building historically, I augment some of my simplifying assumptions made earlier. First, commodity booms do not affect all economic actors in a given country, so I focus narrowly herein on "export-oriented actors," a subset of economic actors. Export-oriented actors are involved directly in the production or marketing of export commodities. Other economic actors have lesser connections to exporting, so commodity booms are felt unevenly within a political economy. Some economic actors are indirectly associated with export sectors, as suppliers of foodstuffs to workers in mining enclaves, for example, and thus inclined to support the promotion of export sectors. Others lack any noteworthy connection to exporting. "Economic actors" therefore vary in their inclination to politically support export activities. However, the six ruling coalitions I analyze in this book were led either by "export-oriented actors" (with direct stakes in exporting) or political elites; no coalitions were led by economic actors with indirect or absent interests in exporting. Going forward, I conceptually distinguish between export-oriented actors and political elites.

Second, I mark coalitions based on whether they were led by export-oriented actors or political elites but do not claim that a coalition's leader implies homogeneous membership (e.g., that coalitions led by export-oriented actors only encapsulate export-oriented actors, or even just economic actors). Coalitional membership is rarely homogeneous, but the restrictive assumption made earlier was valuable to suggest an evident contrast in the types of side-payments that each coalition leader ought to prefer. This expectation is reasonable, given that a booming export sector affords a luring fiscal target and also that there was insubstantial wealth outside of the export sectors in my case studies. I find in the book's case studies that coalitions led by export-oriented actors crafted side-payments that facilitated exports, whereas coalitions led by political elites devised side-payments that fleeced export sectors.

Third, as a corollary to the recognition that coalitions have heterogeneous membership, I do not presume that export-oriented actors are fully encapsulated within or excluded from any given ruling coalition. Many countries export multiple commodities, so the actors associated with one export commodity could be part of the ruling coalition, while those associated with another commodity may be politically marginalized. There can also be proprietorial and spatial differentiation with respect to a single export commodity. Chile featured such differentiation, for example. The country's wheat-producing landed elites from the northern central valley dominated politics, yet small-scale wheat farmers in the southern periphery were thoroughly marginalized. Thus, commodity booms can simultaneously enrich export-oriented actors within and outside of the ruling political coalition.

Explanatory Implications

These theoretical relaxations enable a fuller appreciation of how international commodity booms influence state building processes. The rudimentary logic presented earlier implied that the two potential state building outgrowths of commodity booms were mutually exclusive. First, I argued that a coalition led by economic actor A would provide public goods to assist its economic aims, with favorable implications for the growth of state capacity, but not strengthen institutions since it was the beneficiary of boom times. Second, I noted why a coalition led by economic actor B would not provide public goods but would build stronger institutions to frustrate the rise of economic actor A. Third, I argued that coalitions led by political elites would not embark on either state building project because of their flexibility in coalition building. But, in actuality, commodity booms can yield "dual enrichment"—situations in which a boom's direct economic benefits accrue to export-oriented actors encapsulated within the ruling coalition, as well as to exporters who are excluded from political power. This recognition makes it theoretically possible for a commodity boom to induce both public goods provision and institutional strengthening (see table 2.4).

Table 2.4 summarizes how international commodity booms affected state building in my six case studies. In the three cases where export-oriented actors led the ruling political coalition, the state provided new public goods, with positive effects on state capacity. Mauritius expanded its state capacity as a result of politically dominant sugar planters demanding and receiving new public goods, like the coercive "regulation" of the island's labor force. In Chile and Argentina, which featured situations of dual enrichment, governments supplied new public goods to ruling coalition members when asked. They also designed new impure public goods in ways that provided lesser relief of the economic bottlenecks facing exporters who were excluded from political

Table 2.4 **Commodity Booms, Coalitional Politics, and State Building**

Boom's Benefits Accrue	*Public Goods Provision*	*Institution Building*
Within ruling coalition	**Yes**[a] *Mauritius*	No *Mauritius*
Dual enrichment	**Yes**[a] *Chile, Argentina*	**Yes** *Chile, Argentina*
Outside of ruling coalition	No *Colombia, Ghana, Nigeria*	No *Colombia, Ghana, Nigeria*

Note: Bold text and shading designate cases featuring a growth in state capacity. Case study outcomes italicized.

[a] Impure public goods provided to the distributive benefit of ruling coalition members.

power. Chile founded a mortgage bank to aid credit access but restricted collateral to agrarian real estate, which shut out political marginal northern mine owners. This practice also advantaged powerful landed elites around Santiago, where land values were higher, compared to politically marginalized yeomen agriculturalists in the south. The Argentine state behaved similarly, establishing a mortgage bank in Buenos Aires province, the ruling coalition's heartland, while declining to authorize similar institutions where the opposition thrived. In Colombia, Ghana, and Nigeria, where political elites led the ruling coalition, governments refused to provide public goods to export-oriented actors. These countries consequently missed an opportunity to expand state capacity from public goods provision.

Each country's institutional trajectory was also influenced by how its commodity boom intersected with coalitional politics. Mauritius' sugar boom narrowly enriched members of the ruling political coalition, who felt no pressing rationale to overhaul institutions since they were the ones who gained relative power from the boom. Mauritian institutions remained largely unchanged. Chile and Argentina experienced dramatic institutional change, however, because their commodity booms produced dual enrichment. Situations of dual enrichment are exceptionally propitious for institutional strengthening. Recall from the prior subsection my reasoning for why economic actor B would feel fundamentally threatened by boom times in economic sector A. First, actor B would fear the rise of actor A because an ensuing coalitional change would make it the target of actor A's side-payments. Second, actor B's potential coalitional exclusion would prevent it from obtaining state-supplied public goods and probably restrict its ability to maximize economic power in the future. The threat is not simply political but rather jeopardizes the source from which actor B generates social power. Such a diametrical threat will convince actor B that it faces potentially catastrophic costs from inaction and provoke the movement toward unmediated institutions.

In the context of resource booms, such an exigent and diametrical threat develops when a boom enriches coalitional insiders and outsiders who derive their social power from the same export activities. Because commodity exports are so easily taxed, countries in which exporters are excluded from political power typically tax them disproportionately. Such was the case for politically marginalized exporters in Chile, Argentina, Colombia, Ghana, and Nigeria. In these countries, resource booms augmented these marginalized actors' collective economic power and prompted them to seek new distributive political power. Boom times destabilized politics. One could imagine a situation in which these marginalized exporters did not supply the pecuniary resources for the ruling coalition's side-payments and could be brought into an enlarged coalition. But ruling coalitions in these cases funded their side-payments with export wealth, which made accommodating surging exporters implausible. Furthermore, these countries had small, undiversified economies that did not lend themselves to myriad side-payment regimes. Rising exporters therefore imperiled the basis upon which ruling coalition members maintained cooperation.

Yet, as I note in table 2.4, institutional strengthening occurred only in Chile and Argentina and not in Colombia, Ghana, or Nigeria—even though commodity booms enriched political outsiders in all five countries. Circumstances of dual enrichment yield a threat that differs fundamentally from situations in which a boom's direct benefits accrue solely outside of the ruling coalition. In situations of dual enrichment, export-oriented actors encapsulated within the ruling coalition anticipate that if they are displaced from power, their economic endeavors will almost certainly fund the new coalition's side-payments. They also recognize that coalitional change will disable them from obtaining public goods, something they regularly regard as necessary to maximize economic power. And, crucially, those export-oriented actors currently in power realize that rising but presently marginalized exporters would be the ones to reap the relative gains from new impure public goods. Coalitional exclusion would imply declining power and relative impoverishment. Rising exporters therefore pose a threat that is diametrical and existential.

The diametrical threats that developed in Chile and Argentina were especially intense because coalitional outsiders gained relative economic power during each country's first major commodity boom. Ruling coalition members funded their side-payments with economic surplus generated by rising exporters, which made accommodating them impossible. Chile levied comparatively high taxes on the copper sector and concentrated expenditures in the northern central valley, home to the ruling coalition. Coalitional insiders in Argentina used their control over the Buenos Aires port to tax trade to-and-fro the interior provinces, where the opposition flourished. Ruling coalition members were also seeking state-supplied public goods and knew that coalitional change would prevent them from fully exploiting ripe export opportunities. Political contention in Chile and Argentina spawned civil war, which further solidified power holders' view that institution building was needed. An 1851 civil war in Chile demonstrated to ruling coalition members that, if they lost power, a new ruling coalition would upend fiscal policy and redirect public goods outside of the northern central valley. Ruling coalition members in 1850s Argentina were convinced that their opponents were collaborating with Indians to conduct raids in southern Buenos Aires province, which had pushed the frontier back to its 1836 limit and halted ranching expansion.

Ruling coalition members perceived that coalitional outsiders posed an elemental danger to their generative aim.

By contrast, when the direct benefits of a commodity boom accrue outside of the ruling coalition—that is, when political elites lead the ruling coalition—the threat posed to coalition insiders is less grave. Political elites worry less about coalitional change because their social power ultimately comes from extra-economic sources. They will not regard themselves as the probable target of a new side-payments regime and are less likely to consider public goods vital to their well-being. Political elites will consequently deem rising exporters to be a political menace but not a basic impediment to generating social power. Even so, political elites have much to gain by holding the reins of political power. Yet the fact that rising exporters do not constitute a diametrical and existential threat will likely convince political elites that institutional change would be imprudent due to its costs and uncertainty.

It was the diametrical threat—not civil war per se—which provoked the movement toward unmediated institutions in Chile and Argentina. In fact, Ghana and Colombia also featured armed confrontations between ruling coalition members and rising exporters—but significant institutional strengthening did not follow. Political elites led the ruling coalitions in Ghana and Colombia, so rising exporters constituted to a serious political challenge but not a diametrical threat. Rather than pursue unmediated institutions, ruling coalition members utilized non-institutional means to inhibit their opponents. In Ghana, the government would occasionally raise the purchasing price for cocoa paid by the state-run marketing board and momentarily temper hostility. And although a vicious civil war decimated Colombia's coffee economy, power holders were not themselves coffee owners and could maintain their coalition with the government printing press. Ruling coalition members in Ghana and Colombia perceived that rising exporters posed a different type of threat than did their counterparts in Chile and Argentina, largely because of the different sources of these actors' social power. Overall, these six countries varied in many ways, but there were consistent patterns in how commodity booms intersected with coalitional politics and influenced their state building trajectories.

Case Selection and Measurement

CASE SELECTION

I illustrate how coalitional politics affected these boom-induced state building opportunities through a comparative historical analysis of three Latin

American and three African cases.[68] Above all, I employ process tracing to indicate the viability of a coalitional approach to explaining state building trajectories during resource booms. Process tracing refers to the illumination of the historical process or sequence through which some hypothesized causal factors produced (or failed to produce) an outcome of interest. A virtue of process tracing and within-case analysis is that one can identify the causal mechanisms responsible for observed outcomes in a particular case. Process tracing can help explain why state building happened as it happened, in other words.[69] There are two ways the reader could view this research design. One might conservatively conclude, as I am inclined to, that the arguments advanced in this book adequately explain the six cases under investigation and should be applied to additional cases to further probe their veracity. Others might draw more aggressive conclusions from this research design, however, since the identification of the relevant causal mechanisms in these cases arguably discounts the plausibility of rival explanatory mechanisms in the larger population to which these cases belong.[70]

The cases I examine were broadly similar to most developing countries historically, as they had been colonized, featured weak institutions, and were agrarian. These boundary conditions serve as the backdrop to my theoretical arguments. First, as I note earlier, these six countries were oriented to primary commodity production during colonialism and should have been sensitive to the economic opportunities afforded by commodity booms. Second, each country was weakly institutionalized and exhibited low state capacity in general, which I discuss further in the following subsection. This initial condition is significant, as much international political economy scholarship (and research on "open economy politics" in particular) considers institutions to be the key force mediating the influence of the international economy, especially in advanced industrial democracies.[71] Studies of the resource curse do likewise, maintaining that strong institutions are the best way that countries can avoid the pitfalls associated with resource wealth.[72] My focus on weakly institutionalized polities eliminates the possibility that robust institutions account for the way in which a country managed its commodity boom. I furthermore

[68] See Mahoney and Rueschemeyer (2003) on comparative historical analysis.

[69] See especially George and Bennett (2005: 6–7, 135–149, 205–232); Hedström and Swedberg (1998: 21–23); and Mahoney (2012). My approach has affinities with what Hall (2003) terms "systematic process analysis," Sil (2010) calls "cross-regional contextualized comparison," and Skocpol and Somers (1980: 176–178, 191–192) refer to as a "parallel demonstration of theory."

[70] Waldner (2007).

[71] See Lake (2009) and Acemoglu, Robinson, and Verdier (2004).

[72] Mehlum, Moene, and Torvik (2006) and Robinson, Torvik, and Verdier (2006).

examine these countries' first major commodity booms, as a means to eliminate potential prior "learning effects" that might have affected policymakers during subsequent booms.[73] Third, I limit my analysis to agrarian societies, even though some industrialized countries, like Norway, are noteworthy primary commodity exporters. I exclude industrial states from consideration because they are more likely to possess strong institutions. A focus on developing societies helps to isolate the influence of coalitional politics.

My case studies conform to these basic boundary conditions, despite their manifest differences. Their disparateness makes it easier to emphasize what these countries shared—principally, a reliance on primary commodity exporting for their economic vitality and exporters requesting state support of their economic and political endeavors. I chose these particular cases because they display variation in my independent and dependent variables: political coalitions and state building trajectories. By analyzing coalitional variation within and between each region, these case studies suggest the fruitfulness of my arguments to better understanding state building variation throughout Latin America and Africa. Overall, these case studies amount to a group of "diverse" cases, which analyze variation in explanatory and dependent variables and thereby hopefully "enhance the representativeness of the sample of cases chosen by the researcher."[74]

MEASUREMENT

I utilize a multifaceted measurement scheme to illustrate how coalitional variance led to state building divergence in the six countries under investigation. Recall that I conceptualize state capacity as the ability of state managers to penetrate society by extracting resources, exercising coercion, and deploying authority via political alliances, the military, or an administrative apparatus. Whereas many studies of state building try to account for changes in revenue extraction, this book strives to explain instances of public goods provision and institutional strengthening.[75] The provision of new public goods and the building of stronger institutions are more closely connected to coercive and

[73] Of my cases, Colombia had the most experience with commodity exporting before its coffee boom, having undergone small and ephemeral booms in other commodities during 1850–80. Yet this experience did not help Colombia adroitly manage its coffee boom. Rather, a coalition of political elites encapsulated within the Conservative Party preyed on coffee, in sharp contrast to the support that the export-oriented Liberal Party had lent incipient exporters between 1850 and 1880. Chapter 6 elaborates this theme.

[74] Seawright and Gerring (2008: 300–301).

[75] However I do discuss extractive capacity in each case study in order to gain leverage over alternative hypotheses.

penetrative power than extractive capacity (see table 2.1). My measurement scheme accordingly probes only those facets of state capacity in which I attempt to explain change, including the establishment of territorial control, the invigoration of penetrative capacity, and the elaboration of the state's regulative functions. Below I describe my measurement proxies and then briefly summarize how these indicators fared during each country's first major commodity boom. The result, I believe, is a nuanced assessment of the extent to which state building did, or did not, occur in each country.

Measures of Public Goods Provision

As I note earlier, there are myriad public goods that can be supplied by the state or private actors. My three indicators of public goods provision probe the particular public goods that exporters regularly asked the state to provide in the book's case studies. (I discuss public goods that were unique to a particular case study in its respective chapter, though their provision or lack thereof paralleled the trends depicted in table 2.5.) These three proxies suggest whether state managers enhanced their coercive and penetrative capabilities as a result of exporters' public goods seeking. First, I assess if states pacified their national territories, which signals coercive power. Second, I measure the density of railroads and, in some cases, roadways; both proxies indicate the logistical infrastructure available to and suggest the penetrative capacity of the central state. Third, I measure a country's perceived investment climate, as indicated by bond yield spreads versus British Consols. I use this proxy as an indirect measure of a country's ruling coalition and whether its government assisted exporters, such as by promoting credit availability. Table 2.5 reveals that the countries with export-oriented coalitions—Chile, Argentina, and Mauritius—repeatedly provided public goods, while the countries led by political elites—Colombia, Ghana, and Nigeria—did not.

A first measure of public goods provision assesses if a country has achieved territorial pacification, the process through which state officials eliminate "rival claimants to the national territory" and establish that only they "may have access to the means of violence."[76] Territorial pacification indicates state coercive power. I mark territorial pacification by the absence of significant regional revolts and regional warlords. Warlords (e.g., *caudillos*) signal a governmental inability to control the national territory, even if a tenuous alliance between state leaders and regional power holders prevails. In Chile and Argentina, exporters pressed for and received territorial pacification to advance their economic interests. In Colombia and Nigeria, by contrast, regionalist violence

[76] Centeno (2002: 108–109).

Table 2.5 **Indicators of Public Goods Provision and Institutional Characteristics at Beginning and End of Each Case Study**

		Chile (1848–1883)	*Argentina (1852–1886)*	*Mauritius (1825–1895)*	*Colombia (1880–1905)*	*Ghana (1945–1966)*	*Nigeria (1945–1966)*
Indicators of public goods provision	Overall judgment: public goods provided to exporters?	**Yes**	**Yes**	**Yes**	No	No	No
	Territorial pacification? (date of last regional rebellion)	No → **Yes** (1881)	No → **Yes** (1881)	Yes → Yes	No → No (1950s)	No → **Yes** (1956)	No → No (ongoing)
	Logistical resources: railroad and/or road density	RR: None → **.0029**	RR: None → **.0022**	RR: None → **.0895**	RR: .00004 → .0006	RR: .0035 → .0042 Road: .05 → .13	RR: .0034 → .0038 Road: .04 → .08
	Investment climate: bond yield spread vs. British Consols (%)	**2.4**	**3.2**	**“1.7”**	4.8 (8.9)	—	—

continued

Table 2.5 **(continued)**

		Chile (1848–1883)	*Argentina (1852–1886)*	*Mauritius (1825–1895)*	*Colombia (1880–1905)*	*Ghana (1945–1966)*	*Nigeria (1945–1966)*
Indicators of institutional characteristics	Overall judgment: institutions mediated or unmediated?	Mediated → **Unmediated**	Mediated → **Mediation waning**	Mediated → Mediated	Mediated → Mediated	Mediated → Mediated	Mediated → Mediated
	Mayors: state controls appointment?	No → **Yes**	No → **Yes**	None → **Yes**	No → No	No → No	No → No
	Municipal fiscal affairs: controlled from center?	No → **Yes**	No → No	None → No	No → No	No → No	No → No
	Local elections: central state intervention?	No → **Yes**	No → **Somewhat**	None → No	No → No	No → No	None → No
	Judicial system: discernible strengthening?	**Yes**	**Yes**	**Yes**	No	No	No

Note: Bold text and shading indicate a significant improvement of proxy. Data sources listed in the paragraphs and case study chapters that follow.

was common. Colombia fought a catastrophic civil war from 1899 to 1902. Nigeria experienced a secessionist civil war in 1967–70, and its oil-rich Niger Delta region today remains beset by insurgent groups.[77] I consider Ghana to have achieved territorial pacification during its boom period, after deflecting a violent challenge from cocoa farmers in 1956. But, in general, countries with export-oriented ruling coalitions were more likely to pacify their territories than those governed by political elites.

My second measure of public goods is the density of transportation infrastructure, indicated as the amount of railroad and/or roads relative to a country's overall territory. Exporters routinely sought improved transportation infrastructure to facilitate their economic goals, and new transportation infrastructure qualified as a local public good when it was part of an integrated network. Transportation infrastructure can have spillover effects for state capacity, as it can enable the government to rapidly deploy agents to suppress an internal disturbance, for instance. I measure railroad density for my nineteenth-century cases, as railroads were the key new means through which governments then reached into their interiors.[78] I measure railway and road density for my two twentieth-century African cases, because the data are available and because African governments emphasized road building after the Second World War. I provide qualitative judgments in the case studies regarding the extent to which a country's transportation infrastructure was integrated, which is vital to enhancing penetrative capacity.[79] Overall, I find the greatest gains in logistical infrastructure in the countries ruled by export-oriented coalitions, even though there was analogous demand for improved infrastructure in all six countries.

My most difficult measurement challenge is connecting state assistance with credit accessibility to a growth in state capacity. There is no plain and direct measurement proxy that clearly indicates if governments aided credit accessibility, which is one reason why the case study narratives are so valuable. But in the interest of a summary presentation of case study outcomes, I have selected a highly indirect measure that implies if policymakers supported exporters, including through beneficial credit market intervention. I list the

[77] International Crisis Group (2009).

[78] Migdal (1988: 73–79). Moreover, good data on roads in nineteenth-century Latin America are not available.

[79] And quantitative metrics can be deceiving. What qualifies as an African "road" might be a footpath passable only during the dry season (Herbst 2000: 85). My railroad data are from Mitchell (1998a, 1998b) and road density measures are from Herbst (2000: 86). Herbst's latter road density figure for Ghana may be high: the International Road Federation (1978) pegs Ghana's 1973 road density at 0.09, of which 20 percent was tarred.

yield spreads between debt issued by my four nineteenth-century cases versus British Consols, perpetual bonds issued by the British government, between 1877 and 1913.[80] I compare the Latin American countries' spreads to other countries that had also previously defaulted on their sovereign debt; the peer group average was 3.4 percent above what British Consols paid. Countries whose debt scored below the peer group mean, including Argentina and Chile, were regarded as comparatively safe investments in the London bond market.[81] I have accordingly shaded and bolded their scores in table 2.5, as I do with other indicators that imply comparatively impressive outcomes. Colombia scores above the peer group average, meaning that its debt was regarded as riskier. In fact, Colombian bond yield spreads periodically exceeded 20 percent during this era, leading some scholars to treat these data as outliers and exclude them from analysis.[82] If one includes all observations for Colombia during the 1870–1913 period, its average yield spread versus British Consols rises to 8.9 percent.[83]

I believe that variance in bond yield spreads implies differences in ruling coalitions and, more tangentially, government behavior in domestic credit markets for one simple reason.[84] Sovereign debt was not denominated in domestic currencies, but instead in the creditor's currency (or gold). Debtors had to come up with pounds (or francs, or gold) to pay their creditors, and the best way to do so was by exporting. Indeed, countries with higher exports per capita featured lower bond yields and smaller spreads versus British Consols.[85] These findings suggest that investors found countries with flourishing exports to be safer investments. Many factors affect export levels, of course, but export-oriented coalitions contribute positively to them. Moreover, Flandreau et al. find that underwriters played an important informational role in nineteenth-century debt markets. The largest firms, such as Rothschild, tended to underwrite relatively safe bond issues as a way to offer solid products, acquire prestige for the firm, and attract capital. It is perhaps telling that much of Argentina's and Chile's debt issues were underwritten by Baring Brothers,

[80] The Latin American data come from Mauro, Sussman, and Yafeh (2006); Mauritius' data are from Accominotti, Flandreau, and Rezzik (2011).

[81] Mauro, Sussman, and Yafeh (2006: 93).

[82] Accominotti, Flandreau, and Rezzik (2011: 392 n. 25).

[83] Calculations based on data from Mauro, Sussman, and Yafeh (2006).

[84] Stasavage (2011: 90–93) supports the notion that such financial data can indicate political coalitions, as he finds that city-states in early modern Europe in which merchants enjoyed formal political representation featured lower long-term borrowing costs than countries in which these capital-rich actors were politically marginalized.

[85] Tomz (2007: 61–63) and Mauro, Sussman, and Yafeh (2006: 95–97), respectively.

the second largest underwriter in Latin America, while Colombia's issues were handled by the smaller London and Country Bank.[86]

I also indicate the spread on Mauritian debt ("1.7" percent), though this datum should be read as suggestive and not straightforwardly comparable to the Latin American statistics. Scholars agree that colonies like Mauritius borrowed more cheaply in capital markets during the first wave of global capital expansion (1880–1913) because they were "subsovereign" entities of the British Crown. I arrive at the "1.7" percent figure by taking the average yield spread between Mauritian bonds and British Consols (0.93 percent) and adding to it 0.75 percent, which is the difference in the average spread versus British Consols between British colonies and sovereign debtors during 1880–1913.[87] My point is that Mauritian debt was relatively well regarded, as was Chilean and Argentine debt. Finally, I have not made similar measures for twentieth-century Ghana and Nigeria, as such comparisons would be even more fraught with pitfalls, in part because average bond yield spreads have varied throughout time.[88]

I use the measures of bond yield spreads to suggest variation in coalition type, as well as government assistance to exporters in general. One would expect countries with export-oriented coalitions to do more to facilitate exports, including making credit more widely available when exporters wanted it. Among my four nineteenth-century cases, the three countries with export-oriented coalitions displayed considerably lower bond spreads than Colombia, the country governed by political elites.[89] And, as table 2.5 indicates, the countries with export-oriented coalitions had more remarkable gains in logistical infrastructure, even though it was uniformly sought after by exporters. The measurement proxies of public goods in table 2.5 display a remarkable consistency with respect to coalition type.

[86] Flandreau et al. (2010) and also Marichal (1989: 243) and Mauro, Sussman, and Yafeh (2006: 168–169).

[87] Data from Accominotti, Flandreau, and Rezzik (2011) and available at http://eh.net/databases/finance. Mauritius' bond yields were slightly below the average of other British colonies at the time (3.71 versus 3.77 percent). Ferguson and Schularick (2006) find an even larger "empire effect" of 1.75 percent. Yet even if one uses the larger rebate, Mauritian debt was still well regarded, especially compared to Colombian debt. Finally, if one measures Mauritian bond spreads only during the years of my case study with available data (1880–1895), the country's average spread rises slightly, to "1.8" percent.

[88] Flandreau et al. (2010).

[89] Peru also featured enormous bond spreads in the 1880s (Accominotti, Flandreau, and Rezzik 2011: 392 n. 25). I elsewhere suggest (in Saylor 2012: 320) that Peru, like Colombia, was ruled by a non-export-oriented coalition.

Measures of Institutions

The second set of measurement indicators probes the movement toward unmediated institutions.[90] Central states establish unmediated rule as they supplant local notables as the pivotal administrative force at the local level. I measure such a development with four proxies: if central state officials control mayoral appointments; their oversight of municipal fiscal affairs; if they directly intervene in local elections; and the strengthening of a national judicial system. These four indicators collectively suggest the extent to which central state officials are increasing their oversight and influence of local affairs. These proxies are not the only conceivable markers of unmediated institutions, of course, but they help to signify the growth of state capacity where it occurred in the cases under investigation.

One indicator of the movement toward unmediated institutions is whether the central government controls mayoral appointments.[91] I specifically have de facto, not just de jure, power in mind. Sometimes central state officials possess the legal right to unilaterally appoint mayors but, in practice, only appoint those individuals regarded as palatable by local notables. Such de facto limitations signal mediated institutions. For instance, Colombia passed a constitution in 1886 which ostensibly overhauled local administration and centralized power, but presidents continued to exercise only qualified authority at best over mayors.[92] Before 1854, the Chilean president possessed the authority under an 1844 law to unilaterally appoint Intendants, who were formally endowed with comprehensive powers. But, in actuality, the Interior Minister negotiated with local elites over who would be appointed.[93] When Chile truly began usurping local prerogatives in 1854, people protested in the streets.[94]

I similarly gauge the state's influence over municipal fiscal affairs. Local notables often entrench themselves with patronage networks, which hamper the ability of central state officials to exert their authority in localities. As central states gain power over municipal taxation and spending, they improve their ability to curtail the influence of local powerbrokers. As with mayoral appointments, however, oftentimes municipalities rely on government subsidies for their operations but still operate autonomously. I therefore code this proxy

[90] Unlike my indicators of public goods, which are drawn from the handful of sources listed in the footnotes above, most of my measures of institutional characteristics come from sources specific to each case study. The sources for the summary judgments I provide in table 2.5 are identified in the following chapters, particularly when I assess each country's state capacity at the beginning and end of its chapter.

[91] Hagopian (1996: 47).

[92] Posada-Carbó (1996a: 222).

[93] Cáceres Muñoz (2005) and Valenzuela (1996: 237–238).

[94] Sotomayor (1856: 29).

conservatively. Localities in Ghana and Nigeria, for example, depended heavily on grants from the central state but retained considerable spending discretion. Similarly, by the 1880s Argentine President Julio Roca could align mayors' interests with his own due to his control over credit from the Banco Nacional, but his influence was not hegemonic.[95] Only in Chile did central state authorities domineer municipal fiscal activities,[96] which indicated unmediated institutions.

A third indicator of institutions examines the extent to which central state officials influenced local elections, particularly when ruling coalition members wanted to neutralize opposition candidates. All six countries under investigation featured elections, although they were not serious mechanisms of democratic accountability.[97] But when ruling coalition members desired to manipulate electoral outcomes, their ability or inability to do so indicated if they could extend the state's tentacles into local affairs.[98] Indeed, Steven Levitsky and Lucan Way note that "Whereas some state institutions . . . uphold a democratic rule of law, others provide mechanisms to suppress opposition and maintain political hegemony."[99] Five of the six ruling coalitions examined in the book faced political opposition concentrated in regional strongholds. (The exception was Mauritius.) Elections were thus moments when ruling coalition members would try to engineer electoral victories in opposition areas, such as by controlling the local election boards that made judgments on voter eligibility. The ability to produce electoral victories in opposition strongholds signaled noteworthy institutional power, particularly since government manipulation was generally subtler than outright ballot stuffing. In Chile, the ruling coalition's presidential candidate in 1851 was resoundingly defeated in the regional peripheries; but once the central government began to usurp the functions of local electoral boards after 1854, it was able to defeat opposition candidates. Similar but less dramatic control developed in Argentina. In Ghana, by contrast, Kwame Nkrumah's government tried to curtail opposition in the Asante heartland but was unable to sway elections. Election results help to establish which countries witnessed unmistakable strides in institutional control, especially in opposition areas.

My final measure of institutional strengthening examines judicial institutions. Courts are "procedural institutions par excellence . . . [and help] define relations between state and society."[100] Where one finds evidence of a

[95] Rock (2002: 117–119).

[96] Soifer (2006: 271–274).

[97] On elections in non-democratic contexts, see Gandhi (2008); Levitsky and Way (2010); and Posada-Carbó (1996b).

[98] Cf. Slater (2008: 259–260).

[99] Levitsky and Way (2010: 57).

[100] Skowronek (1982: 27).

strengthening national court system, one finds local notables being displaced from their de facto judicial roles by actors more beholden to the central state. Although a budding national court system does not suddenly eliminate the influence of local notables, it does create a means to curtail their power. I assess whether a country's judicial system underwent discernible strengthening during the case study period, which I discuss in each respective chapter. Summary judgments are necessary for table 2.5 because of the trickiness in differentiating de jure from de facto judicial development, as well as the relative underdevelopment of research on state building and judicial systems, something scholars working in this area often lament.[101] My admittedly rough appraisals of these countries' judicial systems are meant to help bridge that gulf and provide a further indication of institutional change, where it occurred.

The seven indicators I employ generally align with my overall assessment of which countries experienced palpable gains in state capacity following their first major commodity booms and which ones did not. This measurement scheme is meant to descriptively evoke the meaning of the concepts under investigation, and one should not regard it as a straightforward assessment of my causal arguments. Measurement is an endeavor separate from explanation. I have simply selected indictors that scholars recognize as capable of making pertinent distinctions in the concepts under investigation.[102] Accordingly, my causal arguments are not intended to explain discrete changes in each measurement indicator. I am merely striving to explain change in an overarching concept, the content of which is probed in different ways by my indicators. So, for instance, I do not purport to explain why Argentine state builders chose to exert their influence through local electoral processes, rather than over municipal fiscal affairs. But I do have an argument for why they moved in the direction of unmediated rule. Overall, these measurement proxies collectively suggest the gain in state capacity, or lack thereof, in each case. Assessing the explanatory veracity of my arguments is best left to the process tracing in each case study chapter, as it is the evidence linking commodity booms, coalitional politics, and state building.

Alternative Hypotheses

Another means to judge my arguments is by evaluating alternative approaches to state building and how well they explain the six cases under investigation.

[101] E.g., Chambers (2013). Tilly (1975: 9) considered the judicial system to be the "chief omission" of his seminal edited volume on European state formation: "it is easy to forget how large a part certain kinds of courts played in the day-to-day construction of Western states."

[102] I discuss these themes in Saylor (2013).

I conclude this chapter by briefly considering four prominent explanations of state building: bellicist models, the resource curse, colonial legacies, and ethnic diversity. I discuss these alternative explanations and find them to be less compelling accounts of the state building observed in each case study chapter. I also illustrate, in table 2.6, that none of these rival hypotheses' predictive expectations align with the state building vicissitudes in my six case studies as a whole. That said, this book does not claim to be a simple refutation of competing theories. There are nevertheless reasons why one might find these general theoretical frameworks wanting, which serves as part of my justification to advance an alternative theory of state building in the developing world.

BELLICIST THEORIES

Many studies on state formation take as their point of departure the work of Charles Tilly, who memorably wrote that "war made the state, and the state made war." Incessant warfare in Europe between the sixteenth and eighteenth centuries gradually led to standing bureaucracies and the institutions today associated with the modern state, largely as a functional outgrowth of

Table 2.6 **Expectations of Rival Hypotheses**

	Argentina	*Chile*	*Mauritius*	*Colombia*	*Ghana*	*Nigeria*
Bellicist (bellicist pressures → stronger state)	Stronger	Stronger	*Weaker*	Weaker	Weaker	Weaker
Resource curse (minable resources → weak state)	Stronger	*Weaker*[a]	Stronger	*Stronger*	*Stronger*	*Stronger*
Colonial legacies ("high liberalism" → stronger state)[b]	*Weaker*	*Weaker*	Stronger	Weaker	Weaker	Weaker
Ethnic diversity (ethnic diversity → weak state)[c]	Stronger	*Weaker*	*Weaker*	Weaker	Weaker	Weaker

Note: Italicized text indicates misprediction by rival hypothesis.

[a] Due to copper.

[b] Expectations derived from Lange, Mahoney, and vom Hau (2006: 1419–1420, 1437–1438), who compare Spanish and British colonialism.

[c] I assume countries scoring above Fearon's (2003) global mean of ethnic fractionalization are inclined to have weak states, and vice versa.

preparing for war and servicing wartime debts afterward.[103] The revenue imperative serves as the prime mechanism linking geopolitical competition to state building.

The lack of such endemic warfare in the non-European world suggests why many developing countries have not followed the path carved by European state builders. Indeed, early modern Europe was "an unusually warlike multistate system."[104] Moreover, once powerful countries developed in Europe, they could dissuade war-making elsewhere, as during *Pax Britannia* and the Cold War. Outside of Europe, the relative lack of warfare has severed a chief pathway to new state capacity. And even when states in Latin America or Africa have gone to war, they could generally fund their activities with foreign aid or loans. The revenue imperative was thus less acute, which forestalled state building projects.[105]

My arguments are not direct competitors with this bellicist logic, although I do note its shortcomings in each case study. As I discuss earlier in the chapter, I am investigating facets of state capacity other than extractive (or taxing) capacity. Yet there are nonetheless reasons to question the applicability of bellicist logic to parts of the world that have featured little warfare but exhibit considerable state building variation, such as along South America's west coast, in the Middle East, and in Southeast Asia.[106] And even where researchers have found variation in state capacity among such countries, they find that their extractive capabilities are quite similar. Virtually all countries in Latin America and Africa historically depended on customs duties for revenue, regardless of if they were enmeshed in geopolitical competition.[107] For example, Chile was known as the Prussia of Latin America and a "land of war," but its revenue mix did not differ substantially from its neighbors. The observable implications of bellicist theory simply have not developed as manifestly as they did in early modern Europe.

THE RESOURCE CURSE

The importance of the government's revenue imperative has also been highlighted by scholars advancing the notion of a resource curse. This literature

[103] Tilly (1975: 42, 1992).

[104] Mann (2006: 268).

[105] Centeno (2002) and Herbst (2000). See Thies (2005, 2007) for a revisionist take which argues that external rivalries have positive state building byproducts, by way of the revenue imperative.

[106] Kurtz (2009: 490–491); Barnett (1992); and Slater (2010), respectively. See also Kacowicz (1998).

[107] See Centeno (2002: 116–126) and Herbst (2000: 113–121).

investigates various pathologies associated with natural resource wealth, including economic underperformance, feeble state institutions, authoritarian regimes, and civil war.[108] The conventional wisdom maintains that these problems are largely restricted to contemporary fuel and mineral exports, because they produce extraordinary rents that often accrue directly to the state. Rents eliminate the need to build taxing institutions; sever the democratizing impulses that come from bargaining over taxation; and encourage rent-seeking and corruption.[109] Scholars have long argued that spatially concentrated export activities, epitomized by mining, can be deleterious. These "enclave" sectors establish few linkages to other economic sectors and are tempting revenue targets, given asset immobility. Hence, mining enclaves tend to produce lower levels of state capacity, since revenue windfalls obviate the need for strong fiscal institutions. Agricultural exports, conversely, are considered to be comparatively auspicious because they render greater economic linkages and are spatially diffuse, which arguably impels the development of extractive capacity.[110]

However the fiscal pitfalls associated with fuel and mineral exports are a matter of degree—not kind—since it is easy to tax any commodity export.[111] Indeed, some researchers have found that the institutional debility found among fuel and mineral exporters is present in countries exporting spatially concentrated plantation crops, as well as coffee and cocoa.[112] Similarly, Robert Bates's study of African marketing boards suggests that institutional weakness in postwar Africa resulted partially from the ease with which agricultural exports could be taxed.[113] The fiscal pitfalls of natural resource wealth are arguably found in varying degrees in all commodity-dependent economies, even if these fiscal pathologies are most obvious and acute among contemporary fuel and mineral exporters.[114]

Although fuel and mineral commodities produce rents to a degree not found among agricultural commodities, the state building pathologies associated with fuel and mineral exports often elide the fact that rent capture by the government is ultimately a matter of fiscal policy. It can be avoided "when a

[108] Seminal statements respectively include Sachs and Warner (1995); Karl (1997); Ross (2001a); and Collier and Hoeffler (2002).

[109] Karl (1997: 48, 60); Leite and Weidmann (1999); Sala-i-Martin and Subramanian (2003); and Ross (2012: 4–6).

[110] Cardoso and Faletto (1979: 69–73); Gallo (1991); Hirschman (1977); and Shafer (1994: 35–36).

[111] E.g., Doner, Ritchie, and Slater (2005) and Smith (2007: 54).

[112] Isham et al. (2005).

[113] Bates (1981).

[114] Cf. Dunning (2008: 39–52).

concentrated and powerful domestic elite that is independent of the state owns and controls the natural resources"—as was the case with Bolivia's powerful *la Rosca* tin barons.[115] Similarly, during Chile's nitrate era (1880–1930), the state taxed but never nationalized the sector because nitrate interests were part of the ruling coalition, through pressure from the British (who controlled nitrate production) and domestic interests (considerable Chilean capital was invested in nitrates via domestic banks). When President José Manuel Balmaceda seemed poised to nationalize nitrates in 1890, ruling coalition members overthrew him.[116] These examples are remarkable because export-oriented actors tempered governmental acquisitiveness. Unfortunately, such cases are often regarded as anomalies, rather than consistent with a certain type of ruling coalition. Too many studies implicitly presume that political elites lead ruling coalitions in countries rich in fuel and minerals (or, more precisely, in countries that export fuel and minerals[117]). This coalitional dimension is often overlooked because the literature on the resource curse was energized by studies of oil producers since 1970, when state ownership has predominated.[118]

The comparatively sanguine outlook for agricultural producers likewise has much to do with implicit coalitional expectations. Export-oriented agriculturalists historically headed coalitions in Argentina, Brazil, and Chile, Latin America's most successful state builders.[119] Botswana and Mauritius are often cited as African countries that have avoided the resource curse,[120] and they happen to be governed by export-oriented coalitions. Consider, alternatively, what happened when coalitions of political elites presided over agricultural booms in postwar Africa. Governments used marketing boards to impose astounding taxes on export producers. They then directed agricultural surplus to fledgling urban industries and, through a variety of market manipulations, created administratively generated rents. The revenue derived from marketing boards functioned quite like the rents associated with mineral producers: they were determined largely by international price swings and fiscal policy. These policies, while economically damaging, made sense for African rulers, who relied on urbanites for political support.[121] None of my case studies featured rent-generating commodities, but their trajectories diverged in accordance to

[115] Dunning (2008: 38, 231–253).

[116] Zeitlin (1984: 71–131).

[117] Plenty of developed countries consume, rather than export, their fuel and mineral production (Schrank 2011).

[118] Jones Luong and Weinthal (2010: 6, 322–323).

[119] Cardoso and Faletto (1979: 40–69).

[120] E.g., Acemoglu, Robinson, and Verdier (2004: 166).

[121] Bates (1981: 96–103).

the coalitional logic described herein. Overall, one of my basic arguments is that greater examination of coalitional politics may enrich our understanding of why a resource curse takes hold in some countries but not others. I develop this argument more fully in the book's conclusion.

COLONIAL LEGACIES

A third approach to understanding state building in the non-European world emphasizes colonial legacies. The strongest version of this approach maintains that colonial legacies determine postcolonial trajectories. For instance, some scholars portray African colonialism as particularly vicious and debilitating, given the technological advantages European powers enjoyed at the time of colonization, and thus responsible for Africa's contemporary woes. Colonial rule in Latin America arguably created similar but less extreme obstacles to state formation, including *caudillos* and patrimonial bureaucracies. Colonialism was sometimes a force for good, however. Atul Kohli has singled out Japan's highly bureaucratized colonial rule to account for why South Korea has fared so well over the past fifty years.[122]

Scholars have begun to favor less deterministic claims about colonial legacies, however, since most countries have featured significant breaks from their colonial past. In Latin America, the Wars of Independence largely destroyed colonial institutions.[123] By 1850, postcolonial change had "destroyed the most important traits of the colonial heritage and had triggered new political alliances, institutions, and styles of leadership and organization."[124] In Africa, the administrative reliance on tribal chiefs waned after the Second World War, as some colonial overlords expelled chiefs from ruling coalitions and tried to co-opt the leaders of burgeoning urban nationalist movements. The key administrative group in colonial Africa was sidelined, making it tough to directly connect colonial chieftain rule to postcolonial maladies. Critics of Kohli's thesis on South Korea similarly point to institutional discontinuities following Japanese rule and before the inauguration of South Korea's developmental state.[125] The significance of colonial legacies seems to ebb and flow.

[122] Kohli (1994, 2004) and Young (1994). Acemoglu, Johnson, and Robinson (2001) maintain that settler mortality rates determined the types of institutions that became implanted in colonies. When Europeans settler mortality rates were high, colonial powers established extractive institutions, which hinder growth and development. But when settler mortality rates were lower, Europeans built inclusive institutions that promoted growth and development.

[123] Mahoney (2010: 191, 203).

[124] López-Alves (2000: 27–28, 35–36).

[125] Haggard, Kang, and Moon (1997) and Waldner (1999).

Most scholars now claim that colonialism shaped but did not determine a country's future. James Mahoney, for instance, believes that colonialism mattered in how it conditioned social structures, which incline but do not guarantee certain developmental pathways.[126] Matthew Lange likewise maintains that direct colonial rule encourages postcolonial success, but not deterministically so.[127] In Mauritius, Lange argues that direct rule was brought about by the British clamping down on labor unrest in the 1930s and 1940s. I find, alternatively, that the movement toward direct rule began much earlier and was propelled by the Franco-Mauritian sugar planters, who wanted a greater colonial state presence in the countryside to "regulate" the workforce. In my African case studies, which partially cover the colonial period, coalitional politics—not colonial doctrine—forged just what sort of colonial inheritances were present at independence. In sum, mainstream views on colonial legacies currently acknowledge that postcolonial politics influence a country's developmental trajectory.

STATE BUILDING AMID ETHNIC DIVERSITY

A final rival hypothesis maintains that ethnic diversity accounts for the state building underperformance of many non-European countries. This claim is bolstered by the sizable literature on the undersupply of public goods in ethnically diverse societies.[128] Many studies of African politics also regularly bemoan the arbitrary territorial boundaries drawn by European powers, arguing that the resulting ethnic heterogeneity impeded the development of cohesive polities and well-functioning government institutions. These scholars imply that boundaries which better adhered to long-standing cultural groups would help improve governance on the continent.[129] Their implicit referent is Europe, where one finds higher levels of state capacity and less ethnic fractionalization than in the developing world.[130]

Yet in none of my cases do I find ethnic diversity at the root of state building failures. This finding is perhaps most striking with respect to Nigeria, commonly depicted as hostage to ethnic factionalism. In the case study I illuminate how the salience of ethnicity was increased by a decentralization of power

[126] Mahoney (2010: 123). See also Lange, Mahoney, and vom Hau (2006).

[127] Lange (2009). See also Gerring et al. (2011).

[128] E.g., Alesina, Baqir, and Easterly (1999) and Habyarimana et al. (2007).

[129] E.g., Jackson and Rosberg (1982: 15). For a critical review, see Sambanis and Schulhofer-Wohl (2009).

[130] Fearon (2003: 212).

in 1954, which indigenous nationalist leaders demanded.[131] Regionally dominant ethnic groups came to control regional governments, which meant the centers of power in Nigeria were nestled in fairly ethnically homogeneous contexts. But Nigeria's regional governments nonetheless failed to supply public goods to their ethnic brethren, and state building foundered. Colombia and Mauritius are curious as well. They feature nearly identical levels of (significant) ethnic fractionalization but embarked on opposite state building trajectories. Even Chile, the most remarkable state builder examined herein, today scores above the global mean for ethnic fractionalization.[132]

There are general theoretical reasons to believe that ethnic diversity has been overblown as a cause of political underdevelopment.[133] Robert Bates, for instance, argues that ethnic conflict tends to be a product, not the cause, of political disorder.[134] And the idea that ethnic diversity imperils state building glosses over the historical forces that have enabled, or reduced, ethnic diversity. Today, France scores low on measures of ethnic fractionalization. Historically, however, "France" was a conglomeration of distinct cultural and linguistic communities in Burgundy, the Languedoc, Provence—areas that often violently resisted amalgamation with Paris. But Parisian state builders eventually incorporated them and deliberately forged a national identity.[135] This process occurred generically throughout Europe, as parochialism abated, and fairly homogeneous cultures formed. Yet to attribute state building underperformance in the non-European world to ethnic diversity is to associate Europe's state building successes with cultural invariability, and the suggestion is anachronistic.

The next six chapters provide evidence to find these competing hypotheses wanting, at least for explaining the state building developments in the countries and time periods in question. I find the links between commodity booms and coalitional politics to offer greater explanatory insights. The next three chapters are the "positive" cases, in which resource booms and export-oriented coalitions spawned state building. Chile and Argentina (chapters 3 and 4) featured situations of dual enrichment and the most substantial gains in state capacity among the six countries. Mauritius (chapter 5) experienced a growth in state capacity from public goods provision, but it lacked a coalitional threat to provoke the creation of unmediated institutions, and its state building lagged

[131] There is a compelling literature on how colonial policies imbued ethnic identities with new meaning (e.g., Horowitz 1985: 147–166; Posner 2003).

[132] Fearon (2003).

[133] Slater (2010: 44).

[134] Bates (2008: 132–134).

[135] Scott (1998: 25–82) and Tilly (1992: 107–114).

by comparison. By contrast, in Colombia, Ghana, and Nigeria (chapters 6, 7, and 8, my "negative" cases), political elites led ruling coalitions, fleeced exporters to fund their side-payments, and squandered state building opportunities. State capacity did not grow in these countries. These cases collectively suggest that state building in resource-rich countries hinges on coalitional politics, perhaps more so than any other factor.

CHAPTER 3

Striking State Building Due to Chile's Double Boom, 1848–1883

In recent decades, Chile has been among Latin America's best economic performers, with some calling it Latin America's "Tiger," a laudatory nod to the developmental states of East Asia. Chile performed well in the nineteenth century, too, avoiding the intractable civil wars and *caudillismo* that plagued other Latin American states. Some scholars maintain that the country's narrow terrain and concentrated population in the central valley made it tough for *caudillos* to establish regional strongholds. Hostile Indians in the southern frontier provided a further rationale for cooperation, rather than infighting, among power holders. Wise leaders, such as Diego Portales in the 1830s and Manuel Bulnes in the 1840s, also helped foster as island of institutional stability in a sea of regional instability. According to the conventional wisdom, the reasons for Chile's successes are, in short, distinctly Chilean.[1]

Although these factors may have aided Chile's development, they cannot explain the particularities of the country's formative state building era between 1848 and 1883. The coalitional politics amid a double boom in copper and wheat can. Export opportunities propelled the country's politically dominant stratum of landed elites, from the northern central valley around Santiago, to move into export-oriented wheat production. The state provided them complementary public goods, such as state-backed railroads and new lending institutions to facilitate credit accessibility. These public goods were carefully designed to maximize landed elites' gains relative to small-scale wheat producers in the south and northern copper mine owners, both of whom were politically marginalized. As southern yeomen and northern miners gained economically from the booms, their political frustrations boiled over in two civil wars during the 1850s. The rise of southern wheat agriculturalists was particularly troubling to northern central valley landed elites, as southern

[1] See Coppedge (1998: 180) and Loveman (2001: 1–7).

yeomen were gaining more from the wheat boom than were existing power holders. This threat propelled the ruling coalition to build unmediated institutions to enhance its control of local affairs and ensconce ruling coalition members' existing advantages. These actions collectively led to a substantial growth in Chilean state capacity.

Chile at Mid-Century

Chile's mid-century commodity booms transformed its economy from subsistence-oriented to one with thriving international connections. Chile had incipient links to world markets before its booms, through some limited exports of wheat to Peru and minerals to Europe. Minerals accounted for about 60 percent of total Chilean exports, while agriculture contributed about 15 percent.[2] Much of the land in the countryside lay fallow, and the central valley was "an area with plentiful if idle hands."[3] Capital was scarce, as it was throughout Latin America at the time. In 1848, Chile was on the margins of global commerce.

Four social actors jockeyed for power in nineteenth-century Chile: landed elites in the northern central valley, foreign merchants in the port city of Valparaíso, small-scale agriculturalists in the southern central valley, and copper mine owners in the desert north. Landed elites (*hacendados*) from the northern central valley around Santiago sat at the apex of the country's political hierarchy and derived their power from *haciendas* dating to the seventeenth century. Most estates "lay in isolated neglect populated by droves of cattle and casual workers," due to limited demand.[4] Landed elites maintained homes within a small section of Santiago, attended the same schools, and participated in the same social clubs. *Hacendados* constituted a small and homogeneous group and translated their economic prestige into political power by serving in the Chilean Senate and Chamber of Deputies. They also mobilized through the Sociedad Nacional de Agricultura (SNA), an advocacy group dating to 1838 that was reinvigorated in the 1850s. The SNA served to bring "together sociopolitical elites to decide matters of state and economy outside the public halls of the Congress."[5] Northern central valley landed elites dominated Chilean society and politics as of the late 1840s. Manuel Montt, president during the 1850s, owned one of the country's wealthier landed estates, "Mercedes," near

[2] Oppenheimer (1976: 458–460).

[3] Bauer (1975: 148).

[4] Bauer (1975: 27). The relatively few *hacendados* who exported wheat were in the Aconcagua valley, part of the northern central valley northeast of Valparaíso.

[5] Loveman (2001: 130).

Santiago. One of Montt's Interior Ministers, Francisco Javier Ovalle, was perhaps the richest landowner in the export-oriented Aconcagua Province, near Valparaíso.[6]

Foreign merchants in Valparaíso served as *hacendados'* coalitional partners. After independence, foreign, especially British, merchants came to control the wholesale trade and moneylending in Chile. They lent directly to northern central valley landed elites for the purchase of imports and indirectly to mine owners through intermediaries known as *habilitadores*. Chile's capital market was "informal" and lacked publically authorized lending institutions. The merchant community was tight-knit. As of mid-century, there were only seventeen British merchant firms in Valparaíso, situated in close proximity on the port. British merchants attended the same churches, associated in the same social clubs, and would come to share interlocking directorships on banks and insurance companies in the 1850s and 1860s.[7] They were reportedly "united by a common philosophy, by a common interpretation of Chile's role in the world economy, [and] by the common goals and aspirations they shared as merchants."[8]

The other main social actors stood outside of this ruling coalition. There were small-scale agriculturalists in Chile's southern central valley, including Maule and Talca provinces, where egalitarian land tenure prevailed. Most of these yeomen possessed uncommercialized farms, though some of them farmed wheat for export through the Concepción port.[9] Southern agriculturalists were politically marginalized, something facilitated by their large group size, physical dispersal, and paltry communication and transportation networks.[10] During the 1840s, for example, area residents asked government officials in Santiago to improve the area's transportation infrastructure, to no avail.[11] Southerners mostly wanted autonomy from Santiago because they felt ill-served by state policy, which concentrated expenditures in the northern central valley.[12] Southern agriculturalists' antipathy toward Santiago would rupture into armed conflict in the 1850s as a direct consequence of the wheat boom.

Copper mine owners in the northern desert were also politically marginalized. Chile's Norte Chico was rich with copper deposits, so rich that

[6] Bauer (1975); Bengoa (1988, 1990); and Pregger Román (1979).

[7] Mayo (1987) and Pregger Román (1978).

[8] Pregger Román (1978: 88).

[9] Bauer (1975: 30–34, 64–66, 145–146). As of 1854, only four of Chile's 145 highest-earning estates were located outside of the northern central valley.

[10] Daitsman (1995: 72–76, 124–127).

[11] Pregger Román (1979: 204–205) and Zeitlin (1984: 37–38).

[12] See Valenzuela (1977: 184).

high-grade copper ore existing just below the surface could be extracted with simple, labor-intensive techniques. Small-scale mines predominated in the Norte Chico, though larger mines existed as well.[13] A number of proto-industrial enterprises had developed alongside humble mines and, by 1850, mining elites controlled 40 to 60 percent of Chilean copper production, especially in capital-intensive smelting and refining.[14] These capital needs led to dependency on British merchants' *habilitadore* intermediaries.[15] All mine owners were politically sidelined.[16] In 1840, for example, the state raised export taxes on copper while simultaneously lowering them on wheat and flour.[17] The copper sector contributed disproportionately to state revenue, but received few policy benefits, which would provoke rebellion in the 1850s.

The coalition between northern central valley landed elites and Valparaíso merchants required few side-payments because neither actor's economic activity infringed upon the other's. Chilean *hacendados* derived power from land and their control over labor, while merchants controlled capital. Both actors benefitted from the country's informal credit market: merchants gained as lenders, and landed elites secured loans with appreciating land values. Tariffs, insofar as they existed at all, were used to shift the tax burden onto weak social actors. Northern central valley landed elites could craft such distributive policies because they held about two-thirds of the seats in the legislature.[18] The ruling coalition also controlled educational access and thereby influenced bureaucratic staffing patterns. Most bureaucrats graduated from the Instituto Nacional (Santiago's elite secondary school), and the Instituto Nacional effectively barred entry to anyone without an upper-class patron.[19] Ruling coalition members dominated the state.

Yet the state possessed low levels of state capacity as of 1848. From 1810 to 1830, disorder reigned with the collapse of Spanish authority, with *hacendados* responsible for what order prevailed in the countryside. In 1833, the "Portalian" state was established, which brandished a constitution that ostensibly centralized power—and something which commentators often claim caused Chile's ensuing political stability. In fact, mediated institutions typified the

[13] Przeworski (1980: 62–63) and Volk (1988: 71–74; 1993: 71–73).

[14] Culver and Reinhart (1989: 724–732); Volk (1988: 78); and Zeitlin (1984: 141–157).

[15] Mayo (2001).

[16] Scholars often depict the Chilean elite as well-integrated among agricultural and mining interests (e.g., Véliz 1963). This integration had largely not begun by 1850, however (Bauer 1975: 37–38; Zeitlin 1984: 22–23).

[17] Volk (1988: 88).

[18] Congressional representation did not require district residency (Pregger Román 1975: 228–230; 1979: 210–212).

[19] Campos Harriet (1960) and Yeager (1991).

Portalian state.[20] The state deployed Intendants and other functionaries outside of Santiago only after negotiations with local elites, which gave local notables de facto control over provincial administration.[21] There was no uniform municipal code. (Congress rejected a proposal to overhaul municipal administration in 1848.) Localities were instead governed by a hodgepodge of rules inherited from the colonial period. The government had not yet established Courts of Appeals in Concepción and La Serena, the two main regional centers outside of the northern central valley.[22] And the National Guard units were headed by local *hacendados*, not state agents, which was significant because the Guard functioned as the government's electoral machine. (Artisans and small property holders, around 5 percent of the population, were enfranchised at the time.)[23] The Chilean state possessed limited institutional capacity.

The state's structure of tax revenue also indicated low state capacity. Custom duties formed the majority of ordinary revenues, with another 20 percent coming from state monopolies. A tithe on agricultural property, the third most important revenue source, was collected by clerical tax farmers, not government agents. Widespread evasion had effectively rendered the tithe a voluntary contribution by the 1840s.[24] The state possessed limited coercive power, despite having won the War of the Bolivian-Peruvian Confederation (1836–1839). The war did not create "the institutional infrastructure needed for further development of state capacity."[25] The country was not "pacified," as Araucanian Indians controlled significant territory south of the Bío Bío River. Overall, the state exhibited little capacity on the eve of Chile's first major commodity boom.

The Revenue Imperative and Chilean State Building

Chile's growth of state capacity after 1850 was not due to the revenue imperative. But, consistent with resource curse theories, the government relied fiscally on the copper sector, as northern mining areas "paid for the bulk of imports" between 1848 and 1883, when import duties constituted the leading source of state revenue.[26] State policy also imposed relatively high duties

[20] E.g., Cáceres Muñoz (2005); Encina (1949b: 433–434); and Loveman (2001: 101–118).

[21] Cáceres Muñoz (2005: 114–121).

[22] Encina (1949a: 341–342).

[23] Datisman (1995: 127–131) and Valenzuela (1996).

[24] Dirección de Contabilidad (1914) and Edwards (1932: 143–146).

[25] Centeno (2002: 27).

[26] Loveman (2001: 115).

on copper exports.[27] However, Chile's nineteenth-century copper production did not generate sizable rents due to the prevalence of small-scale mines based on simple extractive techniques.[28] Chilean copper therefore was more like an agricultural commodity, so one might expect a diversified taxing apparatus in order to preserve copper's international competitiveness.[29] Yet, after 1850, Chilean taxation became less diversified, and "landowners enjoyed an ever-decreasing tax burden." Even stagnating government revenue between 1864 and 1879 did not trigger a substantial change in the state's fiscal profile.[30] Chile continually leaned on mining for revenue because copper exporters were excluded from the ruling political coalition.

Chile's revenue-raising strategy similarly confounds bellicist hypotheses. Chile was arguably a "land of war" and "perennially insecure" throughout the nineteenth century, partly because of external rivalries with Argentina (beginning in 1843), Bolivia (1836), and Peru (1832).[31] Chile's only international conflict between 1848 and 1879 was a brief naval war with Spain during 1865–66. But rather than build a stronger state to confront Spain, Chile relied on a cunning diplomatic strategy to prohibit Spanish refueling in regional ports. Spanish aggression exposed the weakness of Chile's "pitiable fleet,"[32] but the war "did nothing to stimulate Chilean shipbuilding even in the face of the obvious lesson of the nation's vulnerability to one of Europe's third-rate powers."[33] Most important, Chile did not strengthen its extractive apparatus to service its new wartime debt, which is at odds with perhaps the key observable implication of bellicist theory.[34]

The War of the Pacific (1879–83) against Bolivia and Peru—designed to capture nitrate wealth in the Atacama Desert—may have aided state legitimacy but did not trigger considerable state building.[35] At the outset, Chile's small, 3,000-man army "lacked training in modern warfare, had no experience with large-unit maneuvers, and was practically without auxiliary services."[36]

[27] Humud Tleel (1969: 130) and Volk (1988: 57; 1993: 93–94).

[28] Dunning (2008: 216 n. 5).

[29] Cf. Shafer (1994: 35–36).

[30] Bauer (1975: quote from 118) and Dirección de Contabilidad (1914). Legislators implemented a national income tax only amid economic depression in 1876 but repealed it in 1884 (Sater 1976).

[31] Quotes from Góngora (1986) and Resende-Santos (2007: 156), respectively. Rivalries from Thies (2005: 457).

[32] Burr (1965: 97–106, quote from 98).

[33] Loveman (2001: 132).

[34] Humud Tleel (1969: 73).

[35] Kurtz (2009).

[36] Loveman (2001: 146).

During the war, the army ballooned to 45,000 men, but quickly shrunk below 5,000 afterward.[37] Chile's superior logistical resources, particularly its railroads, enabled its victory.[38] (As I discuss below, these railroads were products of public good seeking by coalition members.) Chile funded the War of the Pacific with paper money emissions, which amounted to roughly 60 percent of ordinary state revenue over 1879–80, when the fighting occurred.[39] Afterward, the state did not enact new taxes or deepen existing revenue but instead began to live off of nitrate rents and "systematically reduced the burden of non-nitrate taxes"—contra bellicist theory.[40] Overall, Chile's reliance on customs duties, as a percentage of ordinary revenue, increased from 49 percent (1848) to 65 percent (1883) during the case study period, which implies state weakening and thus underscores that revenue-raising played little role in Chile's formative state building era.[41]

Chile's Double Boom in Wheat and Copper

Two international commodity booms struck the Chilean economy around 1848. First, a boom in global wheat demand began with gold rushes in California and Australia and dovetailed into a prolonged rise in European wheat demand. The period after 1848 was "a time of economic euphoria" that came to be known as Chile's "Great Wheat Trade." The average annual value of agricultural exports rose from $0.9 million pesos (1844–45) to $13.2 million pesos (1871–75). Between 1845 and 1871, wheat production expanded twentyfold and flour production grew by fourteen times.[42] Growing production also stimulated Chile's agricultural machinery imports (used mostly for wheat cultivation) from 200 pieces of imported machinery during 1846–50 to 1,449 in the second half of the 1850s.[43] Copper demand also intensified around 1850, due to the growing use of electric power in Europe. Chile became the leading worldwide copper source between the 1850s and 1883, when copper production was about nine times its 1830s level.[44] Copper led all mineral exports, which typically accounted for 50–60 percent of total exports between 1844

[37] Cordero (1992) and Resende-Santos (2007: 164–168).

[38] Sater (2007: 354).

[39] Hostilities largely ended by early 1881 but the concluding treaty was not signed until 1883.

[40] Bowman and Wallerstein (1982: 446–448). See also Dirección de Contabilidad (1914: 22–27) and Sater (1976).

[41] Centeno (2002: 124–125).

[42] Sepúlveda (1959: 50) and Bauer (1975: 67).

[43] Robles-Ortiz (2009: 506).

[44] Pederson (1966) and Przeworski (1980).

and 1880.[45] Copper remained the bedrock of the Chilean export economy, even with expanding wheat production.

In response to these booms, *hacendados* in the northern central valley either increased existing wheat production or made their initial transition into commercialized agriculture. Estates could commercialize easily because they were hand-sown and did not have to be laboriously cleared.[46] The wheat boom also wrought changes in the southern central valley. The region then had most of Chile's commercialized wheat production because of its inland fluvial waterways, which made it easier to transport wheat to the ports of Constitución and Tomé, compared to the overland routes used to reach Valparaíso in the northern central valley.[47] Exploding wheat production near the southern central valley town of Talca helped spawn a modern milling industry "almost overnight,"[48] and *talquino* elites also moved into mercantile activities and moneylending.[49] The southern central valley's social formation was increasingly bifurcated between a narrow elite and numerous small-scale producers, just like in the Norte Chico. In the north, state policy continued to frustrate miners. Smelters were particularly aggrieved, as the state refused to protect them against their competitors in England and the United States, who received government protection.[50] Chile's double boom constituted the country's first major commodity boom, and it enriched actors both within and outside of the ruling political coalition.

Public Goods Provided, but Only to Ruling Coalition Members

Export-oriented actors developed preferences for state-supplied public goods as they strove to exploit the wheat and copper booms, but the state provided public goods to the distributive benefit of ruling coalition members. First, the state subsidized railroads in the northern central valley, but provided no financial assistance for Norte Chico mining railroads and vetoed proposals for a southern central valley railway. Second, the state scuttled efforts by northern mine owners to eliminate Valparaíso merchants' stranglehold on the country's credit supply, while helping northern central valley landed elites formalize the country's credit market to stimulate lending. Finally, as I discuss toward the

[45] Volk (1988: 89).

[46] Sepúlveda (1959: esp. 57–68, 78, 81–95).

[47] Bauer (1975: 65–66).

[48] Collier and Sater (1996: 81).

[49] Bengoa (1990: 103–104) and Daitsman (1995: 43–72).

[50] Zeitlin (1984: 60–66) and Culver and Reinhart (1989).

end of the chapter, the wheat boom created new incentives for central valley peons to migrate south into Indian territory to establish small wheat farms. Northern central valley *hacendados* pressed the state for territorial pacification to facilitate the creation of haciendas in the frontier instead and stem labor flight. The provision of these public goods augmented state capacity.

PREFERENCES FOR NEW PUBLIC GOODS

Chile's existing transportation infrastructure constituted a major barrier to production for existing and potential exporters. For landed elites in the northern central valley, high transport costs rendered them uncompetitive global producers, aside from those estates in the Aconcagua valley close to Valparaíso. Landed elites saw railroads as the solution.[51] Wheat producers in the southern central valley felt likewise. Although fluvial networks around Talca provided some agriculturalists cheap, reliable transport, most area wheat farmers used burros and colonial-era cart paths for transportation. This costly method of transport spawned preferences for a railway linking the Maule basin to a nearby port, a widespread desire reflected in local newspapers and Intendant reports.[52]

High transport costs also plagued northern mining areas and made it cost-ineffective to extract anything other than the highest grade ores.[53] Transportation depended on the burro, something particularly limiting to copper elites wanting to further proto-industrialization.[54] Mining elites discussed ways to finance and construct area railroads as early as 1845, and the copper boom increased these desires.[55] Finally, Valparaíso merchants found railroads attractive because importing the inputs would be "big business to the commission houses."[56] But British merchants shunned directly financing Chilean railroads, as Europe's 1848 political turmoil had stunted overseas investment.[57] Railroad building therefore necessitated state involvement.

The other major economic bottleneck in mid-century Chile stemmed from limited credit availability. High interest rates prevailed, and domestic capital sources could not to meet the demands of northern mine owners. Merchants extended loans to them through the "credit-option system," which permitted lenders to purchase commodities at the prevailing price during harvest or at

[51] Bengoa (1988: 203–204) and Oppenheimer (1976).
[52] E.g., *El Correo del Sur*, December 28, 1854 (Vol. 5, No. 432) and Sotomayor (1856: 92–94).
[53] Pederson (1966: 213–222) and Przeworski (1980: 211–212).
[54] Culver and Reinhart (1989: 724–732).
[55] Marín Vicuña (1916: 172).
[56] Mayo (1987: 217).
[57] Alliende Edwards (1993: 24).

the retrospective price when their loan had been extended and thereby shifted risk onto producers. Merchants also lent to small mine owners through intermediaries known as *habilitadores,* so integral to the copper sector that in many respects they controlled the level of production.[58] Historically, northern central valley landed elites had found this situation acceptable because they received credit-based loans from merchants to purchase imports and effectively repaid these loans with appreciating land values.

Northern mine owners' opposition to these lending practices intensified after 1848, particularly since capital shortages prevented them from using steam power to aid drainage in their mines, which were prone to flooding.[59] A liberalized lending environment could help mine owners access capital for railway construction, too. Southern agriculturalists supported credit reform because they wanted capital to irrigate their properties but depended on "onerous" British firms.[60] During the 1840s, northern miners and southern agriculturalists sponsored legislation to create a national bank to end this "informal" credit system, but the measure failed due to opposition from Valparaíso merchants.[61] Northern central valley landed elites altered this status quo once they developed preferences for modern banking institutions, brought about by their desire to irrigate and commercialize their estates due to the wheat boom.[62] Informal merchant lenders, facing "rapidly expanding demand for credit," could not respond satisfactorily.[63] The state became involved in procuring capital and establishing the legal strictures for a modern credit market, once politically dominant *hacendados* began pressing for credit market formalization.

THE POLITICAL LOGIC OF RAILROAD PROVISION

Railroad policy typified the distributive logic underlying the state's posture toward exporters. During the 1840s, northern mine owners in the Atacama Desert lobbied the government to assist with a proposed railway project to connect the mining town of Copiapó with the Caldera port. But "despite the repeated requests of the mineowners," the state offered no direct financial aid.[64] Financing was left to private economic actors; when the first financing efforts failed, the state refused to directly provide or assist in raising capital.

[58] Pregger Román (1978: 76–81); Przeworski (1980: 99–101); and Volk (1988: 78–87).
[59] Volk (1988: 81).
[60] Bengoa (1988: 204–207).
[61] Encina (1949a: 362).
[62] Robles-Ortiz (2009: 500–506).
[63] Pregger Román (1979: 81–82).
[64] Zeitlin (1984: 40).

Eventually, an American entrepreneur named William Wheelwright raised sufficient capital in October 1849. Wheelwright would play a key role in financing railroads in Chile's mining areas, where privately financed railroads became the norm.[65]

State posture differed dramatically toward proposed railways in the northern central valley. A railroad linking Santiago with Valparaíso had been suggested as early as 1842, but the project received state assistance only when it was economically sensible for ruling coalition members. Following the start of the wheat boom, the state granted Wheelwright a concession in 1849 for a railroad linking Santiago with Valparaíso (the Ferrocarril de Santiago á Valparaíso, or FCSV). Wheelwright failed to raise adequate private capital, at which point landed elites "more or less forced [a state-backed solution] upon the government."[66] The state pledged $2 million pesos of the anticipated $7 million pesos needed for construction and formed Chile's first joint stock company to provide the legal framework needed to raise complementary private capital. The legal framework limited investors' liability, served as a focal point for investment, and thereby facilitated capital accumulation.[67]

Investment patterns in the FCSV reveal the criticalness of this state action. A few prominent Chileans invested sizable sums in the FCSV: Matías Cousiño, Angel Custodio Gallo, and Joshua Waddington each bought between 530 and 800 shares, for a total of $2 million pesos. But all other investors purchased fewer than 50 shares, with 73 percent of them buying five shares or less. Judicial and notarial records on stockholders reveal that they generally hailed from the northern central valley. The return on investment was not particularly good (around 4 percent), which indicates that investors saw the FCSV as a means to advance their export interests and not as a speculative venture.[68]

The other principal Chilean railway built in the nineteenth century was the Ferrocarril del Sur (FCS). Although the FCSV made export-oriented wheat production viable near Santiago, it did not alleviate the high transportation costs facing *hacendados* south of the city in the northern central valley departments of Caupolicán, Rancagua, and San Fernando. In fact, as much as half of the land on Caupolicán haciendas lay fallow after the onset of the wheat boom because transport costs rendered area elites internationally uncompetitive.[69] Landowners saw the FCS as the solution, though capital was in short supply. The government therefore contributed $1 million pesos of the anticipated

[65] Alliende Edwards (1993: 16–20) and Encina (1949a: 343–344).

[66] Mayo (1987: 222).

[67] Alliende Edwards (1993: 24–25); Marín Vicuña (1916: 167–169); and Oppenheimer (1976: 157–158).

[68] Oppenheimer (1976; 1982: 59–60).

[69] Bauer (1972).

$3–5 million pesos needed to build the railroad. Another joint stock framework encouraged broad participation, as 72 percent of investors bought five shares or less. The FCSV and FCS reduced transport costs by approximately 40 percent for most northern central valley landed elites and enabled them to become internationally competitive.[70]

The design and sequencing of the FCS underscore the distributive dimensions of transportation policy. Ruling coalition members designed the FCS to emanate from Santiago, which would enrich northern central valley landed elites before the railroad reached the southern central valley. This design was at once politically sensible and economically questionable. Wheat production flourished initially in the south near Concepción and Talca, so it made economic sense to build a railroad there first. Moreover, such a railroad would have been relatively inexpensive. The Intendant of Concepción, Ramón Sotomayor, noted that Allan Campbell, the British engineer who conducted a feasibility study, estimated the railroad would cost only $260,000 pesos (compared to the estimated $3–5 million pesos for the FCS).[71] But state managers rejected this proposal and instead built the FCS, so that northern central valley landed elites would gain vis-à-vis their economic competitors to the south.[72] By the 1860s, the FCSV and FCS had rendered northern central valley landed elites more internationally competitive than southern agriculturalists.[73]

Merchants in Valparaíso also won big from the FCSV and FCS. When the wheat boom began, just 1 percent of flour exports exited Valparaíso; the rest left through the southern central valley ports where British merchants did not operate branch offices.[74] Valparaíso merchants therefore had reasons to resist railroads designed to serve the southern central valley. As a consequence of railroad policy, Valparaíso displaced Constitución and Tomé as the main entrepôt for Chile's agricultural trade (see table 3.1). In 1861, merchants in Concepción and millers in Tomé pressed the state for a railway in the south linking Chillán to the Talcahuano port. Northern central valley interests in the Chilean legislature vetoed the proposal and only approved it once the railway was redesigned to link up with the FCS in Talca, thus making it part of the budding national network.[75] Similar distributive calculations continued to affect proposed railways in northern mining areas. In 1860, the state authorized a railroad in Coquimbo Province but provided no direct financial backing, forcing miners to rely on foreign capital. These private railroads facilitated the mineral

[70] Oppenheimer (1976).
[71] Sotomayor (1856: 92–94).
[72] Loveman (2001: 141).
[73] Daitsman (1995: 40).
[74] Mayo (1987: 104).
[75] Whaley (1974: 52–69).

Table 3.1 **Flour Exports by Port, Annual Average (metric quintals)**

Year	*Constitución*	*Tomé*	*Valparaíso*	*Valparaíso % of Total*
1851–55	92,000	190,000	4,000	1.4
1856–60	89,000	101,000	20,000	9.5
1861–65	156,000	109,000	109,000	29.1
1866–70	163,000	71,000	262,000	52.8
1875	148,000	63,000	230,000	52.2

Source: Bauer (1975: 65).

trade, as "formerly worthless ores became valuable" from reduced transport costs. Yet mine owners still regarded the region's transportation infrastructure as inadequate and lobbied the government for assistance, without success.[76] A coalitional logic guided state policy.

State capacity nonetheless grew from new railroads. The FCSV and FCS augmented the logistical power available to state managers: the trip between Santiago and Valparaíso now took a matter of hours, not two or three days.[77] Railroads also promoted the development of complementary infrastructure, such as telegraphs, which were built alongside rail track.[78] Local communities would build roads to create railroad access points, which stimulated the country's road network. Railroads (and telegraphs) helped state managers pacify the national territory, as I discuss below, and were critical in helping Chile win the War of the Pacific (1879–83). New specialized bureaucratic administration developed and employed 2,318 bureaucrats by 1880 (up from 686 in 1863).[79] Overall, railroads enhanced state capacity while serving the economic goals of export-oriented power holders.

THE WHEAT BOOM AND CREDIT MARKET FORMALIZATION

A similar distributive logic guided the formalization of Chile's credit market. Before the commodity booms, Chile had an "informal" credit market controlled by Valparaíso merchants, who blocked two attempts to loosen their control over capital in the 1840s.[80] In 1848, Manuel Camilo Vial, the powerful

[76] Alliende Edwards (1993: 86–91); Pederson (1966: quote from 220); and Przeworski (1980: 213–247).

[77] Thomson and Angerstein (2000: 24).

[78] Johnson (1948). Chile had 3,500 km of telegraph line by 1876.

[79] Oppenheimer (1976: 496).

[80] Pregger Román (1978: 80).

Interior Minister, remarked: "I would not have hesitated to prefer the establishment of a bank by the government, were I not aware of the almost insuperable opposition which many of the most distinguished citizens of the country have to such an idea."[81] But, after 1848, this situation changed, particularly as northern central valley landed elites transitioned into export-oriented agriculture.[82]

Hacendados pressed government officials to alleviate their credit bottlenecks as informal networks struggled to meet surging demand for capital. The government responded to their preferences as it had with railroad policy. The first major development was the creation of Chile's mortgage bank, the Caja de Crédito Hipotecario, in 1855. The bank provided borrowers credit up to one-half of their land value at low interest rates, which advantaged *hacendados* near Santiago because of the area's relatively high land values. The bank directed the vast majority of its early loans to Santiago and Colchagua provinces, the heart of the northern central valley where the coming FCSV railroad made commercial agriculture attractive.[83] The bank was a boon to *hacendados* and has been characterized as a "docile instrument in the hands of landed elites."[84] The accessible, advantageous credit source for northern central valley landed elites was arguably the most important factor in the development of Chile's commercial agriculture.[85]

However, the transformation of Chile's credit market potentially threatened Valparaíso merchants. They feared the bank would be a precursor to a paper money regime and stimulate inflation. Legislators recognized this fear and designed the mortgage bank in a way to assuage merchant opposition.[86] The bank was not authorized to have paid-in capital, nor could it lend directly. Instead, it issued fixed-value, interest-bearing letters of credit, known as *cédulas*; the borrowing landowner then sold the letter on the open market for cash (i.e., his loan), which effectively determined the loan's interest rate.[87] Such letters of credit can have a serious inflationary potential, but mostly when used to purchase additional land (and thus essentially becoming a revolving line of credit). But most land was already privately titled in Chile's central valley, unlike countries with expansive frontier territory, such as Argentina, which reduced this inflationary pitfall.[88]

[81] Quoted in Fetter (1931: 9).
[82] Robles-Ortiz (2009: 500–506).
[83] Bauer (1975: 90–96) and Garreaud (1981: 170).
[84] Borde and Góngora (1956: 126).
[85] Edwards (1932: 150).
[86] Pregger Román (1978: 80–83).
[87] Bauer (1975: 90).
[88] Ferns (1960: 370–371).

The Caja de Crédito Hipotecario was pivotal to the development of commercial agriculture near Santiago, yet simultaneously of little benefit to wheat producers in the southern central valley. Since one's land value determined his loan, southern agriculturalists were disadvantaged by their smallholdings and distance from the capital city. When Ramón Sotomayor, the Intendant of Concepción, filed his periodic report to the Interior Minister in 1856, he noted that small property owners had received little benefit from the new mortgage bank.[89] Furthermore, the mortgage loan application process "could be trying and lengthy," giving influential elites an "imponderable advantage" over lesser agriculturalists in obtaining loans.[90] Even so, the Caja de Crédito Hipotecario was not a private good, despite these distributional features. Some agriculturalists from Concepción, Maule, and Talca provinces in the southern central valley managed to obtain loans from the bank, and even a few landowners in the northern mining provinces of Atacama and Coquimbo received loans.[91] The new mortgage bank is properly characterized as an impure public good.

As northern central valley landed elites, Chile's coalition leader, developed preferences for a formalized lending environment, Valparaíso merchants adapted to preserve their power. In 1854, merchants formed the Banco de Valparaíso, the first and most important lending institution they would come to dominate.[92] Southern agriculturalists were among the bank's main customers, given their difficulties obtaining loans from the Caja de Crédito Hipotecario. Not only did commercial banks lend at higher interest rates than the state mortgage bank, but southern yeomen typically paid less favorable rates to commercial lenders than did *hacendados* nearer to Santiago.[93] Moreover, these new financial institutions used agrarian real estate as standard loan collateral, so banks "did not make direct loans for copper ventures." Credit-hungry copper producers remained dependent on informal *habilitadore* lenders.[94] Merchants also refused to extend credit to nascent manufacturers for fear of upsetting the economic status quo and solidity of the ruling coalition.[95]

[89] Sotomayor (1856: 17).

[90] Bauer (1975: 90–91).

[91] Garreaud (1981: 170).

[92] To inhibit inflation, the Banco de Valparaíso was disallowed from emitting bills, revolving loans, or transferable certificates of deposit. Between 1855 and 1885, merchants dominated Chile's banking and insurance sector, holding about 75 percent of shares in the sector (and never less than 64 percent) and encasing their power through interlocking directorships (Mayo 1987: 190–204; Pregger Román 1978).

[93] Bauer (1975: 90–101).

[94] Przeworski (1980: 112) notes copper miners did not receive noteworthy institutional banking help until 1906.

[95] Pregger Román (1978: 88–91).

Credit formalization directly aided landed elites in the northern central valley and merchants in Valparaíso, while disadvantaging actors outside of the ruling political coalition.

The distributive politics behind Chile's credit formalization was also evident in the state's savings bank, the Caja de Ahorros. The government established the savings bank during an economic downturn in the late 1850s to encourage savings by public employees. It was a lean time for the state and its coalitional backers, and savings bank deposits provided state managers a new resource that could be used to aid the powerful.[96] The state used savings deposits to fund the Caja de Crédito Hipotecario, purchase shares of the FCSV and FCS, which had fallen on tough times, and service debt accrued during the naval war with Spain in 1865–66.[97] Credit formalization aided the ruling coalition in direct and indirect ways.

But unmet credit demand persisted in Chile, and influential landed elites and merchants responded in 1859 by founding the Banco Nacional de Chile, which provided important indirect benefits to ruling coalition members. Unlike other banks, the government authorized the bank to issue notes, which foreshadowed a liberal banking law passed in 1860 to further expand credit accessibility. Again, the British invested heavily in the Banco Nacional de Chile and established interlocking directorships between it and the Banco de Valparaíso, the country's other leading private financial institution. These banks collectively accounted for about two-thirds of bank deposits nationwide.[98] British merchants, in other words, maintained their control over lending despite the formalization of Chile's credit sector.

The state also accrued benefits from credit liberalization. The Banco Nacional de Chile became the state's de facto banker, not unlike (but on a scale less than) the Bank of England during England's formative state building era.[99] Just prior to Chile's war with Spain in 1865, credit dried up, and people began hoarding currency. In response, the state authorized the issuance of inconvertible banknotes through the Banco Nacional de Chile to meet its expenses, a stopgap measure arranged between the state, the Banco Nacional de Chile, the Banco de Valparaíso, and other domestic banks. This action enabled the

[96] At this time, the state was making deposits in the Banco de Valparaíso to guarantee its solvency (Mayo 1987: 193–194).

[97] Bauer (1975: 109–110) and Encina (1949b: 452–454). The state began purchasing shares of the FCSV and FCS in an economic downturn in the late 1850s, which led to state ownership by the 1870s. The government paid above-market prices for FCSV and FCS shares while refusing to buy shares of the northern Copiapó-Caldera railroad (Oppenheimer 1982: 69–73).

[98] Mayo (1987: 195) and Subercaseaux (1922: 70–81). The Banco Nacional de Chile was known as the Banco de Chile until 1865. It merged with the Banco de Valparaíso in 1892.

[99] Carruthers (1996).

state to continue functioning during the conflict, just as the Bank of England did for the Crown during a war with France in 1797. During Chile's conflict with Spain, the Banco Nacional de Chile secured a foreign loan for the state and, when foreign lenders became jittery during the war, supplemented the treasury with a significant domestic loan.[100] In ten short years, ruling coalition members radically transformed the financial landscape of the Chilean economy, and the source of these changes lay in the expanding export economy.

These developments promoted the growth of state capacity. Modern banking institutions enabled state managers to quickly underwrite war costs, subsidize the country's transportation infrastructure, and facilitate the growth of the export economy.[101] Government leaders created bureaucratic oversight of the banking and insurance sector, which marked new administrative power, particularly through the provincial branches of institutions of the Caja de Ahorros.[102] Overall, the formalization of Chile's credit markets and the development of a modern transportation infrastructure marked palpable gains in state power. What is more, these developments were not functional responses to the emergent needs of the export economy, as politically marginalized actors were consistently punished in the design of new impure public goods. Such distributional policies contributed to civil conflict led by southern agriculturalists and northern mine owners, and the burgeoning threat constituted by rising exporters spawned the movement toward unmediated institutions.

An Opposition Enriched, Civil War, and Institution Building

Chile's commodity booms featured "dual enrichment," and rising exporters from the country's regional peripheries constituted a diametrical threat to ruling coalition members. Miners and southern yeomen were unable to translate their growing economic power into political gain and launched a civil war in 1851. Although the ruling coalition prevailed relatively easily, northern central valley landed elites recognized that coalitional change would disable their ability to exploit the commodity boom, particularly given the importance of state-supplied public goods to their generative aim. They accordingly strengthened institutions, which provoked another round of civil insurrections in 1859. The ruling coalition's ongoing institutional response helped ensconce

[100] Fetter (1931: 7–16); Mayo (1987: 195); and Subercaseaux (1922: 82).

[101] The Banco Nacional de Chile also provided much of the capital the state used to purchase outstanding FCSV and FCS stock, which transformed Chile's central valley railroads into a state-owned network by 1873 (Alliende Edwards 1993: 54–55; Oppenheimer 1976: 230–244).

[102] Encina (1949b: 548–551) and Subercaseaux (1922: 63, 212).

their power and constituted the most striking institution building anywhere in nineteenth-century Latin America.

MUNICIPALITIES, ELECTIONS, AND POWER AT MID-CENTURY

Chilean institution building after 1850 centered on municipalities and local elections, which were pivotal to the ruling political coalition's dominance. A surprising number of artisans and small property owners around urban areas, roughly 5 percent of the population, were enfranchised and represented the majority of eligible voters in Chile circa 1850.[103] Municipal authorities were expected to "manage" their votes, by overseeing voter registration, voting, and the declaration of winners. Once local election officials, who were chosen by municipal authorities, deemed a prospective voter eligible, they issued him a *calificación* (voting registration card). Local elites then toiled to make sure that voters cast their ballots for the government slate. Decisions made at the registration table over voter eligibility were therefore crucial to determining electoral outcomes.[104]

After issuing *calificaciones,* local elites manipulated voting under the auspices of the National Guard, which served mostly as an electoral machine, not a repository of military power. For example, Domingo Santa María, the Intendant in the northern central valley province of Colchagua, reported in the late 1840s that when guardsmen gathered each Sunday for drills, they were seemingly oblivious to their military responsibilities.[105] Local officials understood the Guard's electoral rationale. José Francisco Gana, the Intendant of Atacama Province in 1850, reported to the Minister of the Interior that the local Guard commander, José Ampuero, was responsible for not only imbuing morality and discipline in guardsmen but also ensuring their "correct" election of officials.[106] Unit commanders would "safeguard" their guardsmen's *calificaciones* until the election, at which time they returned guardsmen's ballots marked for government candidates—and with a distinguishing mark to ensure that guardsmen submitted the slate, rather than another ballot.[107] Those who voted against the government's slate faced what period observers regarded as credible threats of personal ruin, imprisonment, or exile.[108] With around 50,000 registered guardsmen by the late 1840s, manipulation by municipal officials was vital to producing the ruling coalition's desired electoral results.

[103] The rural poor were ineligible to vote and under the dominion of landed elites.
[104] Valenzuela (1996: 224–232) and Wood (2002: 446–50).
[105] Santa María (1848: 48–52).
[106] Francisco Gana (1851: 32–33).
[107] Valenzuela (1996: 243–244).
[108] Vicuña (1870: 20–21).

This manipulation occurred in the context of mediated institutions, despite a constitutional structure that ostensibly endowed the state with sweeping leverage over localities; in actuality, municipalities functioned autonomously at mid-century.[109] Potential central state appointees at the local level typically had to be judged palatable by local elites, though there was some clientelistic control of local appointments. Local Governors, who were appointed by the president, selected municipal authorities, which gave municipal authorities an indirect stake in manipulating elections to please officials in Santiago. But, if municipal authorities wanted to deviate from the whims of representatives in Santiago (which was uncommon but not unprecedented), they faced few institutional constraints. Nevertheless, the system of electoral manipulation functioned serviceably for ruling coalition members until mid-century.[110]

CHILE'S BOOMS, THE 1851 CIVIL WAR, AND INSTITUTION BUILDING

Chile's double boom in wheat and copper upset this prevailing order by creating an exigent threat to the ruling coalition. Chilean wheat and flour exports grew from 122,960 metric quintals (qq) in 1846 to 501,643 qq in 1850—a 400 percent increase in four years. This exploding production was concentrated in the southern central valley, when more than 75 percent of wheat and flour exports exited the southern central valley ports of Constitución and Tomé.[111] Yet southern agriculturalists were politically marginalized. Their tax revenue was diverted to the northern central valley. Many yeomen were indebted to Valparaíso merchants through the *habilitación* system, and these lending practices intensified with the boom. Indeed, almost immediately after the boom, merchants and northern central valley landed elites began acquiring area farms as indebtedness grew among local residents.[112] Maurice Zeitlin maintains that *hacendados* were working to initiate "the transformation of small holders . . . into a subordinate agrarian tenantry."[113] The 1851 presidential election exacerbated these grievances, as the government's electoral chicanery delivered an easy victory for Manuel Montt and a stinging defeat for the south's candidate, General José María de la Cruz. The presidential defeat, in combination with

[109] Valenzuela (1977: 184).

[110] Cáceres Munoz (2005: 114–137) and Valenzuela (1996). Municipal authorities were often candidates for election and thus had a personal stake in manipulating outcomes.

[111] Bauer (1975: 65) and Sepúlveda (1959: 127).

[112] Bengoa (1988: 204–207) and Cerda-Hegerl (1997: 115–117).

[113] Zeitlin (1984: 36–37).

"the frustration of important economic interests in the provinces made it impossible . . . to swallow the election results."[114]

Meanwhile, northern mineral exports doubled from $6.1 million pesos in 1844 to $12.4 million pesos by 1850. At mid-century, mining accounted for 63 percent of Chile's total exports; agriculture contributed 25 percent.[115] Although heavy indebtedness plagued copper miners, state legislators vetoed a plan by northern miners and a Spaniard named Antonio Arcos to found a national bank in 1849.[116] Miners were also frustrated in their quest to obtain financial assistance for the proposed Copiapó-Caldera railroad, even as the state was poised to assist the Ferrocarril de Santiago á Valparaíso. Finally, in August 1851, the government raised mineral export duties from 1.5 to 4 percent.[117] Shifting relative economic power and ongoing political marginalization ruptured the veneer of tranquility in Chile the following month.

In September 1851, northern mine owners and southern agriculturalists launched a civil war. The insurrection began on September 7 in the northern port city of La Serena, followed a week later by an uprising in Concepción, the principal city of the southern central valley. Intendant reports had indicated percolating discontent in these areas, but state managers lacked the institutional resources to prevent insurrections.[118] Once the insurrections began, General Cruz assembled a rebel army of 4,000 men, including National Guard members, in the south. By November, his army was in open military confrontation with the government. War plainly threatened the exports that buoyed the ruling coalition and state. Stephen Henry Sulivan, the British chargé d'affairs, believed that if Cruz's forces prevailed, Chile would "soon fall into a state of utter confusion and anarchy, and that confidence, so essential to Commercial transactions will be entirely destroyed."[119] But Cruz's army was no match for government forces, and the state also offered generous amnesty to Cruz's officers, leading some to defect. The civil war in the south ended by mid-December, and the insurrection in La Serena ended in early January 1852. The ruling coalition celebrated. On March 9, 1852, British merchants honored President Montt with a banquet in Valparaíso.[120]

Nevertheless, the challenge had been "the worst faced by the Conservative regime in its twenty years of power."[121] The civil war demonstrated the

[114] Loveman (2001: 141).
[115] Oppenheimer (1976: 458–460).
[116] Volk (1993: 91–93).
[117] Vitale (1971a: 8).
[118] E.g., Francisco Gana (1851: 33).
[119] Quoted in Mayo (1987: 69).
[120] Vicuña Mackenna (1862: 191–192).
[121] Collier (2003: 102).

diametrical, exigent threat facing ruling coalition members. Had the insurrections succeeded, they would have, first, overturned fiscal policy. Second, rebel victory would have ended *habilitación* lending and the credit-option system, which allowed merchants to shift the risk associated with commodity price fluctuations onto producers. Third, coalitional change would likely terminate the government's support for ruling coalition members' desired public goods; the government would have probably instead supported a southern central valley railroad, thereby imperiling northern central valley nascent movement into export-oriented agriculture. Finally, an opposition victory would have ended electoral manipulation, which was one of its stated aims.[122] The threat to the ruling coalition was diametrical and fundamental.

Fearing such developments, the government repressed opponents in the 1852 and 1855 local elections.[123] The state complemented this short-term strategy with a long-term institutional solution to regional opposition. In January 1853, President Manuel Montt traveled south to assess the threats facing coalition members. According to Montt's personal correspondence, he was exploring institutional solutions to ensure the ruling coalition was not displaced through its own electoral system.[124] The ineffectiveness of electoral manipulation in opposition strongholds during the 1851 presidential elections worried Montt and his allies.[125] In Concepción Province, for example, the newspaper *La Reforma* reported that Cruz had defeated Montt by 5,000 votes to 179.[126] The government's electoral machinery needed an overhaul.

The government passed the 1854 Law of the Municipalities to address its tenuous local control. The law transformed municipal administration and included broad new executive powers at the municipal level, including greater control of electoral processes. Intendants and their local agents could now suspend existing municipal regulations and ordinances and unilaterally replace them with ones to their liking. Local mayors could be replaced arbitrarily, a change that fortified clientelistic bonds to power holders in Santiago. *Intendentes, Gobernadores,* and *Subdelegados* gained new powers over municipal budgeting and were empowered to pass laws at municipal meetings called on short notice (as little as 48 hours), even if only a portion of the municipal corporation attended. Municipal authorities who missed these meetings could be fined, a deterrent used to improve attendance and create a façade of consensus

122 Valenzuela (1996: 225–228).

123 Barros Arana et al. (1861: 50–51) and Barros Arana and Sotomayor Valdés (1858: 29–30).

124 Bravo Lira (1990: 153–154) and Vicuña (1870: 8–11).

125 Barros Arana et al. (1861: 62–63).

126 Collier (2003: 97). Although probably embellished, the point is clear. Vitale (1971a: 21) puts the tally at 2,011–142.

and legitimacy for the local population. Most important, there was no legal recourse to oppose these actions. The law usurped municipal autonomy, and scholars unanimously regard it as a watershed moment for Chilean institution development.[127]

The 1854 Law of the Municipalities vested new powers in the central state to control local affairs, elections, and the National Guard. The Consejo de Estado (Council of the State), which was appointed by the president, became the ultimate arbiter of elections, giving the executive branch final say over *calificaciones*. The council could illegally exclude voters before elections and, when results proved undesirable, invalidate municipal elections by forcing overall turnout below the two-thirds required through a post hoc disqualification of voters. Furthermore, the state had broad latitude to call new elections.[128] The state and its allies smothered local autonomy.

The state also expanded the number and improved the quality of state agents in the countryside to heighten its social control. The government nearly doubled the number of *Intendentes* and *Gobernadores* in the interior (from eighty-nine in 1850 to 150 by 1860) and increased their salaries as well, hoping to align their interests more closely with power holders in Santiago. Officials in Santiago demanded more and better information about activities in the countryside, and Intendants became less office-bound, moving throughout the provinces to exercise greater oversight.[129]

The state created new provinces and subdivided existing ones to facilitate local administrative control. Lawmakers subdivided Concepción Province into the provinces of Arauco (1852) and Llanquihue (1861) as part of a "divide and rule" strategy toward southern dissidents.[130] The government created a third department in Colchagua (Santa Cruz) to heighten its control of the population there.[131] Subdivision requests came from local state appointees as well. Ambrosio Camus, the governor of Putaendo (north of Santiago), asked that his subdelegation be divided in 1856 to foster better policing and social control.[132] This overriding concern pervades the correspondence between Interior Minister Antonio Varas and the Intendant of the Arauco Province, created from Concepción Province in 1852. Varas pressed the Intendant to implement the

[127] This consensus includes Barros Arana et al. (1861: 62–73); Figueroa Escuti (1953: 416); Gustavo Silva (1931); Moya Figueroa (1901); Letelier (1907: 80); Madrid (1911: 7); Orrego Luco (1890: 158–170); and Valenzuela (1977: 184–186).

[128] Madrid (1911: 4–16) and Moya Figueroa (1901: 13–22).

[129] Bravo Lira (1990: 155–156) and Humud Tleel (1969: 246–247).

[130] Barros Arana et al. (1861: 51) and Bravo Lira (1990: 154–155).

[131] Cacéres Muñoz (2005: 167).

[132] Camus (1856: 27).

1854 Law of the Municipalities as vigorously as possible, expressing particular interest in the electoral process, *calificaciones*, and the actual limits to municipal state power in Arauco.[133] Citizens in opposition strongholds regarded the new law as oppressive. Concepción-based newspapers ran editorials opposed to it, and Concepción's Intendant, Ramón Sotomayor, noted the law's implementation had triggered popular protests.[134] The new municipal ordinances were more than formal rules; they translated into enhanced state control at the local level.

The government exerted more power through fiscal policy as well. It repealed the colonial-era tithe (*diezmo*) on agricultural assets and replaced it with a tax on agricultural production, known as the *contribución territorial* (and later the *impuesto agrícola*). The tax did not generate much income—it was, after all, part of the decreasing tax burden on landed elites throughout the nineteenth century. But the way it was collected is noteworthy. Whereas clerical tax farmers collected the tithe, state agents directly extracted the new *contribución territorial*.[135] Municipal taxation also grew steadily after 1854 and fell under the purview of the central state. Municipal authorities "had to obtain permission from the national government for (tax) collection, and the funds were earmarked for particular purposes" that required state approval. These provisions "meant that the national government oversaw the collection of these taxes to a significant extent."[136] The state increasingly interacted with the populace directly, rather than indirectly overseeing citizens via local notables.

A RESPONSE TO FORTIFIED INSTITUTIONS: THE 1859 CIVIL WAR

The 1854 Law of the Municipalities proved efficacious. Prior to elections, Intendants "seized" registration cards of suspected government opponents and remitted them to Santiago with neither "cause nor process." At election time, National Guard troops would be called to their barracks and cajoled into voting for government candidates. The opposition Liberal Party found itself "defeated and persecuted tenaciously."[137] Voting irregularities and coercion were normal. In 1858, government critics maintained that, during the vote count in Santiago, "the municipality had not become an organ of the law, but

[133] Intendency archives (Arauco Province, Vol. 7), Archivo Nacional de Chile, Santiago.

[134] *El Correo del Vapor*, December 12, 1854 (Vol. 5, No. 425) and *El Correo del Sur*, December 16, 1854 (Vol. 5, No. 427). Sotomayor (1856: 29).

[135] Bauer (1975: 118) and Edwards (1932: 143–147).

[136] Soifer (2006: 272).

[137] Barros Arana et al. (1861: 50, 567–568).

rather an interpreter of the wishes and interests of the government."[138] Local officials regarded their duties as such. Vincente Izquierdo, the Intendant of Santiago Province, reported with great pride in 1865 that he had used the 1854 municipalities law with "all the zeal and patriotism possible" to identify new candidates for the National Guard, contact them via the police, and add their names to the electoral registry.[139] The "abuses, frauds, violence, forgery" that accompanied elections were supplemented with election nullification when results were undesirable, as in the districts of Chillán, Freirina, Illapel, San Fernando, and Vallenar in 1868. The root problem, critics argued, was that municipalities had been subjugated to the central state.[140] The government carefully controlled elections and sequestered competition to elite circles.[141]

In 1858, President Montt's National Party used the government's adept electoral machinery to "spoil" opposition candidacies, who captured only fourteen of seventy-two seats in the Chamber of Deputies, the lower house of Congress.[142] Against this backdrop, a new political party, the Radicals, emerged. The Radicals were Chile's first non-elite party, representing northern miners, southern agriculturalists, and artisans. The party thrived in Concepción and the Norte Chico towns of Caldera, Copiapó, La Serena, and Ovalle.[143] The Radical Party was a response to both electoral manipulation and the economic marginalization of the regional peripheries. By the late 1850s, Chile's Santiago-Valparaíso railroad pushed eastward from the port city, enriching *hacendados* in the northern central valley and canceling the transport cost advantages once enjoyed by wheat farmers near Talca. Northern mining interests remained aggrieved as well. But Chile's main political parties made no serious attempt to address the basic political and fiscal issues that had spawned the 1851 civil war.

In January 1859, civil war again broke out, with the largest insurrections in Talca and the northern mining city of Copiapó. Northern miners, southern wheat farmers, and artisans formed the core of the insurrections, as many of them had participated in the 1851 war. In Talca, the prominent miller and merchant Juan Antonio Pando provided material and organizational assistance to

[138] Barros Arana and Sotomayor Valdés (1858: 29–59, quote from 44).

[139] Izquierdo (1865: 22).

[140] Arteaga et al. (1868: 6–21, quote from 7).

[141] Chilean party politics, which emerged after 1857, was largely a competition among the Conservative, Liberal, and National (or Montt-Varista) parties. Scully (1992: 28, 212 n. 29) considers it "an incumbency struggle," or "a struggle at the level of political elites with little necessary extension to a larger social base."

[142] Barros Arana et al. (1861: 568).

[143] Gazmuri (1992: 129–149).

rebels. The mining magnate Pedro León Gallo led the movement in the north and had covertly trained artisans in Copiapó for the coming military fight. Founding members of the Radical Party were also among the opposition leaders. The rebels targeted Intendancies and dispatched roaming guerrilla forces, known as *montoneras,* into the northern central valley to antagonize *hacendados* and stir up peasant resistance. Yet the government proved too powerful and extinguished the insurrections by late April 1859.[144]

The political settlement after the war featured landed elites and merchants closing ranks and reconciling their differences on clerical issues, for instance, in order to maintain the marginalization of regional interests. A series of "complex intraelite accommodations and compromises" led to the Liberal-Conservative "Fusion" from 1861 to 1891.[145] Northern central valley landed elites and Valparaíso merchants remained the country's preeminent sociopolitical forces, and successive presidents refused to curtail state prerogatives vis-à-vis municipalities. New state capacity proved durable. Elections remained rife with manipulation, greatly inhibiting the Radical Party.[146] Ruling coalition members solidified their power, which would have been considerably more difficult without the institutional initiatives of the 1850s.

CODA: THE WHEAT BOOM, FRONTIER SETTLEMENT, AND TERRITORIAL PACIFICATION

The final state building development spawned by the wheat boom was the pacification of national territory by the early 1880s. Before 1850, the Bío Bío River, south of Concepción, was the effective southern border of Chilean territory, beyond which were the Indian lands of Araucanía. The state had largely preserved peace north of the river by stationing military troops on the frontier and paying subsidies to Indian tribes. But new export possibilities "upset the previous equilibrium on the Frontier." During the 1850s, more than 14,000 settlers moved south of the Bío Bío River to farm wheat.[147] Valparaíso merchants welcomed frontier settlement for its economic potential and encouraged the government, partly through editorials in their mouthpiece, *El Mercurio,* to colonize the south. The state initially adopted a hands-off policy toward frontier settlement. However, "the southern frontier attracted a heavy migration of impoverished landless laborers" from the central valley, which "deeply

[144] Collier (2003: 223–228); Daitsman (1995: 208–258); and Vitale (1971b: 257–272).
[145] Scully (1992: 45). The National Party died out after the 1850s.
[146] See Arteaga et al. (1868) and Vicuña (1870).
[147] Collier and Sater (1996: 95).

disturbed" landed elites.[148] Smallholdings emerged as the land tenure norm in frontier areas, which also served as refuge for anti-government elements during the 1859 civil war. *Hacendados* believed frontier areas jeopardized their economic interests, and state managers increasingly regarded Araucanía as "a permanent danger to interior peace."[149]

Hacendados concluded that territorial pacification would enable them to control settlement patterns in the frontier, stem labor flight, and perpetuate their dominance. The state moved to militarily subjugate the Araucanian (a.k.a. Mapuche) Indians and tackled land-related issues through administrative action. First, the military incrementally extended the frontier of national territory. By 1862–63, the state created a permanent presence south of the Bío Bío River by establishing forts at Mulchén and Angol. Soldiers on the frontier not only fought Indians but also helped clear woods, construct roads, bridges, and telegraph lines, and erect warehouses and hospitals.[150] In 1867–68, the military extended the frontier to the Malleco River, which marked the fifteenth fort in Araucanía.[151] Along the way, government forces built complementary logistical infrastructure like telegraph lines to enhance their coordination and effectiveness in frontier areas.[152] The military surged south to Traiguén in 1878–79, which bifurcated remaining Indian tribes, portending their ultimate defeat in 1883.[153]

The government toiled throughout to ensure that a yeomanry would not take root in Araucanía. The government thwarted the budding yeomanry by regulating land transactions to the advantage of northern central valley landowners. Some settlers reported being "violently dispossessed" of their farms by landed elites seeking to colonize the south. The government did little to help these settlers, with dispossession claims often stagnating in the bureaucracy. (Early settlers ultimately became part of the floating regional peasantry.) The state revealed its indifference toward settlers through an auction system it adopted in 1873–74. Indians became viewed as illegal squatters on frontier lands, and the state began to auction off the lands.[154] The auction system required a down payment of one-third the sale price of property, rather than the prior 2 percent requirement. The larger down payments restricted land purchases

[148] Quotes from Solberg (1969: 118) and Whaley (1974: 78), respectively.
[149] Edwards (1932: quote from 367) and Ruiz-Esquide (2000: 122–132).
[150] Ferrando Keun (1986: 350–358).
[151] Estado Mayor General del Ejército (Chile) (1980: 251–272).
[152] Ruiz-Esquide (2000: 228–229).
[153] Fernando Keun (1986: 434–477).
[154] Pinto Rodríguez (2003: 221) and Ruiz-Esquide (2000: 219–224, 267–269, quote from 219).

to the wealthy.[155] The government held these auctions in Santiago, not in the frontier, and tax rolls confirm that many emerging landed elites in Araucanía hailed from the northern central valley. Over 1875–87, the state distributed 84 percent of frontier lands through these auctions. Auctions forestalled the emergence of a frontier yeomanry and eliminated the incentive for central valley peasants to migrate south.[156] After landed elites consolidated their grip on frontier lands, their new estates lay fallow—well into the 1930s in some areas.[157] Once again, state policy proceeded according to a political, not economic, rationale.

Chile in 1883: A Precocious Latin American Leviathan

The pacification of the national territory marked the end of Chile's formative state building era, during which state capacity grew impressively. Leading theories have difficulty accounting for this growth in Chilean state capacity. As I note above, Chile became more reliant on customs duties (from 49 percent of revenue in 1848 to 65 percent in 1883), which suggests that the revenue imperative did not propel state building.[158] Chile was also a perennial colonial backwater and its trajectory was "underdetermined by Spanish colonialism. (One) must therefore look to postcolonial nineteenth-century events to explain" its development.[159] Indeed, both the 1833 constitution and the 1854 Law of the Municipalities marked sharp breaks from the colonial past. Finally, it may be tempting to attribute Chilean state building its lack of ethnic diversity. But it was only with the pacification of Araucanía that Chile assuaged ethnic antagonism; during colonialism, the Araucanians were notoriously violent toward the Spanish.[160] Today, "ethnic boundaries" are not central to Chilean politics,[161] partly because of efforts to imbue a sense of national identity, or *chileanidad*, through the military and public education.[162] To credit Chile's state building success to a lack of ethnic diversity is to confuse cause and effect to a significant extent.

[155] Solberg (1969: 119) notes that landed elites paid installments on auction purchases interest-free with "rapidly depreciating" paper money.

[156] Ruiz-Esquide (2000: 245, 275–276) and Solberg (1969: 120). The state gave lands not purchased at auctions to military officers as concessions.

[157] McBride (1936: 294).

[158] Centeno (2002: 124–125).

[159] Mahoney (2010: 123). Lange (2009: 203) shares Mahoney's assessment.

[160] Mahoney (2010: 83–85). In fact, today Chile scores just above the global mean of "ethnic fractionalization" (Fearon 2003).

[161] Lieberman (2009: 284, 291).

[162] Centeno (2002: 256) and Mahoney (2010: 198, 224).

The subjugation of Araucanía marked one of the earliest territorial pacifications in Latin America. Even more impressive was the movement toward unmediated rule, epitomized by the 1854 Law of the Municipalities. State agents gained new despotic powers to control elections, and local autonomy withered. Mayors were subordinated to central state prerogatives, as were municipal fiscal affairs. The burgeoning national judicial system was one sign of the growth of central state capacity.[163] The state established Courts of Appeals in Concepción and La Serena, the two main regional centers, in 1849 and later added one in Iquique (Tarapacá Province), seized during the War of the Pacific. Whereas the Chilean Supreme Court and Courts of Appeals handled 1,724 cases in 1856, they handled 5,234 cases in 1885. Public schooling was another sign of the growing state presence in Chilean society: the nationwide school system expanded from 186 schools in 1850 to around 750 by 1883.[164] Administration in Santiago strengthened, too. The size of the state grew from 2,211 public functionaries in 1850 to 3,048 in 1880 (and 13,119 by 1900), and administrators generally adhered to rationalized bureaucratic precepts.[165] The state's institutional power was wholly unlike that which prevailed at mid-century.

New public goods also contributed to the growth of state capacity. The formalization of Chile's credit market led to direct oversight of the financial sector, as well as direct involvement in it through new institutions like the Caja de Crédito Hipotecario and the Caja de Ahorros. State administrators also benefitted from loans from the Banco Nacional de Chile when foreign credit dried up during the run-up to the conflict with Spain in the 1860s. The Banco Nacional de Chile similarly provided capital needed to transform the FCSV and FCS into state-owned enterprises. Railroads gave state managers new logistical power, and by 1873, the state owned the FCSV and FCS, then over 500 km of track (which would grow to 950 km by 1880).[166] A national telegraph service developed alongside railroads and improved communication with state agents throughout the countryside—which proved vital to coordinate military forces during the pacification of Araucanía.[167]

These developments are best explained by how Chile's booms in wheat and copper intersected with the country's coalitional politics. The booms spurred northern central valley landed elites to seek new public goods. It also gave

[163] On general developments in the Chilean judiciary, see Couso (2005: 214–216) and Hilbink (2007: 46–55).

[164] Encina (1949b: 436–438, 1950: 13, 1951: 240).

[165] Humud Tleel (1969: 80–88, 176–181, 246–249). See also Heise González (1974: 300–303) and Urzúa Valenzuela and García Barzelatto (1971: 29–32).

[166] Oppenheimer (1976: 492–493).

[167] Pinto Rodríguez (2003: 197–202).

rising exporters outside of the ruling coalition new reasons to press for political power, which prompted deep anxiety among ruling coalition members, who turned to a long-term strategy of institutional elaboration in municipalities to fortify their existing advantages. Neither of these developments were functional outgrowths of export production but were rather conditioned by coalitional politics. The following chapter on Argentine state building details how dual enrichment across the *cordillera* led to similar growth in state capacity. These analogous processes yielded by 1900 what were arguably Latin America's two strongest states.

CHAPTER 4

Seizing State Building Opportunities during Argentina's Wool Boom, 1852–1886

As of the mid-nineteenth century, "Argentina" had ceased to exist as a single entity. The country had degenerated into two competing reservoirs of power: the government of Buenos Aires province and a rival confederation of *caudillo* leaders from surrounding provinces. The government in Buenos Aires controlled an area of just 102,000 km^2, roughly the size of Iceland and about 4 percent of the landmass that would constitute Argentina by the early 1880s.[1] Cattle ranchers, more so than state agents, were responsible for maintaining law and order within this limited sphere of influence. The government in Buenos Aires province was weak by any measure. Between 1852 and 1886, however, power holders in Buenos Aires dramatically altered this state of affairs. They subjugated the confederation of *caudillos*, extended state institutions into the country's interior, and pacified the national territory. Argentina was transformed from a port city to a modern state.

These striking accomplishments have long been regarded as part of the country's good economic fortune in the second half of the nineteenth century, when export-led growth made Argentina one of the wealthiest countries outside of Europe. The concurrent growth of state capacity was not a functional outgrowth of boom times, however, but hinged on coalitional politics. Export-oriented ranchers in Buenos Aires led the ruling coalition and impelled the state to provide public goods like new transportation infrastructure, credit sector reform, labor market regulation, and territorial pacification. Yet, even though the boom enriched ranchers in Buenos Aires, its relative gains accrued to upstart ranchers in the rival Argentine Confederation. Economic competition exacerbated political rancor and begot civil war in 1859. Buenos Aires

[1] Zimmerman (1945).

prevailed, reuniting Argentina. But the steadily rising power of ranchers outside of Buenos Aires posed a diametrical threat to ruling coalition members, who initiated institution building to constrict their rivals and forged a substantial increase of central state power in the hinterland.

Argentina at Mid-Century

Four principal actors affected Argentine state building: ranching elites in Buenos Aires province, urban merchants in the port city of Buenos Aires, provincial elites, and the rural masses. Ranching elites in Buenos Aires province were the major economic and political force in nineteenth-century Argentina. Before 1850, they were mainly cattle ranchers who exported salted meat to Brazil and hides to Europe, albeit in limited quantities. After 1850, ranchers diversified into wool production, the basis of Argentina's economic vigor in the second half of the century. Ranchers exhibited "a great deal of group cohesion and solidarity."[2] Urban merchants located in Buenos Aires were their junior partners in the ruling political coalition. State revenue came mainly from customs duties, which shielded landed property from taxation, and pastoral products were subject to relatively low duties.[3] Fiscal policy was the chief side-payment maintaining the coalition of Buenos Aires ranchers and *porteño* merchants.

Provincial elites beyond Buenos Aires province were the main opposition force. Many provincial elites were ranchers with embryonic links to external markets, and the provinces were ruled by *caudillos*, local strongmen or regional warlords. The provinces were organized collectively as the "Argentine Confederation" but in actuality each province "continued to be ruled by caudillos, even if they were called governors, and the confederation was essentially a network of personal loyalties to its president."[4] Finally, labor was relatively scarce in Argentina, so ranchers within and beyond Buenos Aires perennially worried about the prospect of insufficient labor supplies. Labor concerns made the rural masses an economic consideration and a political target, though the rural poor were not consequential political players in their own right.

At mid-century, Argentina was linked to external markets through trade in cattle hides and salted meat, but this activity was not weighty. Real prices of pastoral products in Buenos Aires experienced a secular decline from 1833 to 1850, even as absolute levels of cattle hide exports rose. Cattle exports grew

[2] Lynch (1981: 97).

[3] Chiaramonte (1971: 85–90).

[4] Lynch (1993: 39). See also Scobie (1964a: 202).

largely because of internal dynamics. Foreign merchants were crowding out native *porteño* merchants in Buenos Aires, which propelled Argentine merchants to employ their assets in cattle ranching. The development of Argentina's pastoral sector was thus incipient, though this nascent organization helped ranchers respond quickly to changing price signals in the 1850s.[5]

Argentine politics was in flux after the fall of Juan Manuel de Rosas in 1852, who had ruled Argentina since 1829, mainly as an agent of cattle ranchers and urban merchants. Ranchers led the political coalition and were "the life-blood of the Rosas state." The interior provinces and rural masses stood outside the coalition.[6] During the 1830s and 1840s, Rosas advanced ranchers' interests by eliminating state ownership of huge tracts of land in the pampas and privatizing these holdings for them. Rosas also enacted internal passport restrictions to facilitate control of the small rural labor force.[7] These actions reflected Rosas' responsiveness to ranchers' economic pursuits, though they rendered modest state building byproducts.

State capacity in general was unimpressive around 1850. Over 90 percent of revenue was generated at the Buenos Aires port, and colonial era cart paths functioned as the country's paltry transportation infrastructure. Rural administration was carried out largely by the Justices of the Peace, who were typically local landowners, not state employees.[8] The Justices were the bedrock of the state's judicial arm, though it was ad hoc, personalistic, and embryonic.[9] Electoral practices were similar to Chile, and in Argentina the Justices of the Peace appointed local election officials, who set up the registration tables and thereby controlled elections. Networks of personal loyalties, rather than bureaucratized administration, were how Rosas exerted his influence.[10] More generally, "local government remained embryonic."[11] Indeed, even before Rosas' fall, "Argentina" was something of a fictitious entity: the effective frontier of government-controlled territory was just beyond the Salado River, or roughly half of what would constitute Buenos Aires province by the 1880s. To the south of this frontier lay hostile Indian tribes; to the west were the interior provinces; and to the north were the littoral provinces—areas all historically at odds with Buenos Aires.

A coalition of disaffected provincial interests, with backing from Brazil and Uruguay, overthrew Rosas in 1852. During the 1840s, Rosas tried to

[5] Brown (1979: 69–96).

[6] Burgin (1946); López-Alves (2000: 41); and Lynch (1981: quote from 124).

[7] Lynch (1981: 52–67).

[8] Díaz (1959).

[9] Lynch (1981: 169, 210–212) and Zimmermann (1998: 131–133).

[10] Zimmermann (2009: 19–21, 37 n. 82).

[11] Rock (2002: 24).

monopolize area trade by blockading the Paraná River, which served as a crucial trade link between the Río de la Plata and Argentina's littoral provinces, Brazil, and Uruguay. Britain and France objected to Rosas' blockade and imposed a blockade of their own on Buenos Aries. Urban merchants and some cattle ranchers defected from the ruling coalition and weakened Rosas. Among the defectors was Justo José de Urquiza, a *caudillo* from Argentina's Entre Ríos province and one of Rosas' army commanders. Urquiza turned his forces on the government and, with Brazilian and Uruguayan support, defeated Rosas at the Battle of Caseros in 1852.[12]

After Rosas' defeat, Argentina ceased to exist as a single entity for a decade. Buenos Aires province remained the most powerful economic force in "Argentina," but it stood apart from the newly formed Argentine Confederation. Ranchers remained the preponderant economic and political power in Buenos Aires and continued to lead the ruling political coalition.[13] Entre Ríos, the province immediately north of Buenos Aires, was the nerve center of the Argentine Confederation. The Confederation functioned akin to the United States under the Articles of Confederation, with substantial provincial autonomy and similar obstacles to trade, including inter-provincial tariffs on goods en route to the Confederation's main port in Rosario, on the Paraná River.[14] The Confederation's social and economic characteristics paralleled those of Buenos Aires in key respects. Large ranching estates predominated in the Confederation's leading provinces of Corrientes, Entre Ríos, and Santa Fe, and area landowners were tenuously linked to external markets via pastoral exports.[15] These embryonic links positioned them as potential rivals to *estancieros* in Buenos Aires, and economic competition between them would spawn remarkable state building during the coming wool boom.

The Revenue Imperative and Argentine State Building

As in Chile, Argentina's formative state building was not propelled by the revenue imperative. Argentina's reliance on non-rent-generating pastoral exports arguably inclines a diversified taxing strategy so as to not hinder exports' international competitiveness. On the one hand, Argentina's taxing strategy emphasized import duties, rather than export duties, which shifted the tax burden toward consumers and away from pastoralists. From 1863 to 1886, import

[12] Rock (1987: 111–113).
[13] See López-Alves (2000: 141) on Argentina's coalitional continuity.
[14] Scobie (1964a).
[15] Chiaramonte (1986).

duties supplied 69 percent of state revenues, while export duties contributed 14 percent.[16] But, on the other hand, this dependence on volatile trade duties did not amount to a diversified fiscal strategy. Customs and royalties never accounted for less than 70 percent of ordinary income during the case study period.[17] Even after the costly War of the Triple Alliance (1864–70), when Argentina faced gaping budget deficits, *estancieros* "paralyzed" efforts to tax rural wealth.[18] Coalitional politics, not the characteristics of pastoral products, dictated fiscal policy.

Argentina's taxing profile remained unchanged despite the War of the Triple Alliance, the closest Latin America has "come to the modern notion of total war."[19] Argentina entered the war after the Paraguayan aggressor, Francisco Solano López, moved into upper portions of the Paraná River area as a staging ground for attacks against Brazil. Argentina suffered heavy casualties in the conflict, which accelerated an ongoing effort to incorporate rural labor within the national army.[20] The war roughly doubled public debt, but policymakers did not strengthen fiscal institutions.[21] In fact, state officials found only "skin-deep (support) among the porteño oligarchy" to fund the war partly with new internal taxes.[22] The war, like most wars in Latin America, yielded "blood and debt and not much more."[23] External rivalries had similarly little influence on Argentine state building. Argentina's border dispute with Chile, for instance, began in the 1840s but the two sides waited twenty-five years to hold formal diplomatic discussions on it. Meanwhile, Argentina did not attempt to colonize or permanently deploy state officials into the disputed area of Patagonia. As in Chile, the revenue imperative was not central to Argentina's state building after mid-century.

Argentina's Wool Boom

Argentina's first major commodity boom was a prolonged upward secular trend in wool prices due to expanding European textile manufacturing. This boom dwarfed Argentina's existing exports of cattle hides, tallow, and salted meat, which had grown from about F$3 million (*pesos fuertes*) in the

[16] Calculation based on data in Oszlak (1982: 204–205) and Cortés Conde (1989: 150).
[17] Centeno (2002: 124–125).
[18] Oszlak (1982: 214–215).
[19] Centeno (2002: 54–56).
[20] López-Alves (2000: 190–191).
[21] Chiaramonte (1971: 90). See also Centeno (2002: 133).
[22] McLynn (1984: 89).
[23] Centeno (2002: 127).

mid-1820s to F$10 million by 1850, despite an ongoing secular price slump. The wool boom was more consequential. The boom began abruptly, when Russian wool exports halted due to the Crimean War. Between 1856 and 1857, the average price paid for wool in Buenos Aires rose about 40 percent.[24] The cattle ranching elites of Buenos Aires province, who were "always alert, gradually shifted from cattle to sheep raising." A sheep, "whose price even in the 1840's was hardly equivalent to that of an egg, had finally become valuable."[25] The number of sheep in Argentina grew quickly, from about 15 million head in 1857 to 47 million head by 1865.[26] By then, wool and sheepskin exports passed F$13 million and climbed to F$35 million by 1881.[27] Sheep exports constituted 60 percent Argentine exports in the early 1880s, up from 10 percent circa 1850.[28] Productivity improved as well, as better methods and stock improvements enabled a more thorough extraction of wool.

But there were obstacles to expanding sheep production within Buenos Aires province. The most viable lands in Buenos Aires were located north of the Salado River,[29] as much of the rest of the province was afflicted by Indian raids and inhospitable to ranching. Land access constituted a barrier to production and would be among the triggers of public goods seeking after 1857. Competition for land also created conflict between Buenos Aires and the littoral provinces of the Confederation, especially Corrientes, Entre Ríos, and Santa Fe, where ranching expansion was less precarious. The wool boom thus presented barriers to expanded production and shifted relative economic power between ranchers in Buenos Aires and their competitors in the littoral provinces of the Argentine Confederation.

New Public Goods for Powerful Ranching Elites

The pursuit and provision of new public goods paralleled the Chilean case. Many of the public goods were similar as well. Some of the collective goods sought by Buenos Aires ranchers, such as new banking institutions, necessarily had to be supplied by the state, while others, such as railroads, hinged on state involvement because of the reluctance of foreign investors. Like Chile's Sociedad Nacional de Agricultura, Argentine *estancieros* organized themselves through the Sociedad Rural Argentina, a tight-knit and long-lasting interest

[24] Sabato (1990: 205).
[25] Scobie (1971: 159, 83, respectively).
[26] Chiaramonte (1971: 43).
[27] Sabato (1990: 31).
[28] Scobie (1971: 83) and Slatta (1983: 195).
[29] Sabato (1990: 10–14).

group that advanced the interests of export-oriented ranchers.[30] Buenos Aires ranchers succeeded in obtaining their desired public goods and simultaneously pressured the state to design them to their distributional benefit.

PREFERENCES FOR NEW PUBLIC GOODS

First, Argentine *estancieros* sought improved transportation infrastructure to facilitate sheep exports. Unlike cattle exports, which were sold dried or salted, sheared wool was transported by cart, likely to dampen when exposed to the elements, and therefore susceptible to rotting. *The Brazil and River Plate Mail* lamented that wool arriving by cart in downtown Buenos Aires from Luján, a town 40 miles away, was almost always partially damp, at a cost of "millions" to "poor sheep farmers" every year. Transport costs for estancias north of the Salado River to the port constituted 4 to 5 percent of total production costs.[31] These costs would have been even higher south of the Salado River or in the Confederation's littoral provinces. Railroads could ameliorate such costs but would have to involve the state: potential foreign investors were wary of capital-intensive projects in Argentina not backed by government profit guarantees.[32]

Capital accessibility was another concern. Compared to cattle ranching, which required little capital investment, sheep raising was capital-intensive, involving shearing equipment, boiling vats, and other inputs not needed for cattle production. As the value of wool rose, so too did the capital needed to begin raising sheep. The capital requirements to establish a 10,000 hectare sheep estancia in Buenos Aires (a typical large-scale estate) more than doubled from 1845–1854 to 1855–1864. By the 1880s, it was five times as costly to initially establish a good sized sheep farm as it had been before to the boom.[33] Merchant houses were the country's main creditors.[34] Banks did not exist, aside from the Banco de la Provincia de Buenos Aires, though it only issued currency and did not make loans.[35] The growing appetite for capital exerted "increasing demands on the primitive financial networks" that existed.[36]

[30] See Hora (2001: 8–23); Slatta (1983: 98–99); and Sabato (1990: 163–164).

[31] Sabato (1990: 221–225).

[32] Lewis (1983: 8–12).

[33] Brown (1979: 133) and Sabato (1990: 138–148). In 1864, about half of the land in Buenos Aires province was part of estates larger than 5,000 hectares. A mere 44 families, or 3.5 percent of landowners, controlled 37 percent of the best land in Buenos Aires province, north of the Salado River (Sabato 1990: 44–48).

[34] Reber (1979).

[35] Ferns (1960: 357).

[36] Sabato (1990: 253–254).

Part of this capital demand was due to labor costs, as sheep raising was comparatively labor-intensive to cattle ranching. Labor costs were roughly 60 percent of a typical estancia's annual expenses, and aggregate labor demand in the pastoral sector increased tenfold in Buenos Aires province by 1885, in spite of rising productivity. There were chronic seasonal labor shortages, particularly for shearers, indicated by the fact that Argentine peons earned twice the wages paid to rural workers elsewhere in South America.[37] *Estancieros* resorted to advancing cash to potential ranch hands, not as a means to indebt them but simply as a means to attract them. Nongovernmental solutions to labor scarcity were unlikely because there was something of a collective action dilemma facing ranchers. Some *estancieros* permitted peons to rent portions of their estates throughout the year in order to meet seasonal shearing demand. But there were not enough rural laborers for all estancias to employ this practice, so other ranchers wanted peon families resettled from their competitors' estates to towns or frontier areas. What ranchers could agree on was that the state should continue to enforce internal passport requirements, as it had under Rosas. Public solutions seemed best to mitigate the economic risk associated with a transitory labor supply.[38]

Finally, land-related concerns stimulated public goods preferences. First, rising land prices added to ranchers' credit demand. For instance, a hectare of land north of the Salado River sold, on average, for $1.11 "golden pesos" ($oro) before the boom (1850–1854) but rose precipitously, to $12.04, following the boom (1860–1864).[39] Second, ranchers wanted the state to open up new ranchlands. One option for ranching expansion was the southern and western portions of Buenos Aires province, then controlled by the Araucanian, Pampas, and Ranqueles Indian tribes. Rosas had secured a tenuous peace with them via subsidies, though this policy paradoxically let Indian communities strengthen themselves, and by the 1850s, they were more formidable than twenty years prior.[40] In 1872, the newspaper *La Prensa* claimed that "in the period 1820–1870 the Indians had taken eleven million cattle, two million horses, and two million sheep; they had killed fifty thousand people, destroyed three thousand houses, and stolen twenty million dollars' worth of property."[41]

[37] Amaral (1998: 161–179); Newland and Poulson (1998: 332); and Sabato (1990: 70–73). Progressively raising wages to attract urban dwellers was apparently ineffective. In 1854, an editorial in *La Tribuna* was confounded that street vendors, earning $2–4 pesos daily, did not migrate to earn the $15 daily pesos offered on rural estates (Slatta 1983: 112–113).

[38] Sabato (1990: 84–88).

[39] Sabato (1990: 55).

[40] Lynch (1998: 10–16).

[41] Article summary from Lynch (1998: 11). Newland and Poulson (1998: 330) consider the Indian raids during the 1850s "particularly harmful" to ranchers.

As of the mid-1850s, these lands were not viable for ranching expansion. The other candidate lands were in the littoral provinces of Corrientes, Entre Ríos, and Santa Fe, which featured some incipient ranching.[42] Later, I discuss how ranching expansion shifted to these littoral provinces and impelled institutional strengthening. Once Buenos Aires institutionally asserted its control over these provinces, policymakers turned to pacifying the country's Indian tribes to enable ranching expansion in southern Buenos Aires province.

PUBLIC GOODS SEEKING AND PROVISION IN BUENOS AIRES PROVINCE

There were remarkable similarities in public goods seeking and provision in Argentina and Chile. In the transportation sector, the Argentine state regularly supplied profit guarantees to make railway projects possible; sometimes, it directly subsidized railroad construction, and other times the government tempted financiers with sizable land concessions alongside new railroads. Railroad investment came from Britain, as well as William Wheelwright, who financed some Chilean railways. Domestic investors tended to have export-oriented interests and purchased railway shares in limited liability companies established by the state.[43] The first Argentine railroad, the Ferrocarril Oeste, began operating in 1857, and its next section stretched to Chivilcoy, "the heart of the sheep-raising district." Railways lessened ranchers' transport costs: whereas cart transport cost ranchers about $0.12–0.14 ($oro) per ton of wool per kilometer, railroad transport was just $0.09 as of the early 1870s and fell to roughly $0.05 by the 1880s.[44] Although railways developed initially in Buenos Aires, ruling coalition members sometimes welcomed them in the interior provinces. The Central Argentine Railway, for example, linked Rosario (in Santa Fe province) with Córdoba and served to facilitate central state penetration of the interior and deepen its economic reliance on Buenos Aires.[45]

The state's actions to foment credit accessibility advanced the interests of ranchers from Buenos Aires and impinged on upstart ranchers from Entre Ríos and Santa Fe. In 1862, the government authorized Argentina's first joint stock enterprises and passed a new banking law, which paved the way for the 1863 opening of the London and River Plate Bank, the first British joint stock bank in Latin America. Foreign capital flowed into Argentina, partly as loans to the state that were, in turn, used as profit guarantees for British-funded

[42] Rock (1987: 123) and Chiaramonte (1986).
[43] Lewis (1983: 8–22).
[44] Sabato (1990: 220–225).
[45] Rock (1987: 145).

railroads. The new banking framework freed the existing Banco de la Provincia de Buenos Aires to make loans, which it did widely to pastoralists.[46] Nicholas Bouwer, Baring Brothers' representative in Argentina, wrote in 1877 that *estancieros* viewed the bank as "an institution specially created to supply them with funds without they [*sic*] being compelled to refund in due course."[47]

In 1872, the government formed the Banco Hipotecario de la Provincia de Buenos Aires, which functioned like the mortgage bank in Chile. The Argentine mortgage bank issued mortgage bond letters of credit (*cédulas*), which attracted noteworthy British investment and helped relieve the capital constraints facing sheep raisers.[48] The Argentine mortgage bank and the Banco de la Provincia de Buenos Aires were largely extensions of export interests, with wool raisers, cattle ranchers, and merchants "among [their] organizers, directors, and board members." Moreover, the large, rich, and powerful *estancieros* benefited more than smaller scale pastoralists because they could more readily and cheaply obtain loans from the newly authorized lending institutions.[49]

The government also assisted ranchers in Buenos Aires by taking steps to frustrate their rivals in Entre Ríos and Santa Fe. In the early 1860s, Buenos Aires ranchers defeated a proposal for a "free" banking system, which would have eliminated the need for new banks to receive specific authorization from the central government. (Free banking was not authorized until 1887.) The defeat of free banking constrained credit availability in Argentina's other provinces.[50] And though the government formed the Banco Hipotecario de la Provincia de Buenos Aires in 1872, it did not establish a commensurate national mortgage bank until 1886.[51] Meanwhile, *estancieros* in Buenos Aires obtained cheap credit from the provincial mortgage bank, while landowners in Entre Ríos and Santa Fe had to rely on commercial banks. The most important of these commercial banks was the London and River Plate Bank's branch office in Rosario. But the bank did not make mortgage loans, limiting pastoralists to short-term and relatively expensive credit instead.[52] As in Chile, credit sector reform constituted an impure public good, as Argentina's limited banking liberalization led to the establishment of some commercial branches in the interior. Overall, though, banks "offered very few credit facilities to private individuals or at least to individuals without political connections."[53]

[46] Lynch (1993: 43) and Sabato (1990: 254–266).
[47] Cited in Jones (1977: 32).
[48] Ferns (1960: 370–371).
[49] Sabato (1990: 273–274).
[50] Cortés Conde (1999: 228–243).
[51] Williams (1920: 73).
[52] Joslin (1963: 28–50).
[53] Reber (1979: 30).

State action in the labor market was similarly responsive to ranchers' preferences. The Buenos Aires government strengthened vagrancy statutes in 1858, just as the wool boom was taking hold. Two years earlier, the "government began soliciting suggestions from prominent ranchers" for a comprehensive reform of rural statutes, and in 1865, the state pressed austere restrictions onto gauchos and peons. Only local Justices of the Peace could grant peons permission to travel outside of their assigned region, and justices adjudicated disputes with absolute authority. The law was the zenith of Argentine rural legislation and created a legal labyrinth intended to reduce worker mobility. The new code resulted from close collaboration between *estancieros* and the state. The government presented the Sociedad Rural Argentina—the chief interest group of export-oriented ranchers—a draft of the legislation for its extended comment before the legislative vote on it. Society members "scrutinized the code in thirty-eight sessions and offered no substantial modifications" to it.[54]

The provision of new public goods contributed to the growth of Argentine state capacity. New transportation and communications infrastructure facilitated the deployment of state agents, and new lending institutions promoted bureaucratization and greater oversight of the economy in general. Labor "regulation" was draconian but nonetheless led to a greater state presence in the countryside. Eventually, the state helped ranching expand southward from Buenos Aires to Patagonia by pacifying the national territory. Before that, however, ruling coalition members dealt with a burgeoning threat from the country's other littoral provinces and moved toward unmediated rule in order to ensconce their existing advantages. It was the watershed era of Argentine state formation.

Enriching Exports, Inter-Provincial Conflict, and Institution Building

After Juan Manuel de Rosas' defeat at the Battle of Caseros in 1852, "Argentina" became two separate entities. This institutional profile changed drastically over the next two decades. In 1852, the littoral and interior provinces formed the Argentine Confederation, with Rosario functioning as its trading entrepôt and commercial lifeblood. Justo José de Urquiza, the Confederation's president, was intent on expanding trade between the littoral provinces and Europe as a means to offset the economic power of Buenos Aires. Buenos Aires, for its part, remained defiantly independent of the Confederation throughout

[54] Slatta (1983: 112–115).

the 1850s because it had the financial strength to do so.[55] Yet, despite Rosas' despotic rule, his "institutional legacy was almost nil."[56] Beyond Buenos Aires province, the Confederation was governed by a network of personal loyalties, not bureaucratic administration.[57] In other words, mediated rule prevailed throughout "Argentina."

In the aftermath of the Battle of Caseros, relations between Buenos Aires and the Confederation remained contentious and rooted in economic competition. Economic conflicts dated to the Rosas era. Rosas had hoarded customs revenue in Buenos Aires and occasionally blockaded the Paraná River to funnel Argentine trade through the Buenos Aires port.[58] The Buenos Aires government used these tactics intermittently after Rosas' fall to frustrate the Confederation from directly trading with external markets. Even when the Paraná River was not obstructed, the Confederation government was perennially on the verge of bankruptcy.[59]

THE WOOL BOOM AND INTER-PROVINCIAL ANTAGONISM

A key issue driving inter-provincial conflict after 1857 was access to land, which was increasingly valuable due to the wool boom. *Estancieros* in Buenos Aires province sought to use their existing landholdings north of the Salado River for sheep raising and, ideally, wanted to displace their cattle herds southward into the province's frontier areas. But frequent Indian raids made this strategy unworkable.[60] The best candidate lands for ranching expansion were in Corrientes, Entre Ríos, and Santa Fe, the core of the Argentine Confederation. Wool production thus had the potential to disrupt the existing balance of power between *estancieros* in Buenos Aires and their budding competitors in the Confederation.

The changing spatial distribution of sheep within Argentina indicated that a shift in economic power began as the wool boom commenced. Prior to the boom, there were about 15 million head of sheep in Argentina, almost all of which were located in Buenos Aires province north of the Salado River. Between 1857 and 1865, the absolute number of sheep in "Argentina" grew to 38–40 million head, but Buenos Aires' relative share of them declined to 80–85 percent. Most of the rest were being raised in Entre Ríos and Santa Fe. This trend continued such that, by 1875, only 63 percent of all Argentine

[55] Rock (1987: 120–122).
[56] Merquior (1986: 268).
[57] Lynch (1993: 39).
[58] Burgin (1946: 282–287).
[59] Scobie (1964a: 118–123).
[60] Lynch (1998: 10–16).

sheep were located in Buenos Aires province.[61] A redistribution of relative economic power was underway in Argentina, which inflamed the tense relationship between power holders in Buenos Aires and upstart ranchers in the Confederation.

Historically, ranchers and merchants in Buenos Aires dealt with economic challenges from the interior by blockading the Paraná River and funneling trade through Buenos Aires. The Argentine Confederation therefore tried to create incentives for external trading partners to make the trip upriver to Rosario. As the wool boom began in 1857, Urquiza tried to attract trade away from Buenos Aires by undercutting its tariff rates. The measure was instrumental in improving the Confederation's economic position. William Christie, a British foreign officer, noted that the lowered tariffs had led to a considerable growth of trade at Rosario throughout 1857. He characterized the growth between June 1856 and December 1857 as rapid, sizable, and surprising. Christie speculated that the new customs law could mean the end of the Confederation's financial difficulties. Expanding trade also enabled the Confederation government to obtain a small loan from Brazil, noteworthy because it had been unable previously to obtain external financing.[62]

The economic changes were remarkable to Wilfrid Latham, a British expatriate raising sheep in Argentina, who wrote:

> Not many years ago, the "Santa Fecinos" were little better than a band of plunderers . . . but at the present time the humanising influences of steam, commerce, and industry . . . have fairly done their work. The governor, Señor Oroño, a man of large and liberal mind, embraces every opportunity of furthering the material interests of his province. Very extensive purchases of state and other lands have been made in the southern portion of the province [near the Rosario port], which is now studded with the sheep-farms of intelligent settlers from the educated classes of Great Britain and other countries.[63]

Latham expected that Santa Fe would inevitably become "the second nerve centre" of Argentina.[64] Similar changes were afoot in Entre Ríos and Corrientes. During the 1850s, "the wool, cattle, and agriculture boom had transformed Entre Ríos, which in many ways had become a miniature replica of the province of Buenos Aires."[65] Correntino trade was expanding considerably,

[61] Calculations based on data in Chiaramonte (1971: 42–43) and Sabato (1990: 36).
[62] Scobie (1964a: 158–162).
[63] Latham (1868: 337–338).
[64] Latham (1868: 338).
[65] Gibson and Falleti (2004: 252 n. 22).

too, and by the middle of the 1850s, over one hundred, mostly foreign, merchants resided in Corrientes.[66] The relative economic improvement throughout the littoral provinces was palpable.

The littoral provinces posed a rising, diametrical threat to Buenos Aires and its *estancieros*. Urquiza, the leader of the Argentine Confederation, was a rancher, leading merchant, and largest landowner in Entre Ríos. He had also demonstrated his military prowess by defeating Rosas in 1852. His stance toward Buenos Aires remained hostile, aggravated no doubt by continuing economic blockades. Urquiza wanted direct access for the Confederation to external markets, which would end Buenos Aires' stranglehold on customs revenue. (Export duties on products originating outside of Buenos Aires province largely remained within the province.) Throughout the late 1850s, Urquiza relentlessly cultivated allies against Buenos Aires. He sought to enlist Brazil, Paraguay, and Uruguay in his cause, touting the economic advantages from backing his rule of a unified Argentina.[67] By 1859, Urquiza was using promises of future customs revenue from the Buenos Aires port to secure external financing as he prepared for conflict.[68] The Confederation was strengthening economically, appeared resolved to go to war with Buenos Aires, and had a track record of defeating *porteño* forces.

Ruling coalition members in Buenos Aires were unnerved by the growing threat in the Confederation. As ranching expanded in the Confederation, land in Buenos Aires north of the Salado River was becoming saturated with sheep. But hostile Indian tribes prevented *estancieros* in Buenos Aires from extending the frontier southward. What is more, Indian raids had pushed the effective limit of Buenos Aires province to within 40 miles of the city—closer than the 1836 frontier in some places. A perception prevailed in Buenos Aires that Urquiza was encouraging and perhaps even aiding these Indian raids. Some field commanders reported that the Indian attacks were surprisingly skilled and tactically sophisticated.[69] This perception intensified antagonism toward the Confederation, as Indian raids meant sheep raising would stagnate in Buenos Aires while continuing to move into Confederation lands.[70] Moreover, *porteño* merchants "envied" the growing economic power in the littoral,

[66] Whigham (1991: 77–78).

[67] Scobie (1964a: 199–222).

[68] Scobie (1964a: 237). See Ross (2004) on the use of such futures contracts as incendiaries for civil war.

[69] Scobie (1964a: 146–147).

[70] Railway policy also indicated a growing threat to power holders in Buenos Aires. After Buenos Aires province offered its first railway concession in 1854, the Confederation issued a concession in 1855 for what would become the Central Argentine Railway, linking Rosario to Córdoba (Lewis 1983: 8–10).

especially since about 70 percent of the import trade at Buenos Aires was sent to Confederation provinces. Although Urquiza's low tariffs had not yet diverted significant traffic away from the Buenos Aires port, a reorientation of trade would imperil the ruling coalition's side-payments. Against this backdrop, armed conflict seemed ready to ignite at any moment.[71]

Despite the initial success of Urquiza's tariff policies, they did not transform Confederation commerce, and "commercial war therefore gave way to military conflict."[72] In April 1859, the Confederation declared that Buenos Aires should no longer remain independent and must be integrated into a unified Argentina. The British Vice Consul, Frank Parish, noted that public opinion in Buenos Aires preferred war to falling "under the yoke of Urquiza."[73] Urquiza's declaration provoked legislators in Buenos Aires to order Bartolomé Mitre, the Governor of Buenos Aires and future Argentine president, to blockade the Paraná River and attack the Confederation in Santa Fe province. But Urquiza and the Confederation struck first, winning initially at the Battle of Cepeda and extracting a sizable monthly subsidy from Buenos Aires as its spoils. Meanwhile, Mitre cultivated allies within the Confederation—which was still a hodgepodge of personal networks, in spite its forceful leader. Antagonized, the Confederation attacked Buenos Aires again in 1861. This time, *porteño* forces prevailed at the Battle of Pavón, which marked the triumph of Buenos Aires and the federalization of Argentina.[74] The modern Argentine state was born.

INSTITUTION BUILDING IN THE NEW ARGENTINA

A tenuous peace followed, akin to the situation in Chile after its 1851 civil war. *Caudillos* still ruled the former Confederation provinces, and they could muster appreciable military power. Ruling coalition members feared that armed confrontation with interior *caudillos* could erupt at any time. In addition, the growth of the pastoral sector was occurring disproportionately outside of Buenos Aires, where state power was virtually nonexistent. Ruling coalition members and President Mitre reached the same conclusion as had Chilean President Manuel Montt a decade earlier: institution building was

[71] Scobie (1964a: 134–139) and Lynch (1993: 39). Ferns (1960: 329) notes that the resolution of conflict between Buenos Aires and the Confederation in 1862 heightened the perception of investment security in Argentina, thus encouraging foreign capital investment and immigration, two motors of Argentina's rapid growth after 1860.

[72] Lynch (1993: 39).

[73] Quoted in Scobie (1964a: 236).

[74] Lynch (1993: 39–40) and Rock (1987: 122–123).

needed to contain the diametrical threat that was gaining relative economic power, despite the Confederation's military defeat at the Battle of Pavón.

Mitre's state building strategy aimed to lessen the threat posed by interior *caudillos*. Buenos Aires coopted individual *caudillos* with financial subsidies and then gradually encroached on their prerogatives. Those *caudillos* who rebelled were subdued or killed by the budding national army. Militia members were incorporated into the National Guard, which was used to influence provincial elections. The state also heightened its control over provincial affairs by using the Banco Nacional to distribute credit to local politicians, thus helping to align their interests with the central state. Finally, the state developed a national judicial system in order to usurp the power of rural Justices of the Peace, who were usually local notables. Overall, the government strove to institutionally ensconce the prevailing power advantages of *estancieros* and merchants in Buenos Aires.

The delicate peace which prevailed in the early 1860s meant that Buenos Aires had to tread lightly on interior powerbrokers, at least initially. From 1863 to 1876, Mitre disbursed subsidies to local *caudillos*, to encourage them to tolerate Buenos Aires. (The subsidies were fiscally possible due to the growing export economy.) The state also created bureaucratic agencies in provincial areas for *caudillos* to use as patronage outlets. At first, the state had little control over these agencies, but the strategy placated *caudillos* and enmeshed local residents within the central state's patronage network.[75] This tactic is commonplace, having been used to dampen hostility toward the central state in the American South following the Civil War, for example.[76] In Argentina, the subsidies were a sizable portion of provincial budgets, and Buenos Aires used them in a "completely discretionary" manner, which helped align provincial leaders with central state dictates.[77] By 1876, 85 percent of Argentina's nearly 13,000 bureaucrats were employed outside of the city of Buenos Aires, mostly in the budding national army.[78] Building alliances with *caudillos* help them feel secure, even as the state began to elaborate institutions that would heighten its oversight of Argentine society.

The state coupled direct subsidies to *caudillos* with efforts to incorporate local militias into the National Guard. The most delicate of these arrangements was with Urquiza in Entre Ríos, though an agreement was reached that allowed him to return home, financially subsidized, so long as he disarmed his forces.[79] Expanding the National Guard began to sever the link between

[75] Oszlak (1982: 118–133).
[76] Bensel (1990: 396–397).
[77] de la Fuente (2000: 184–185).
[78] Oszlak (1982: 125–126).
[79] Oszlak (1982: 98–110).

caudillos and their armies. Within two years of the Battle of Pavón, the guard was 160,000 strong and grew to 350,000 by 1880.[80] As in Chile, ruling Argentine elites used the Guard to rig elections. When Urquiza ran for president of Argentina in 1868, he had noteworthy support among the rural poor. But even though the "gaucho masses remained loyal to him . . . he had no chance of victory because of the control of the Liberal generals [aligned with Mitre's government had] . . . over the interior provinces."[81] Buenos Aires could sway local elections, even if it did not dictate them.[82] State influence over National Guard units marked an unprecedented intrusion into local affairs, even if government control was imperfect. By 1880, the National Guard was no longer "amorphous and undisciplined." Rather, it had become "a permanent institution, whose existence made possible and accelerated the penetrative capacity of the national state throughout the national territory."[83]

When *caudillos* resisted or revolted against state encroachment, they were subdued or killed by the national army. In the province of La Rioja in 1862–63, the *caudillo* Ángel Vincente Peñaloza rebelled against the central government, which subsequently invaded and killed him. The state neutralized other recalcitrant *caudillos* in Mendoza (Felipe Varela, 1866–67), Entre Ríos (Ricardo López Jordán, Urquiza's successor, 1870), and Santiago del Estero (the Taboadas, 1875).[84] The Argentine Senator Nicasio Oroño estimated the encroachment of the national army into provincial affairs provoked over 100 uprisings against the state between 1862 and 1868.[85] These unyielding conflicts transformed the army into "a fundamental instrument of penetration and territorial control."[86] Indeed, in 1870, National Guard troops fought against López Jordán's forces in defense of the central state. The episode indicated the state's success in incorporating *caudillo* militias into the National Guard and, more importantly, creating something beyond a mere patronage outlet.[87] These developments represented a degree of state penetration that was entirely absent in the 1850s.

The national judicial system was the non-militarized complement to these efforts. The central state created courts, appointed justices in the interior, and established an institutional presence in the provinces. Policymakers initially

[80] Centeno (2002: 229).

[81] Rock (2002: 50). See also Zimmermann (2009: 14–15).

[82] Alonso (1999: 27–32) and Zimmermann (2009: 21–22).

[83] Oszlak (1982: 104–106). This rural incorporation also exerted new control over the relatively scarce rural labor force (López-Alves 2000: 187–192).

[84] Rock (2002).

[85] Cited in Oszlak (1982: 102).

[86] Oszlak (1982: 100 n. 14).

[87] Ibid., 105.

used the courts to punish anti-government rebels, which indicated that standing state institutions, not just the military, would exert Buenos Aires' influence over the interior.[88] In the two years following the 1863 uprisings, for example, only four trials charging rebellion or sedition moved through the lower levels of the justice system. From 1867 to 1875, however, more than 700 such cases were initiated. Similarly, the number of criminal and civil cases tried in the lower levels of the national judicial system in Corrientes, Entre Ríos, and Santa Fe grew from 51 in 1865 to 409 in 1880. And lawmakers steadily eliminated provisions of the justice system they had previously delegated to local elites over time.[89] Export-oriented actors propelled Argentina's legal transformation in general, including by pressing to refashion the country's commercial code and stabilize the monetary system as well.[90]

The decades of the wool boom yielded thoroughgoing changes in the relationship between Buenos Aires and localities. The president was empowered to intervene in provincial affairs—he gained the power to appoint mayors in 1882, for example—similar to the leverage the Chilean president was granted over municipalities. The direct subsidies used by Buenos Aires to align local elites with central state prerogatives gave way to a more indirect, but no less important, means of political influence: the prospect of credit from the Banco Nacional. Provincial elites would lobby the president (sometimes with an explicit, written request) for credit to advance their private economic interests, like building a sugar refinery, for instance.[91] The central state's control over material side-payments helped it purchase provincial quiescence, as provincial elites directed their energies to constructing local patronage networks, rather than fomenting insurrections.[92] State building was gradual but determined and persistent. With greater political stability in place by the 1870s, ruling coalition members turned their attention to the frontier in southern Buenos Aires province, which became possible only after neutering provincial *caudillos*.

CODA: RISING WOOL PRICES, DEMAND FOR NEW LAND, AND TERRITORIAL PACIFICATION

The conflict between Buenos Aires and interior provinces was due in large part to the ongoing shift in relative economic power. Once the state forged greater

[88] de la Fuente (2000: 184).

[89] Zimmermann (1998: 140, 2007: 285–289).

[90] Adelman (1999: 243–277). See also Mirow (2004: 99–100).

[91] Lynch (1993: 41–42) and Rock (2002: 107–108).

[92] Rock (1987: 129) notes that "by 1880 the term *caudillo* was losing its earlier connotation of regional or provincial leader and now referred to the local political bosses who controlled elections on behalf of their elite patrons."

institutional control over the provinces, policymakers turned their attention to subduing the country's Indian tribes. *Estancieros* in Buenos Aires believed that conquering Indian tribes would enable ranching expansion in Buenos Aires province and, thus, assist their economic goals. In 1867, as the state was subjugating *caudillos* like Peñaloza and Varela, the government passed Law 215, which outlined an incremental strategy of territorial pacification. Over the next dozen years, the state gradually extended the frontier and incorporated Indian communities into the expanding Argentine nation. The final pacification of Argentine national territory in 1878–80 marked one of the earliest such accomplishments in Latin America.

Export price signals help explain these developments. Wool prices in Buenos Aires, after falling in the second half of the 1860s, rose precipitously in 1871–72—faster than any time since the initial boom in 1857–58. But "land within the frontier had become overstocked and exhausted, thus restricting production." Crowded ranchlands also harmed cattle exports, as most ranchers owned sheep and cattle. They concluded that they needed inexpensive land for profitable cattle production. Yet cheap land "was available only on the frontier, but the Indian menace posed too great a risk for a general movement toward the frontier to develop. The initiative of the government was required" to secure frontier lands.[93] Pacification could simultaneously promote cattle production and relieve land overuse in sheep-raising areas. Extending the frontier and pacifying the hinterland emerged as a leading concern of the Sociedad Rural Argentina, the advocacy organization of export-oriented ranchers.[94]

President Nicolás Avellaneda, along with his Minister of War, Adolfo Alsina, agreed with the advocacy group. In August 1875, they implored Congress to authorize a campaign against the Indians for the express purpose of expanding the pastoral economy. Existing lands had become "tired or overloaded," they noted. Avellaneda and Alsina warned that, if the pastoral economy stagnated, it would not be "for lack of markets," but rather because the government had refused to subdue Indian tribes. Avellandea's determination to open new ranchlands was clear in his writings to Coronel Álvaro Barros, then Governor of Buenos Aires province and a proponent of pacification. (Barros would later become the first Governor of Patagonia.) Avellaneda claimed that the "border issue is the first question for all. . . . It is the beginning and the end, the *alpha* and *omega*."[95] Meanwhile, wool prices remained robust—about 50 percent higher, on average, than their temporary 1869 low—which provided an ongoing rationale for frontier expansion.[96]

[93] Perry (1971: 118–119).

[94] Slatta (1983: 138).

[95] Quoted in Gasió and San Román (1977: 114–115).

[96] Sabato (1990: 205).

The zenith of pacification efforts was the so-called Conquest of the Desert in 1878–80, led by Julio Roca, the future president of Argentina. Military forces pushed the effective frontier southward beyond the Negro River, while stationing garrisons along Argentina's western border with Chile to prevent Araucanian Indians from retreating across the *cordillera*, regrouping, and then attacking.[97] The campaign added 133 million acres of land to Argentina. The state and ruling coalition members used a mutually advantageous system to fund military pacification. *Estancieros* purchased bonds to underwrite state expenses and later redeemed them in land newly added to the national domain. Ranchers easily circumvented ostensible limits on land purchases through fraud or by using buying agents on their behalf. The bounty was consumed by Sociedad Rural Argentina members, "speculators and terratenientes [landed elites], as all had previous land."[98] In sum, "as much as 8.5 million hectares (passed) into the hands of 381 persons."[99]

Territorial pacification heightened investment security in Buenos Aires province and provided *estancieros* valuable largesse for underwriting frontier operations. Cattle and sheep raising quickly developed in newly conquered territory, from southern Buenos Aires province down into Patagonia.[100] Territorial pacification was the most visible effort to subjugate what had been, at one point, roughly twenty independent Indian tribes in Argentina. The Conquest of the Desert marked a major state building accomplishment, as Argentina had gone from a country divided by rival governments to a coherent state. Above all, the wool boom and its intersection with the country's coalitional politics propelled Argentina's pivotal state building projects between 1857 and 1886.

Argentina in 1886: From Port City to Modern State

Argentine state capacity grew substantially in the second half of the nineteenth-century, but these gains had little to do with the government's revenue imperative. The state continued to rely overwhelmingly on customs duties. Ruling coalition members resisted direct taxes on income or land and preferred that fiscal policy hinge on volatile trade flows, even though the state chronically ran large budget deficits.[101] Power holders refused to substantially alter the state's revenue mix during or after the War of the Triple Alliance, Latin America's grandest conflict. Neither can Argentina's colonial legacies account

[97] Gasió and San Román (1977: 113–135).
[98] Scobie (1964b: 117–118) and Slatta (1983: quote from 138).
[99] Rock (1987: 154).
[100] Aagesen (2000: 209–210).
[101] See Chiaramonte (1971: 90); Cortés Conde (1989: 150); and Oszlak (1982: 204–205).

for its remarkable state building after 1860, though James Mahoney notes how the more liberal economic arrangements in colonial Argentina facilitated its economic growth.[102] The country's administrative machinery largely dissolved after independence,[103] and Rosas' rule (1829–52) was not firmly institutionalized—to say nothing of the country's bifurcation in the 1850s.[104] Finally, ethnic diversity was not a crucial pivot of Argentine state building, though territorial pacification "extinguished" the autonomy of nearly two dozen Indian tribes, while the country was simultaneously assimilating immigrants from Italy, Spain, and elsewhere in Europe.

Public goods provision did contribute to the growth of state capacity. Argentina went from having no railroads in 1852 to around 5,964 km of track in 1886 (and over 9,000 km by the decade's end).[105] And Argentina's railroads approximated something of an integrated network emanating from Buenos Aires, which helped the state radiate power outward from the center. The growing logistical infrastructure aided the coordination of government troops in the hinterland and facilitated territorial pacification, too.[106] The bureaucracy expanded from a small operation of a few hundred under Rosas to 21,756 employees by 1882 and 32,953 by 1890. Early on in the case study period, many of these appointments were made indirectly through provincial elites, but the state progressively heightened its control of these agents over time. The emphasis of bureaucratization shifted away from the military and toward the Interior Ministry, which grew from 913 employees in 1876 to 11,538 by 1890. Whereas the state spent about three times more on military activities than the Interior Ministry during the 1860s and 1870s (the imbalance was even greater during the War of the Triple Alliance), the trend had flipped by 1890.[107]

The growth of the Interior Ministry indicated Argentina's movement toward unmediated rule between 1852 and 1886. The state gained the power to make mayoral appointments, influenced municipal fiscal affairs through its control of credit from the Banco Nacional, swayed political allegiances in the interior, and elaborated a national judicial system. In just over thirty years, the Argentine state went from having no legal claim over provincial areas to exercising decent institutional oversight of them, even if personal loyalties played an important role in administration. This growth of state capacity was

[102] Mahoney (2010: 120–129).

[103] Halperín Donghi (1975: 377–379, 391).

[104] Cf. Lynch (1992a: 84–99). James Scobie notes, in his renowned and aptly titled history, *Argentina: A City and a Nation,* that Argentina was merely the former, not the latter, until the 1880s. On state building under Rosas, see Lynch (1981) and López-Alves (2000: especially 183–184).

[105] Mitchell (1998a: 545–546).

[106] Oszlak (1982: 106) and Rock (2002: 68–69).

[107] Oszlak (1982: 112–114, 264) and Lynch (1981: 171–175).

nonetheless less extensive than in Chile. Yet state building in Argentina and Chile was qualitatively different, especially in institutional terms, than in the book's other case studies. Those countries did not feature the sort of diametrical threat that accompanied dual enrichment in Argentina and Chile and thus lacked such remarkable state building.

CHAPTER 5

Sugar Exporters, New Public Goods, and State Building in Mauritius, 1825–1895

Mauritius is an African success story. Today, it is one of Africa's few upper middle income countries, with a per capita Gross Domestic Product (GDP) six times its regional average. Between 1975 and 1998, Mauritius had annual per capita GDP growth similar to that of Hong Kong, Malaysia, and Singapore. Mauritius' Human Development Index is similar to theirs as well. It is a democratic and well-governed country. Mauritius is one of a handful of African countries to have earned a positive "stateness" measure from the World Bank, an index used to represent its political stability, governmental capabilities, and rule of law.[1] Mauritius is, by all accounts, extraordinary by African standards.

A number of researchers indicate that the Mauritian state, rather than strict adherence to the orthodox economic policies of the Washington Consensus, seems to be at the core of the country's developmental success.[2] Even so, the historical sources of Mauritian state capacity remain an open question. Matthew Lange, for instance, contends that labor unrest in the 1930s and 1940s prompted the British to move toward direct rule in Mauritius, which ultimately promoted the island's distinctive trajectory.[3] Deborah Bräutigam, alternatively, maintains that haggling over taxation between colonial officials and sugar planters positioned Mauritius for success, though she too emphasizes developments in the twentieth century.[4] I reach further into the island's past to accentuate how an export-oriented coalition of sugar planters, in conjunction with colonial officials, promoted the growth of state capacity during the country's first major commodity boom.

[1] Bratton and Chang (2006: Appendix 2); Lange (2003: 402); Subramanian and Roy (2001: 6–9). On the World Bank's governance measures, see Kaufmann, Kraay, and Mastruzzi (2010) and http://www.govindicators.org.

[2] E.g., Meinsenhelder (1997); Minogue (1992); and Subramanian and Roy (2001).

[3] Lange (2003, 2009).

[4] Bräutigam (2008).

Mauritius' sugar boom revealed a number of economic worries, including an insufficient labor supply, rising transport costs, episodic credit shortages, and problems with the island's undiversified cane stock. Sugar elites responded with public goods seeking, and the state repeatedly fulfilled their requests by promoting and subsidizing immigration, "regulating" the island's labor supply, facilitating lending, building railroads, and undertaking research and development initiatives. The most striking, and morally reprehensible, of these endeavors was coercively forcing former laborers back onto sugar plantations. Unlike Chile or Argentina, however, Mauritius' resource boom narrowly enriched members of the ruling coalition, who did not confront a pressing threat and forewent institution building. Nonetheless, Mauritius' export-oriented coalition propelled state building via the provision of new public goods, which substantially enhanced the capabilities of the Mauritian state.

Initial Conditions in Mauritius, 1825

During the nineteenth century, Mauritius was a colonial dependency of Britain, but it was a marginal part of the British Empire. The colonial governor received few directives from London, so he had "considerable discretionary authority" in policymaking and became closely aligned with sugar interests, since the colony's economic viability depended on sugar exports.[5] In actuality, the landowning elites in control of the sugar industry "dominated island politics despite the façade of British rule" and "pulled the levers of the colonial state." Sugar elites controlled most of the seats in the colonial parliament and staffed much of the bureaucracy.[6] British officials may have formally exercised control in Mauritius, but they did so in close collaboration with sugar planters.

Sugar elites formed the upper stratum of Mauritian society, representing around 9 percent of the population in the 1830s but holding most of the island's economic and political power.[7] Some sugar planters had obtained their landholdings as grants during French rule (1715–1810),[8] which preceded British colonialism, and were therefore known as the "Franco-Mauritians." Other sugar planters began as merchants and later diversified into landholding as sugar export opportunities blossomed after 1825. The Franco-Mauritians

[5] Lange (2009: 67, 76–77).

[6] Storey (1997: 37, 55, 57).

[7] Lange (2009: 72–73) and Storey (1997: 19–20).

[8] d'Unienville (1975–1989) is the authoritative source on the French colonial period. I am grateful to Richard Allen for directing me to this valuable source.

were a small group, with a mere 150 large sugar planters as of 1832, with some surnames appearing repeatedly.[9] Their main advocacy group was the Chamber of Agriculture, formed in 1853, though sugar planters mobilized collectively before the 1850s through groups such as the Royal Society of Arts and Sciences.[10] Sugar planters were also given half of the fourteen seats on the colonial Legislative Council in 1831.[11] Their actual power was arguably greater: William Storey maintains that "the early governors of British Mauritius were weaklings who afforded the Franco-Mauritian elite plenty of room for political maneuver."[12]

A group of domestic merchants intertwined with the Franco-Mauritian elite, as merchants invested in agriculture during the waning years of French colonial rule. This trend continued after Britain's repeal on the preferential trade status for West Indian sugar producers, which initiated the Mauritian sugar boom in 1825. Domestic merchants "abandoned their trade and devoted themselves and their capital to agriculture," including investment in land and new sugar mills.[13] Merchants became integrated with the Franco-Mauritian landed elite. British speculators also played a role in the Mauritian sugar industry, though their investment dwindled by 1839 when the island's labor supply, crucial for profitable sugar production, was increasingly in doubt. British investment rebounded in the 1840s but was never a leading force in the sugar economy.[14] Overall, Mauritius' domestic merchants were largely fused with the landowning elite.

The popular classes were marginalized politically throughout the nineteenth century. Around 1830, slaves, freedmen, and Creoles constituted nine-tenths of Mauritius' population. (Freedmen accounted for about two-fifths of the island's population.[15]) The French began importing slaves to Mauritius in the 1720s, and slaves were critical to the island's plantation economy. But Britain abolished slavery in its colonies in the early 1830s, which changed the composition of the laboring classes in Mauritius. Sugar planters accelerated the importation of indentured workers from India, as 338,000 Indian indentured laborers came to the island between 1843 and 1865; another 112,000

[9] Teelock (1998: 297–301).

[10] Storey (1997: 27, 35–37). Sugar planters' earliest advocacy organization was the Royal Society of Arts and Sciences, founded in 1829 by Charles Telfair, a large landowner with British roots. Sugar elites also organized informally during the 1820s to protest Britain's plans to abolish slavery in its colonies (Napal 1984: 34–35, 42–50).

[11] Carter (1995: 13).

[12] Storey (1997: 25).

[13] Napal (1984: 29–30).

[14] Allen (1999: 19–21, 26–27) and Lamusse (1964c: 357–360).

[15] Allen (2011).

Indian and Chinese workers did likewise before 1920. Not all of these workers remained on the plantation, however. Maroonage during slave times and, later, desertion by indentured laborers from plantations were perennial concerns for sugar planters, as laborers often sought a better life in Port Louis as dock-workers, artisans, or in other urban jobs. Some laborers even became small landowners once they fulfilled their service contracts, giving rise to the "Indo-Mauritian" smallholders later in the nineteenth century.[16]

The non-elite segment of Mauritian society was complex and diverse.[17] In general, however, I emphasize three actors in Mauritian society: the Franco-Mauritian sugar elites, colonial administrators, and the laboring masses. My approach undoubtedly glosses over some socio-historical nuance, but it clarifies the politics undergirding Mauritian state building. The relationship between elite sugar planters and the island's non-elites pivoted on planters' desire to secure an adequate labor supply. Many planters suspected that many middle and lower class urban workers had deserted the rural sugar economy and believed the state should compel them to "re-engage" on the plantation. These "subordinate groups—particularly in rural areas—were unable to press their interests upon the colonial administration"[18] and had little voice compared to the ruling coalition of Franco-Mauritian elites and British administrators.

At the beginning of the sugar boom, the Mauritian state was analogously weak to the book's other cases. Mauritius depended heavily on customs duties and other taxes collected in the capital, Port Louis. There was little transportation infrastructure. Much of the island's (then) limited sugar production was transported by boat from coastal points to Port Louis. The main road on the island, which would eventually connect Port Louis on the west coast to Mahebourg on the east coast, was still under construction.[19] Unlike the book's other case studies, however, I consider Mauritius to have achieved territorial pacification because there was neither lawless violence in the countryside nor rival claimants to the island's territory.[20]

Yet peace in the countryside was secured by landed elites; there was no standing state institutional presence outside of the capital city. Port Louis was the island's only municipality, and it featured little formal governance; a period observer noted that "there is not now [1837] any municipal body

[16] Lange (2009: 72–74).

[17] I am indebted to Richard Allen for assisting my appreciation of Mauritius' intricate social history.

[18] Lange (2009: 77).

[19] Lamusse (1964c: 356).

[20] These are Centeno's (2002: 109) criteria of pacification.

to regulate the affairs of the active and wealthy inhabitants of Port Louis." In 1831, a court "system" was established, which comprised two courts (a Supreme Court and a petty court), three judges, and a judge advocate.[21] Although Mauritius featured a civil service examination, *The Mauritius Almanac and Civil Service Register* noted that "a candidate applying for a nomination [for a civil service commission], should be recommended by some person of respectability to whom he is personally known, and supported by a member of the Legislative Council, a head of Department, or a magistrate."[22] Sugar planters, not a bureaucratized apparatus, were the main source of administration on Mauritius.

The Revenue Imperative and Mauritian State Building

Although Mauritius possessed low levels of state capacity, the country featured a relatively diversified structure of tax revenue. From 1825 to 1835, customs duties constituted half of Mauritius' revenue (much less than, say, Argentina, where customs duties accounted for 93 percent of revenue at the start of its commodity boom). Other revenue came from taxes on real estate and slaves held in Port Louis and license, stamp, and registration fees.[23] Mauritius' revenue sources are consistent with the expectation that non-rent-generating commodities demand diversified fiscal policy. Yet sugar planters' political power, not the fiscal properties of sugar, determined tax policy.[24] When planters lost a preferential tariff to the British market in 1846, for instance, they leaned on the state to reduce export duties; colonial officials complied and cut sugar duties by two-thirds.[25] Sugar planters' preferences explain why sugar's relative contribution to state coffers declined over time. Moreover, the quest for revenue was peripheral to Mauritian state building after 1825. Geopolitical pursuits were likewise inconsequential. Mauritius served as a British garrison to safeguard the maritime route to India, especially before the completion of the Suez Canal in 1869, but the island's remoteness meant that it did not face noteworthy bellicist pressures. Overall, the revenue imperative did not propel Mauritian state building.

[21] Martin (1839: 507, 509). There was a "commune council" in Port Louis from 1817 to 1821 that served as a conduit between local notables and colonial administrators.

[22] de Joux (1864: 51).

[23] Data from Kyshe (1870: 30, 1878: 18); MacGregor (1850: 141); and Martin (1839: 507–508).

[24] Bräutigam (2008).

[25] Kyshe (1870: 115).

The Sugar Boom and the Transformation of Mauritius

Mauritius' sugar boom began in 1825 and dovetailed into a long-term upward secular trend until 1865. Britain repealed a preferential tariff on West Indian sugar in 1825, making Mauritian sugar more attractive to British importers. The policy change "revolutionized Mauritian agriculture" and stimulated the doubling of sugar exports between 1825 and 1829. Sugar came to dominate the island's economy, always accounting for at least 85 percent of exports. From the early 1830s to the mid-1840s, sugar prices rose by 45 percent in the London market, from £27.0/ton to £39.2/ton. (There was spectacular growth in British sugar demand during the nineteenth century.) In 1851, when Mauritius was the leading sugar supplier to Britain, the Crown repealed a ban on foreign ships in its colonial ports, opening Mauritius to the wider global economy. Overall, annual exports rose from 11,107 tons before the 1825 tariff repeal to over 123,000 tons by the early 1860s. Land devoted to sugar production expanded from 24,967 arpents in 1826 to 123,000 arpents by 1861. The value of sugar exports rose commensurately, from £170,342 in 1824 to over £2.1 million annually by the early 1860s, when Mauritius accounted for 9 percent of global sugarcane production.[26]

However, the rise of beet sugar production in Europe tempered the bountiful ascent of Mauritius' sugar industry and exerted downward pressure on cane sugar prices after 1850. Prices stagnated from 1860 to 1880, after which they experienced a steady decline (to £13.1/ton in the early 1890s, roughly one-third of early 1840s prices). Slumping prices threatened the viability of Mauritius' sugar exports. The Franco-Mauritian planters pursued new public goods to reduce transportation costs and improve the quality of their cane stocks in order to remain internationally competitive. Subsequent state-supplied public goods helped them remain viable amid hard times, and export production remained steady until the early 1890s (usually around 115,000 tons annually).[27] Mauritian sugar exports increasingly went to India, Australia, and South Africa because of these markets' proximity.[28]

The Franco-Mauritian planters were the principal beneficiary of good times in the sugar industry. New trade opportunities stimulated a growth in production, and sugar planters made productivity investments as well. They used steam power in their sugar factories because global demand was tilted toward

[26] Allen (1999: 12–30, quote from 12); Mintz (1985: 74–150); Storey (1997: 38); and Teelock (1998: 84). An arpent is the landholding measure used in Mauritius. One arpent equals 1.043 acres.

[27] Allen (1999: 23).

[28] Lamusse (1965: 24–25).

the higher-quality and lower-cost sugar produced by steam-powered factories. Steam power also improved sucrose extraction from sugar canes. Whereas, in 1823, 39 percent of Mauritian sugar factories were powered by animals and only 4 percent by steam, by 1848, none were powered by animals and 80 percent ran on steam power. In the 1830s, Mauritian mills extracted 40–45 percent of the juice from the sugarcane; technological improvements enabled mills to squeeze out 70 percent of the cane juice by 1865.[29] Mauritius was a leader in sugarcane production and technology.

Public Goods Seeking and Mauritian State Building

The Mauritian sugar boom revealed assorted economic bottlenecks that spawned public goods seeking and the growth of state capacity. The most dramatic government action involved helping sugar planters ruthlessly secure an adequate labor supply, by way of coercion and intimidation. Other economic bottlenecks included problems of credit accessibility, high transport costs, and the need for technological innovation. The colonial state aided sugar planters by making legal changes to spur mortgage lending, financing new railroads, and spearheading research and development initiatives—which promoted the growth of state capacity in various ways.

"REGULATING" THE ISLAND'S LABOR SUPPLY

Sugar planters considered labor shortages to be their paramount barrier to production. The international competitiveness of Mauritian sugar hinged on abundant cheap labor, and until 1835, African slaves constituted the island's labor supply. Britain banned the slave trade in 1807. (The British governor in Mauritius, Robert Farquhar, lobbied unsuccessfully for an exemption.) Mauritian planters turned to importing slaves illegally, and slavery finally ended in 1835, after the British banned it following a large and deadly slave revolt in Jamaica. London compensated Mauritian sugar planters over £2 million for their losses, yet slavery's abolition created labor supply problems as most former slaves became subsistence farmers.[30] The state assisted sugar planters to stem labor shortages by helping them acquire workers from India and tilting the island's legal system against indentured laborers, thus preserving elite dominance over the island's labor supply.

[29] Lamusse (1964a: 24).

[30] Allen (1999: 14–15); Carter (1995: 14–17); and Northrup (1995: 20).

Immediately after slavery was outlawed in Mauritius, sugar planters took to importing Indian laborers because they believed it would be easier than coercing emancipated slaves back onto their estates. Between 1834 and 1838, nearly 24,000 laborers arrived in Mauritius, or about 35 percent of the slaves emancipated in 1835. Treatment of Indians was as harsh as under slavery, and the colonial state did little to restrain and arguably facilitated planters' zealousness. A group of bureaucrats known as the Stipendiary Magistrates were responsible for overseeing labor relations. Stipendiary Magistrates had originally been appointed to implement the abolition of slavery in Britain's colonies and were retained afterward as the judicial officials overseeing vagrancy and breach of contract cases in plantation economies. Mauritius had sixteen magistrates by 1837.[31] Few had proper legal training, and most were half-time military or naval officers. More important, Stipendiary Magistrates were given "wretchedly low salaries to adjudicate cases arising between masters and apprentices."[32] Low salaries and improper training limited Stipendiary Magistrates' ability to act independently of powerful social actors.

The Stipendiary Magistrates typically sided with planters in their investigations of laborers' circumstances and eagerly awarded corporeal punishment, so much so officials in London inquired about the high rates of corporeal punishment in Mauritius during the late 1830s. Magistrates' sensitivity to planters' interests was due in part to their fear of them. A British missionary noted in 1838 that "it is said that those who have been removed from the office of special magistrate have universally been those who filled it the most efficiently, in the performance of their duty as the protectors of the Apprentices [laborers]."[33] Magistrates' site visits were "cursory and largely ineffective" because they had little de facto power to sanction planters and could not communicate with laborers, as interpreters were chronically lacking. Overall, "stipendiary magistrates and appeal court judges closed ranks against the Indian immigrants."[34]

The harsh treatment of Indians created opposition to the labor trade among abolitionists in India and Britain. In 1838, India outlawed emigration to Mauritius due to planters' labor practices, creating a dire labor supply problem. Sugar production declined by one-third despite rapidly rising global prices.[35] Planters responded quickly by holding public meetings and forming the Mauritius Free Labour Association (MFLA). They desperately wanted to resume the labor trade because indentured Indians cost them about one-third less than employing freedmen. The MFLA outlined plans for improved treatment

[31] Green (1974: 43–44); Nwulia (1978: 91); and Smith (1995: 268).

[32] Green (1974: 43–44).

[33] Nwulia (1978: 95).

[34] Carter (1995: 209–212).

[35] Allen (1999: 23, 55–56); Carter (1995: 18–21); and Lamusse (1964c: 357).

of indentured Indians, from the voyage from India to a free passage back upon the completion of a service contract. The MFLA got the state to pledge to better regulate labor practices, which bolstered confidence in Indian and British officials, and the emigration ban was repealed in 1842. The state subsidized the cost of new labor imports (discussed below in the section on credit bottlenecks), and the subsidies were financed by wine and liquor duties, taxes spread among the population, even though the policy narrowly benefitted planters.[36]

Yet despite the promises of Mauritian officials, the state exercised virtually no oversight of labor treatment on the plantation. It concentrated instead on regulating laborers outside of the plantation system by passing in 1847 anti-vagrancy statues and internal passport requirements, which planters sought in order to intimidate laborers. The harshest policy was the "double cut" system, which imposed a penalty of two days of extra work for each day (or partial day) missed on the plantation. The system effectively extended a typical five-year labor service contract by two years. Subsidized labor imports and regulative actions helped sugar planters alleviate their labor supply problem, as nearly 94,000 indentured Indian migrants came to Mauritius during the 1840s, with another 184,000 following in the 1850s.[37]

Desertion and "vagrancy" perennially concerned sugar planters. Rates of desertion and illegal absences from plantations rose steadily after the abolition of slavery in 1835 and became particularly troublesome, from the planters' perspective, in the 1860s.[38] By that time, many former indentured laborers had fulfilled their service contracts and moved into urban jobs; others became small landowners (i.e., Indo-Mauritian smallholders). The labor supply was shrinking, and although immigration remained an option, planters had come to prefer trained laborers who had previously worked on their estates. Sugar planters therefore lobbied the state to pressure former field laborers to "re-engage" on the plantation. The result was Ordinance 31, a draconian legal code passed in 1867. Internal passports, replete with a photograph, tied Indians to their districts of residence and had to be carried at all times. All Indians, indentured or free, had to carry them, at an annual cost of £1 (roughly two months' pay). Planters also compelled the government to institute fines for early termination of service contracts and special taxes on Indians who worked outside of the sugar industry as domestic servants, petty retailers, or gardeners.[39]

The state complemented its new legal code with a flurry of aggressive behavior to push Indians back onto sugar plantations. Police commonly entered

[36] Lamusse (1964c: 357).

[37] Napal (1984: 88–98) and Northrup (1995: 115–119, 159).

[38] Allen (2008).

[39] Carter (1995: 198–205) and Napal (1984: 109–117).

Indian residences, ostensibly to search for vagrants, and harassment was common, even when one's papers were in order. Throughout the 1860s, the state arrested on vagrancy-related charges approximately 20,000 Indians annually (about 12 percent of the Indian population). The fact that police officers received half of the fines paid by their arrestees undoubtedly encouraged zealous arresting, but police officers' behavior nonetheless illustrated remarkable government activity.[40] Coercion was particularly rife in Port Louis, where 84 percent of contractual laborers were arrested for vagrancy annually, on average, from 1864 to 1871.[41]

State action in the countryside was one-sided, too, as police would pry into the budding nucleated settlements established by former indentured Indians. Indians had little recourse, since the Stipendiary Magistrates were aligned with the planters. In practice, the "Stipendiary Magistrates had made the punishment severe and harsh so as to discourage immigrants in doing liberal jobs [i.e., those outside the plantation economy], urging them to re-engage as a means of protection."[42] Within three years of enacting the anti-vagrancy Ordinance 31, the proportion of Indians engaged on sugar estates rose from 48 to 59 percent.[43] Government intimidation of Indian laborers was coupled with worse repression on sugar plantations. Sugar elites exercised coercion through their estate managers, known as *sirdars*. Private jails were common and used by planters to exact extra-judicial retribution on deserters, freed Indians who would not "re-engage" on the plantation, and those who filed complaints with the authorities.[44]

This situation persisted throughout the century, even as the government established a centralized legal system with district courts and placed police forces under the authority of local magistrates in the 1850s.[45] In 1871, Arthur Hamilton Gordon became governor of Mauritius and "found the judicial

[40] Carter (1995: 196–198, 213, 219–220) and Mishra (2009: 240). Allen (1999: 67) puts the annual arrest rate at 8.8 percent during the 1860s. The conviction rate for arrested Indians was around 45 percent.

[41] Allen (2008: 149–150).

[42] Carter (1995: 198–205); Napal (1984: 109–117, quote from 113); and Smith (1995: 273). Indians did have legal rights and filed thousands of complaints against their employers during the 1860s in particular. Most complaints were for late or non-payment of wages, something of obvious benefit to planters, whose labor costs then accounted for 30 percent of the value of sugar exports (Allen 1999: 67–71; Carter 1995: 201–211). Such contractual violations were easy to demonstrate, and judgments overwhelmingly favored laborers. But Indians secured convictions on more contentious issues like assault at dramatically lower rates (see the data in Carter 1995: 211).

[43] Lamusse (1964b: 120).

[44] Carter (1995: 196–198, 213, 219–220).

[45] Lange (2009: 71–72).

system in Mauritius biased and hopelessly intertwined with the planting interest."[46] Napal concludes that the "labour system was so bad that the labourers were powerless against the employers, the police were corrupt and violent, while some magistrates were said to be ignorant and partial."[47] Throughout the century, the state toiled to serve the narrow interests of planters by diligently repressing laborers. In the process, the state's presence in the countryside became palpable, even if not firmly institutionalized. Government action helped sugar planters hold down labor costs and promoted their international competitiveness.

IMPERMANENT CREDIT BOTTLENECKS, LIMITED STATE ACTION

State action was less pronounced in the credit sector because Mauritian sugar planters had less trouble accessing credit. After Britain's repeal of the preferential tariff for West Indian sugar in 1825, the Mauritian government made two loans to spur sugar production.[48] Soon thereafter, an influx of British capital satisfied credit demand. Slave emancipation in 1835 tempered this investment, and India's prohibition on emigration in 1838 halted it. Times were tough from 1840 to 1843, as little new cane was planted and landowners sold off marginal portions of their estates in a bid to secure a settled, adequate labor supply (a process known as the *petit morcellement*). When Indian immigration resumed in 1842, the state subsidized the cost of each immigrant by £7, costing the government £423,579 and representing one-third of the colonial state budget from 1843 to 1848. Many estates needed to replant cane stock, and the resumption of labor imports reduced investment uncertainty enough that five large British merchant houses invested £500,000 in Mauritian sugar in the late 1840s. Planters faced no prolonged credit accessibility problem before mid-century.[49]

One reason for planters' relatively easy credit access was that the island's prevailing Napoleonic Code (a vestige of the French colonial era) did not require registering property. (A 4.5 percent tax on land transactions further dissuaded registry.) Unsecured loans were the norm, and planters could therefore take out multiple mortgages—and some obtained as many as a dozen loans on a single piece of property. This leverage helped the Franco-Mauritians make considerable improvements in processing before 1850. By mid-century, 80

[46] Smith (1995: 268).
[47] Napal (1984: 71).
[48] Allen (1999: 25).
[49] Lamusse (1964c: 355–357). On the *petit morcellement*, see Allen (1999: 114–127).

percent of Mauritian sugar factories ran on steam power, a precocious development compared to sugar producers elsewhere. Much of this financing was supplied by the British merchant houses. But when the British Sugar Duties Act of 1846 eliminated preferential treatment for Mauritian producers—and prices paid for Mauritian sugar declined by 25 percent in one year—merchants suffered. Without good collateral, four of the five major merchant houses in Mauritius went bankrupt (as did the Bank of Mauritius), ending the era of easy credit.[50]

The sugar industry consequently had to raise capital domestically. Prevailing interest rates were 12 to 25 percent at this time and worried planters. The Franco-Mauritians responded by establishing the Chamber of Agriculture, which became a powerful advocacy group. The Chamber of Agriculture "was in many ways the shadow Government of Mauritius, and it usually succeeded in badgering the colonial state into doing its bidding."[51] The Chamber began studying the problem of credit accessibility in 1856 and, in 1861, proposed modifying Mauritius' mortgage laws to conform to changes made to the Napoleonic Code in France in 1855; the changes stipulated a more detailed system of land registration in order to facilitate secured lending. The state complied with the Chamber's request and altered Mauritius' mortgage law in 1863, paving the way for the opening of three Land Credit Agencies the following year.[52] The planters dispatched a representative to Europe to raise subscription capital in the meantime.[53] This episode marked the only noteworthy barrier to credit accessibility after 1850, save a brief credit shortage in the late 1860s.

The mortgage banks were designed with sugar planters in mind and "doubtless, by their timely aid, saved many a planter from ruin, and enabled him to tide over" during the late 1860s, when a drought, malaria outbreak, and cyclone wreaked havoc on Mauritius. Although the changes to mortgage laws had large planters in mind, there were spillover benefits for all landowners. Nicholas Pike, the US Consul to Mauritius, noted that the new land agencies were "publically celebrated, as not only those who borrowed were benefited, but all estates and land acquired a more solid and certain value."[54] These beneficiaries included the Indo-Mauritians, a budding stratum of small landowners who were acquiring property as planters sold off relatively unproductive portions of their estates (an era known as the *grand morcellement*). Planters used the land sales to decrease uncertainty over their labor supply, as most Indo-Mauritians supplemented their income by working on nearby plantations.

[50] Lamusse (1964c: 355–359).
[51] Storey (1995: 166), cited in Lange (2009: 77).
[52] Lamusse (1964c: 360) and Maigrot (1953: 266–268).
[53] Pike (1873: 391).
[54] Pike (1873: quotes from 401, 393).

Sugar planters also viewed land sales as a way to concentrate production and enhance productivity.[55] Estate subdivision was not a capital-raising scheme, in other words, as planters sometimes financed land purchases.[56] Overall, the Mauritian state was relatively uninvolved in the credit sector but supported planters when they asked for assistance.[57]

TRANSPORTATION INFRASTRUCTURE PLANNED AND FINANCED BY THE STATE

The final two public goods sought in Mauritius came when international and biological factors threatened the sugar industry from the late 1860s on. First, beet sugar cultivation was growing in Europe, with France, Russia, Germany, and others generously subsidizing domestic producers. Beet sugar production exerted downward pressure on global cane sugar prices. Second, the Suez Canal opened in 1869 and rendered Mauritius a more remote sugar supplier to many markets. Third, the island experienced climactic disasters, including a drought in 1866, a malaria outbreak in 1867, and cyclones in 1868 and 1874. Finally, the island had a borer pest infestation that endangered its non-diversified cane stock.[58] These developments jeopardized the international competitiveness of Mauritian sugar, and planters responded by seeking new public goods to assist their viability.

Reducing transport costs was one means to promote sugar exports. Early in the boom period, sugar produced on Mauritius was transported to Port Louis by boat. The government also built roads with convict and slave labor to aid the sugar industry in the 1820s, including one completed in 1832 that linked Port Louis on the west coast to Mahebourg on the east coast. A branch line to Souillac in the south was finished in 1830. This infrastructure sufficed until the 1850s, as high sugar prices dissuaded interest in railroads. Railway entrepreneurs in London considered building a line in Mauritius, taking out ad space in *The Railway Times* in 1845 to raise startup capital for a then-unspecified project on the island.[59] But there was little interest in Mauritius because sugar

[55] Allen (1999: 141–144, 156–170).

[56] Alternatively, Allen (1999: 22) contends that the temporary credit shortage in the late 1860s was the start of perennial credit scarcity. However, testimony by the Chamber of Agriculture's historian (Maigrot 1953: 268) and the US Consul at the time (Pike 1873: 408, 437–438) dispute that conclusion.

[57] For instance, the state bailed out the Commercial Bank of Mauritius when it became over-extended in 1898 and 1908 (Swettenham, Woodcock, and O'Malley 1910: ¶ 296).

[58] Storey (1997: 38–45).

[59] Jessop (1964: 1) and Lamusse (1964c: 356).

prices were at their highest level in twenty-five years and prevailing transport costs were tolerable.

By the 1850s, transport costs were rising as sugar production moved further inland. Expanding sugar production taxed the island's paltry infrastructure, which carried an estimated 4,500 carts and carriages on existing roadways. Inland estates created higher transport costs on both ends of production: first to build and equip a factory, which needed to be located near the point of cultivation, and then to transport refined sugar overland to Port Louis. The boilers used in modern sugar plants were of particular concern to inland planters. At mid-century, transporting three boilers 18 miles inland cost around £1,200, a significant sum for an estate owner; falling international prices after mid-century heightened these cost concerns. In 1856, planters mobilized through the Chamber of Agriculture and asked the government to survey the island for railroads. The government did so in 1858–59, after the colonial secretary in London dispatched an engineer.[60] The government would need to be involved with financing as well, since merchant capital had dried up in the late 1840s. Building railroads in Mauritius, in other words, was necessarily a state building project.

About one year later, the government contributed £200,000 from its Reserve Fund for two railway lines estimated to cost £1 million sterling, and construction began in January 1862.[61] The colonial state also floated seven bond issues in the London bond market between 1862 and 1876. The average rate of interest on Mauritian bonds was 5.5 percent, among the lowest rates secured by any colony or developing country at the time.[62] Mauritius could borrow cheaply in the London bond market because of its "subsovereign" status of the British Crown.[63] The first railway was the North Line, completed in 1864 and stretching north from Port Louis into the island's sugar-producing heartland and then around the northeast coast. The Midland Line was completed in 1865 and tapped into the southeastern portion of the island known as Grand Port. A number of feeder lines were built off of it over the next few decades. The government operated the railroads at a chronic deficit, and the implicit subsidy was a sign of the sugar industry's weight in island politics.[64] The state helped sugar estates remain profitable by coordinating and financing railroad

[60] Jessop (1964: 1–2) and Lamusse (1964c: 359).

[61] Jessop (1964: 2).

[62] Bräutigam (2008: 152). Mauritius' bond yields averaged 3.71 percent during 1880–1913 (calculation based on data from Accominotti, Flandreau, and Rezzik 2011 and available at http:eh.net/databases/finance).

[63] Accominotti, Flandreau, and Rezzik (2011).

[64] Jessop (1964: 2–5) and Napal (1984: 213).

building. In the process, the state gained new logistical infrastructure that could be used to deploy its agents.

RESEARCH AND DEVELOPMENT TO BOLSTER THE ISLAND'S CANE STOCK

Lastly, the colonial state aided sugar exports after 1850 through research and development. Much of what then ailed the Mauritian sugar industry was beyond its control. Planters could not stop the cultivation of beet sugar in Europe, close the Suez Canal, or avoid occasional climactic disasters. But they and government officials could address the island's borer pest infestation. Much of Mauritius' sugarcane stock was non-diversified, leaving it susceptible to a borer that was inadvertently introduced to the island around 1850. The Chamber of Agriculture solicited ideas to eliminate the borer menace in the mid-1850s, but the campaign and other individualized efforts to curtail the impact of the borer failed. Government assistance was preferable to individualized solutions, which were susceptible to collective action problems (i.e., the reluctance any one planter might feel to innovate and search for better cane varietals, given fears that others might copy the innovation without incurring its costs). By the mid-1860s, sugar elites were convinced that "if the sugar industry was to thrive, then (the state) needed to underwrite institutional efforts to discover new canes" resistant to the borer.[65]

The state assisted the Franco-Mauritians through research and development initiatives. At the request of the Chamber of Agriculture, the colonial government devoted its Royal Botanic Gardens in Pamplemousses (a town northeast of Port Louis) to the collection, husbandry, and dissemination of new cane stocks. Improving the island's cane stock entailed significant effort to import cane varieties from around the world. The state financed these efforts upfront, recovering its costs in part through the sale of successful cane varietals later. Sales were robust, which underscored the continuing failure of growers to remedy the borer infestation on their own. By 1875, the Pamplemousses gardens were a recognized international leader in sugarcane research, as the colonial government had substantially improved its scientific capabilities.[66]

The Chamber of Agriculture oversaw much of the day-to-day operations at Pamplemousses and became so integrated with government officials over time that the distinction between them blurred. The cooperation yielded a handful of new, useful cane varieties (out of 250 different types tested). The

[65] Storey (1997: 44–56, quote from 50–51).

[66] Ibid., 44–56.

government's action, directed by the powerful sugar elite, was designed for their benefit. In fact, the records of cane sales from Pamplemousses do not list any small-scale Indo-Mauritian landowners as customers; the new cane varietals were purchased by the Franco-Mauritian elite. Moreover, the state subsidized its research efforts with taxes on the Indo-Mauritians, who "lacked access to the political arena, and . . . were not allowed to participate in debates about new sugar cane varieties."[67] Government assistance helped Mauritian sugar planters to weather deteriorating global price conditions, as sugar exports steadily averaged more than 111,000 tons annually throughout the remainder of the century.

The scientific expertise created at the Royal Botanic Gardens led to new bureaucratization and the growth of state capacity. In 1909, the Franco-Mauritians' Chamber of Agriculture officially requested that the government establish a Department of Agriculture to institutionalize its efforts in scientific husbandry. The Department was founded in 1913, and it was a bureaucratic progeny of the nineteenth-century collaboration at Pamplemousses.[68] Overall, public goods seeking brought about by the sugar boom helped endow the Mauritian state with new technical expertise, better transportation infrastructure, new financial regulative oversight, and an embryonic presence in the countryside as it sought to "regulate" the island's labor supply.

Without a Diametrical Threat, Mediated Institutions Remain

The resource boom in Mauritius narrowly enriched the island's politically dominant stratum of sugar planters, which obviated any momentous projects of institutional change.[69] Sugar estates remained largely independent of government oversight, even as sugar planters impelled the state to enforce anti-vagrancy statutes and internal passport requirements. Planters' pleas for odious labor "regulation" did promote the development of the island's judicial system, one of my measurement proxies of institutional characteristics. This development was an outgrowth of public goods seeking, as I describe above. But it did not amount to a transformative step toward unmediated rule. Such institutional development was unnecessary, given the hegemony of the Franco-Mauritians. Throughout the century, however, policymakers made

[67] Ibid., 55–66, quote from 55.

[68] Ibid., 103–108.

[69] Selvon (2001: 285) notes that there was no significant threat from subaltern classes, either, as former slaves and Indian immigrants did not achieve noteworthy collective mobilization until 1911.

minor institutional modifications, which illustrated how institutions reflect prevailing power balances. At times, the Franco-Mauritians sought greater power on the Legislative Council or the establishment of new municipal councils, and colonial administrators satisfied their requests.

Sugar planters' earliest desires for institutional tinkering stemmed from their fears that Britain would abolish slavery in its colonies. In the late 1820s, planters mobilized behind the leadership of Adrien D'Epinay to lobby the British, both in Port Louis and in London.[70] Planters called for an elected assembly, which they believed would heighten their control of local affairs. (Planters lost their formal conduit to colonial administrators when the short-lived "commune council" was abolished in 1821.[71]) In 1831, London decided that persons "from and out of the chief landed proprietors and principal merchants" would receive half of the seats on the Legislative Council.[72] As I note in the coming case studies of Ghana and Nigeria, Mauritian sugar planters received a considerably larger share of representation on the Legislative Council than did organized interests, like merchants or nationalist leaders, in either of those colonies.

Sugar planters used the Legislative Council to advance their interests and sometimes as leverage against the British. John Jeremie, who was the British Advocate-General on the island in the early 1830s, believed that "many governors practically allowed themselves to be dictated by the unofficial members [i.e., local appointees] of the Council." Indeed, Jeremie was twice the target of the Franco-Mauritians' antipathy. Jeremie was a known sympathizer to abolition, and when he was appointed as the colony's advocate-general in 1832, sugar planters were fearful. (Slavery was not abolished on Mauritius until 1835.) They responded with "armed volunteer bodies" and reduced "the lawful government to a mere shadow, and . . . had effectually taken military possession of (Port Louis)."[73] Jeremie was forced back to England, only to be returned again by the Colonial Office. His second tenure was no more auspicious: lacking support from the Legislative Council and local colonial officials, he resigned his post in 1833. The episode highlighted the extent to which sugar planters directed policy, despite the presence of a colonial overlord.

The British mostly gave sugar planters what they wanted, which was unfettered control outside of Port Louis. There was no institutionalized British presence in the countryside, as "rural parts of the island had no local government whatsoever" throughout the nineteenth century, even as nucleated settlements

[70] Napal (1984: 34–35, 42–50).

[71] Martin (1837: 507).

[72] Quoted from the royal order of July 20, 1831, which is excerpted in Selvon (2001: 284).

[73] Jeremie (1835: 26–28).

of former indentured Indians developed. The colonial police force would conduct vagrancy sweeps in these communities but did not establish standing institutions at the local level.[74] Institutional resources, to the extent they existed, were sequestered in Port Louis.

Planters directed when and where new government institutions were created. The first noteworthy institutional development after the 1831 expansion of the Legislative Council came in response to the Sugar Duties Act of 1846. The act eliminated Franco-Mauritians' preferential access to the British market and thereby created new competition. Planters reacted by forming the Association Mauricienne, which advocated for a new elected municipal council through which planters believed they could exercise greater control over colonial policy. Specifically, sugar planters wanted to reduce their export duties (then 9 pence per hundredweight of exported sugar) to compensate for the lost tariff. In 1849, London permitted formation of the municipal council. George Anderson, the governor of Mauritius, simultaneously increased the slots on the Legislative Council for "unofficial members," ensuring that sugar elites would hold a majority (not just half) of its seats. The new municipal council was elected but the franchise was restricted to 800 property owners.[75] The municipal council proved efficacious: the British cut the export duty by two-thirds, to 3 pence per hundredweight of exported sugar, in 1853.[76] Critics of such cozy relationships between government and elites in sugar colonies charged that bodies like the municipal council "degenerated into corrupt, oppressive, planter-controlled oligarchies" over time.[77]

The next episode of institutional tinkering occurred in the late 1870s, when planters became worried about their property rights. The expansion of the sugar economy had by then eliminated all but 35,000 arpents of the island's forests (down from 406,157 arpents that existed in 1753). Colonial administrators came up with an idea to acquire privately titled land along riverbanks to preserve the remaining forest and protect nearby rivers. The Franco-Mauritians mobilized against the dictate with public meetings and street protests and demanded compensation for any land acquisition. The Legislative Council created a Reform Committee to study the proposal, and planters asked that the Legislative Council be transformed into an elected, not appointed, body. An elected Legislative Council would fortify the Franco-Mauritians' control over it, given the island's restricted franchise. The colonial governor, then John Pope Hennessy, and the Colonial Office in London agreed to replace the Legislative Council with a new Council of Government. The new council featured

[74] Lange (2009: quote from 76) and Toussaint (1977: 68, 79).

[75] Selvon (2001: 285–288).

[76] Kyshe (1870: 115).

[77] Smith (1995: 255).

eight appointed colonial administrators, nine appointed "unofficial" members (in practice, sugar planters), and ten elected slots, which were captured by sugar elites.[78] The institutional change indicated that the "sugar barons were tightening their grip on Mauritian politics, [by] wrestling a measure of control from the British governors."[79]

Not until late in the nineteenth century did sugar planters request governing institutions outside of Port Louis. The colonial government's environmental conservation proposals in part led sugar elites to call for municipal councils in Curepipe, Quatre Bornes, and Beau Bassin and Rose Hill between 1889 and 1895. Each council was located in the Plaines Wilhelms district, the highland area to which sugar elites fled from Port Louis during malaria outbreaks in the 1860s. The town councils were "wholly appointed by the governor" (and would not have a majority of elected members until 1949).[80] But the councils were not ploys by the colonial government to usurp the authority of local notables; rather, local elites sought the new councils for public works maintenance. The councils in Curepipe and Beau Bassin and Rose Hill, which had the largest budgets, received subsidies from the state, while the smallest council, in Quatre Bornes, was funded entirely by local (mostly property) taxes.[81] Nevertheless, most towns at this time "did not enjoy the benefits of local government, and the rural areas were even remoter from central administration." Even around 1950, there was a "lack of contact between the central government and the people of the rural areas."[82]

The absence of a pressing threat helps account for the persistence of mediated rule in nineteenth-century Mauritius. Even so, Mauritius is geographically small, which makes it tempting to attribute its lack of institutional development to the comparative ease with which state agents could be deployed into its hinterland. While I do not want to dismiss the role that geography might have played historically on Mauritius, territorial size is neither a necessary nor sufficient condition for the generation of state power. Another, smaller African island—São Tomé and Príncipe—is notoriously dysfunctional. And the smallest states in continental Africa—Burundi, Equatorial Guinea, Gambia, Rwanda, and Swaziland—are hardly formidable.[83] In my estimation, the counterfactual suggested by the Chilean and Argentine cases is more compelling. Had Mauritius' commodity boom spawned dual enrichment, it seems likely that more palpable institutions would have followed.

[78] Selvon (2001: 275, 288–301).

[79] Storey (1997: 73).

[80] Selvon (2001: 274). See also Mahatma Gandhi Institute (1982: 6–7).

[81] Colony of Mauritius (1898: §E).

[82] Mahatma Gandhi Institute (1982: quotes from 6, 8).

[83] See Herbst (2000) on geography and state building in Africa.

Mauritius in 1895: New Public Goods and a Growth in State Capacity

Although mediated rule persisted in Mauritius, state capacity nevertheless grew impressively in the decades following its sugar boom. But geopolitical competition cannot account for these developments, as Mauritius had no bellicose neighbors. And while the colonial government lowered sugar duties at mid-century, consistent with the expectations of the resource curse literature, this policy change was at the behest of sugar elites and not due to the intrinsic fiscal properties of sugar. The structure of tax revenue reflected planters' power. In 1897, export duties constituted just 8 percent of revenues, while import duties and an excise tax on rum—both of which shifted the tax burden away from planters—made up 67 percent of revenue.[84] Neither can colonial doctrine explain Mauritian state building, as the colonial policies implemented on the island had more to do with the Franco-Mauritians' preferences than dictates from London.

What the Franco-Mauritians sought throughout the century were new public goods to facilitate sugar exports, and public goods provision redounded benefits to the Mauritian state. The state's prowess expanded as it "regulated" the labor supply, and these regulative efforts rendered the laboring masses "legible" to government officials. The Immigration Department became "a nucleus of registration and identification" and supplied vital information to the Stipendiary Magistrates.[85] The growing juridical oversight of subaltern communities spawned growth in the country's judicial system: from two courts established in 1831 to twenty-one functioning courts, including nine Stipendiary Magistracies, by the 1890s.[86] The Mauritian state grew stronger because of its repressive and reprehensible actions to secure low-cost labor for sugar planters.[87]

The state benefitted from the provision of other public goods as well. New railroads enhanced the logistical power at the state's disposal, and the resulting complementary infrastructure, such as local road networks, encouraged

[84] Colony of Mauritius (1898: B1).

[85] Carter (1995: 206) and Smith (1995: 273). On legibility, see Scott (1998) and Slater (2008).

[86] Colony of Mauritius (1898: §L41–58).

[87] These changes in the judicial system were recorded in table 2.5 as indications of Mauritius' institutional characteristics. As I have described, however, Mauritius' judicial system was strengthened as a byproduct of public goods seeking, not in response to a coalitional threat. The fact the public goods seeking affected a measurement indicator I use to gauge institutional characteristics does not imperil my explanation of Mauritian state building or my measurement scheme more generally, since explanation and measurement are separate endeavors, as I note in chapter 2 and discuss more fully in Saylor (2013).

the creation of new municipal councils to oversee these public works.[88] The scientific expertise created at the Royal Botanic Gardens was the forerunner to the Department of Agriculture, a vital bureaucratic resource.[89] In the late 1930s, for instance, planter-owned factories resisted pressing the "Uba" cane varietal used by many small sugar farmers because it was more fibrous and taxing on their pressing equipment than other varietals. The resistance led to a popular uprising in August 1937, which the state repressed. Afterward, the Department of Agriculture defused discontent through the "Uba Replacement Scheme," which distributed other varietals to Uba growers and instructed them in the use of fertilizer as well.[90] The Mauritian state gradually accreted new expertise and capability as it provided and maintained public goods.

Lastly, the provision of public goods in Mauritius confounds the widespread belief that ethnic diversity imperils public goods provision.[91] Public goods provision continued apace throughout the century, even though the country's ethnic makeup was becoming more diverse. (Today, Mauritius scores well above the global mean for ethnic fractionalization.[92]) Scholars often point to a lack of inter-ethnic cooperation and trust to explain the undersupply of public goods in ethnically diverse societies. Although Mauritius has featured such wariness, for reasons obvious enough from the discussion above, the political power of the Franco-Mauritians enabled them to impose their will on other ethnic groups. Coalitional politics transcended ethnic diversity, in a sense. It may thus be alluring to consider Mauritius an anomaly to ethnic-based theories of public goods provision. Yet ethnically narrow ruling coalitions have been common in Africa, but without the provision of new public goods. What distinguished Mauritius was its export-oriented coalition. The coming case studies of Colombia, Ghana, and Nigeria reveal how differently coalitions led by political elites responded to analogous requests for public goods, to the detriment of their countries' state building.

[88] Mahatma Gandhi Institute (1982: 3).

[89] Storey (1997: 103–108).

[90] Ibid., 141–151.

[91] E.g., Alesina, Baqir, and Easterly (1999); Baldwin and Huber (2010); and Habyarimana et al. (2007).

[92] Fearon (2003).

CHAPTER 6

Marginalized Coffee Exporters and Missed State Building Opportunities in Colombia, 1880–1905

At first blush, Colombia appears to be something of a perplexity compared to the other Latin American countries examined herein. After 1850, while Chile and Argentina were institutionalizing order, Colombia "remained weak and maintained only a feeble presence in the countryside."[1] State capacity, when created, proved difficult to sustain, and in the past few decades Colombia has witnessed a "collapse of authority."[2] Some scholars maintain that Colombia "does not fit the stereotypes and 'models' conventionally used in discussions of Latin America."[3] They instead commonly attribute its history of political disorder and instability to the country's "spatial fragmentation, which has found expression in economic atomization and cultural differentiation."[4]

But like Chile and Argentina, Colombia enjoyed state building opportunities during its first major commodity boom, in coffee, late in the nineteenth century. However, Colombia's ruling coalition was led by a group of political elites without direct stakes in exporting. When coffee boomed between 1887 and 1896, the ruling coalition refused to build railroads in coffee areas or tighten monetary policy to facilitate coffee exports. Instead, the government exploited coffee producers, who eventually took up arms against it in the War of the Thousand Days (1899–1902), an enormously bloody and costly civil war. The government prevailed, but ruling coalition members did not subsequently press for institutional strengthening because *cafeteros* did not diametrically threaten ruling coalition members' basic interests; power holders dealt with

[1] López-Alves (2000: 2).

[2] Centeno (2002: 11).

[3] At least in Charles Bergquist's view, as recounted by Bushnell (1993: viii).

[4] Safford and Palacios (2002: ix).

them without moving toward unmediated rule. And with export-oriented actors excluded from political power, policymakers did not provide new public goods, severing that route to new state capacity as well. Colombia's first major commodity boom ended without any meaningful growth in state capacity.

Colombia in the Late Nineteenth Century

Colombia's coffee boom, which began in 1887, provided the first lasting opportunity for prosperity in a country that had suffered economic and political instability since independence. At the time of the boom, politics revolved around five main actors: export-oriented landowners, merchants, artisans, traditional agriculturalists, and the Catholic Church. These groups jockeyed through the country's two main political parties, the Liberals and Conservatives. Although some scholars characterize Colombia's political parties as "multiclass and nationwide,"[5] the parties had an evident divide when it came to exporting. The Liberal Party included export-oriented coffee interests, whereas the Conservative Party relied on a non-export-oriented social base. Accordingly, tariff policy and how the government used the revenue derived from coffee production were central to economic policy and party politics in general.

The Liberal Party represented merchants and export-oriented landowners and championed free trade and an external economic orientation. Domestic merchants invested heavily in coffee production in Cundinamarca and Santander departments, where merchants and export-oriented *hacendados* were largely one and the same.[6] (Departments are the Colombian analog to provinces.) Large landed estates were the dominant social formation in Cundinamarca and Santander, in contrast to the small-scale, family farms that would come to typify Colombian coffee in the twentieth century (especially in the department of Antioquia). In 1888, for example, Cundinamarca and Santander accounted for around 97 percent of coffee exports.[7] Landed elites were organized through the Sociedad de Agricultores de Colombia, which represented large, export-oriented coffee producers. Politically, Cundinamarca and Santander were home to the Radical Liberals, the hardcore of the Liberal Party. The moderate factions of the Liberal Party, known as the Independents, largely hailed from Cauca and the Caribbean coastal zone, areas with a lesser export orientation.[8]

[5] Bushnell (1993: 93). See also Delpar (1981: xi) and López-Alves (2000: 125).
[6] Safford (1965). There was not a sizable foreign merchant community in Colombia.
[7] Delpar (1981: 26–38) and Palacios (1980: 20–43). See also Bergquist (1978: 3–17).
[8] Bushnell (1993: 142) and Ospina Vásquez (1955: 248).

The Conservative Party was more supportive of statism, tariffs, and protectionism because its main economic constituencies were traditional (non-export-oriented) agriculturalists and artisans, who were harmed by free trade. The Catholic clergy also gravitated to the Conservative Party because Liberals had encroached on ecclesiastical prerogatives and expropriated Church lands when they held power from 1850 to 1880.[9] Antioquia most strongly supported the Conservative Party. The department would become Colombia's coffee heartland in the twentieth century but produced just 2 percent of coffee exports in 1874 and only 9 percent as of 1895–1900.[10] Most of Antioquia's inhabitants were small-scale agriculturalists raising foodstuffs for Tolima department to the south.[11] Some *antioqueños* with significant export-oriented, or "capitalistic," interests identified as Liberals; others followed their regional trend and supported the Conservative Party, though they would eventually defect from the Conservatives in the 1890s as a dissident faction known as the Historical Conservatives, or *Históricos*.[12] Overall, Colombia's political parties had a plain divide when it came to exporting, and this dividing line became starker during the coffee boom.

The Liberal Party dominated Colombian politics from 1850 to 1880, when successive small and ephemeral commodity booms in cotton, tobacco, indigo, and cinchona bark (quinine) buoyed its export-oriented partisans. (Gold production, mostly from Antioquia, was steady throughout the period, usually accounting for 20–25 percent of exports.) The growing but nascent external orientation enriched domestic merchants, whose capital would be central to coffee expansion after 1887. Import taxes, especially on low-quality textile imports consumed by the masses, funded the Liberal Party's side-payments. During the 1870s, Liberals planned to use state funds to build the Northern Railroad, an integrated network that would have linked the Liberal bastions of Boyacá, Cundinamarca, and Santander to Bogotá and the Magdalena River. (The project never came to fruition.) Laissez-faire economic policy was otherwise the norm. In fact, Liberals relinquished nearly all other taxing and administrative prerogatives to provincial governments under the 1863 Constitution.[13] Sweeping political decentralization left the Colombian state inchoate.

By the late 1870s, tobacco—Colombia's leading staple export until the rise of coffee—had gone bust. Tobacco really "did not perform well beyond an initial spurt" in the late 1840s, and by 1880, tobacco exports were barely

[9] Bergquist (1978: 51) and Palacios (1980: 78).

[10] McGreevey (1971: 196) and Palacios (1980: 21).

[11] Park (1985: 29). Foodstuffs demand in Tolima developed from modest tobacco and indigo export production during the 1860s and 1870s.

[12] Delpar (1981: 38–42, 159–167).

[13] Bergquist (1978: 8–13); Deas (1982: 289–291); and Delpar (1981: 7–8).

$1 million "golden pesos" ($oro), just one-third their late 1860s apex (in nominal pesos, so the decline was larger in real terms).[14] Imports were likewise declining, which put state revenues under strain. Yet exports were so weak that a significant trade imbalance remained, and rising government spending exacerbated budget deficits. Politicians and other period observers increasingly characterized the economy as paralytic.[15] Amid these macroeconomic difficulties, Rafael Núñez won the presidency in 1880 and inaugurated a period of Conservative dominance, known as *la Regeneración* (the Regeneration). Núñez built a coalition among disaffected Independent (i.e., moderate) Liberals, Conservatives, and artisans. Radical Liberals, trying to stop Núñez's ascendancy, revolted in what was then Colombia's sixth civil war of the century, but Núñez prevailed.[16]

Although Núñez had once advocated free trade, he had become disenchanted with liberal trade policies, which he argued had led to economic weakness and political atomization.[17] Núñez therefore raised tariffs, to the benefit of artisans (especially textile artisans around Medellín, in Antioquia). Núñez claimed that artisans deserved trade protection because they moderated political conflict between the ruling class and the illiterate masses.[18] Núñez also founded the Banco Nacional and instituted a paper money regime, to the dismay of merchants. Loose monetary policy and its attendant inflation benefitted artisans and traditional agriculturalists by making imports more expensive; traditional agriculturalists gained further since they could repay outstanding debts with depreciating currency. Núñez used paper money to fund patronage projects throughout the country and enlarge the bureaucracy in Bogotá. However, loose monetary policy would seem advantageous for coffee producers, since exports become cheaper with depreciation. Yet during the 1880s and 1890s, inflation outpaced depreciation in Colombia, which meant that paper money hurt export-oriented actors. So too did a coffee export tax that the government imposed in 1895.[19] Overall, the side-payment strategy used during *la Regeneración* harmed export-oriented actors.

[14] McGreevey (1971: quote from 157) and Ocampo (1984: 100–101).

[15] Park (1985: 190–196).

[16] Núñez ran as an Independent and later created the short-lived National Party, but it "would become little more than one particular faction of the Conservatives" (Bushnell 1993: 140–143, quote from 143).

[17] Jaramillo Uribe (1964: 297–302) and Martínez Delgado (1970a: 221–224).

[18] Núñez's justification is excerpted in Ospina Vásquez (1955: 289).

[19] Bergquist (1978: 36–56); Ocampo (1984: 326–334); and Palacios (1980: 124–140). Núñez also cultivated support among religious conservatives. After years of relative marginalization, the Catholic Church's status was reinvigorated through the Concordat of 1887, which compensated the Church for property expropriations during Liberal rule and reinstituted its oversight of education (Safford and Palacios 2002: 246).

Núñez led a group of "political elites" without direct stakes in exporting. This coalitional variance, compared to the prior three cases, explains Colombia's divergent response to its first major commodity boom. Rafael Núñez was from a military family; his modest personal fortune came from fees he was able to collect as a diplomat in Europe from 1866 to 1874. His political partner, Miguel Antonio Caro, who was president for much of the 1890s, was a Latin professor. José Manuel Marroquín, who ruled Colombia during much of the War of the Thousand Days, was also a professor. The people "who made the policies of the national government . . . were more or less professional politicians—mostly lawyers and some merchants, military officers, clergy, and literati. Many of these politically active people owned some land, but many, probably most, of these did not think of themselves primarily as landowners, but rather, more honorifically, as public servants or political leaders."[20] Even more important, compared to the Liberals, "relatively few of the Conservative political elite became involved in business ventures to any significant extent," including a pronounced absence from export-oriented agriculture.[21]

La Regeneración began against the backdrop of low state capacity. The central state possessed nothing approaching a monopoly on violence in 1880. Colombia suffered civil wars in 1839–42, 1851, 1854, 1859–62, and 1876–77 and would experience two more during the case study period (1884–85 and 1899–1902).[22] Indeed, López-Alves likens Colombia's departments (called *estados*, or "states," until 1886) to warring Italian city-states: "Lacking a central institution with a monopoly on coercion, the elites in each of these *estados* were forced to resolve issues . . . without much external [i.e., central state] help."[23] Political segmentation, violence, and instability were three reasons among many that the London bond market regarded Colombia so poorly. In 1875, the Corporation of Foreign Bondholders, a group of British investors, announced that its members would refuse to purchase Colombian debt issues due to the country's unsettled outstanding debt; the announcement effectively barred Colombia from foreign debt markets.[24] Colombian bond spreads versus British Consols regularly exceeded 20 percent in the 1880s and 1890s, when the average spread for sovereign countries was 3.4 percent.[25] Yet the state possessed a flimsy extractive apparatus and relied heavily on customs duties, limiting its ability to get its fiscal house in order.[26]

[20] Safford (1995: 119–120).

[21] Delpar (1981: 47–52, quote from 58).

[22] Centeno (2002: 45). López-Alves (2000: 119) considers civil conflicts in 1867 and 1895 to be wars as well.

[23] López-Alves (2000: 97).

[24] Mauro, Sussman, and Yafeh (2006: 155).

[25] Accominotti, Flandreau, and Rezzik (2011: 392 n. 25).

[26] Bustamente (1974: 631). See also Deas (1982).

Colombia's fiscal problems contributed to its paltry transportation infrastructure. In the 1870s, Radical Liberals proposed creating the aforementioned Northern Railroad, which would have linked key Liberal-dominated export zones to Bogotá. But Colombia's export producers could not fund it alone, and the state could offer little more than profit guarantees, which made foreign investors wary.[27] In 1880, Colombia had just 45 kilometers of railroad track, which was "almost insignificant as compared to the networks that countries like Mexico and Argentina were building."[28] Bogotá was not connected to the Magdalena River, the principal transportation route through the central *cordillera*, and the trek from the country's capital to its main port on the Caribbean coast took one to two weeks.[29]

A highly mediated form of rule prevailed. After independence, the central state "disappeared," and Colombia became little more than a conglomeration of *caudillos*.[30] In 1880, the prevailing 1863 Constitution was "the most extreme version of federalism ever known in the Americas."[31] Local administration was autonomous from the central state and embryonic at best. Mayoral posts often went unfilled and had frequent turnover. Municipalities relied mainly on liquor and slaughter taxes and central state subsidies; many local governments "faced acute fiscal penury."[32] Insufficient revenues hampered the development of a justice system. Viable jails were largely nonexistent throughout the *Llaneros* grasslands in the east, for instance.[33] Along the Caribbean coast, the government could not conscript soldiers or stem the contraband trade.[34] More generally, under the 1863 Constitution, the justice system in each regional *estado* was almost wholly independent of Bogotá.[35] Local elections were likewise autonomous from central state interference.[36] Political parties resonated more strongly at the local level than did the Colombian state: "People may not have been willing to kill or die for Colombia . . . but they seemed more than able and ready to do so on behalf of the Liberal or Conservative parties."[37] Nevertheless, Colombia's political parties did not serve as institutional adjuncts to the state.

[27] Molina (1970: 103–107) and Ortega Díaz (1923: 418–429).

[28] Bushnell (1993: 134).

[29] Deplar (1981: 14–15).

[30] Park (1985: 12).

[31] Mazzuca and Robinson (2009: 286). See also Bushnell (1993: 122–126, 130, 141–142) and Safford and Palacios (2002: 243–245).

[32] Posada-Carbó (1996a: 214–222, quote from 216) and Rausch (1993: 127).

[33] Rausch (1993: 125).

[34] Posada-Carbó (1996a: 226–229).

[35] See Rey Vera (2008) for an illustration from Santander.

[36] Posada-Carbó (1997: 257).

[37] Centeno (2002: 67). See also López-Alves (2000).

They had "no permanent structures on the national or regional levels to provide organizational continuity."[38] Colombia exhibited low state capacity in 1880.

The Revenue Imperative and Colombian State Building

The revenue imperative did not strongly influence Colombian state building during *la Regeneración*. Although non-rent-generating commodities like coffee arguably demand a diversified taxing structure in order to preserve their international competitiveness, the government levied an export tax on coffee in 1895.[39] Ruling coalition members used the tax to harm export producers, a move that directly contradicts the expectation for agricultural exporters. Moreover, Colombia's structure of tax revenue was undiversified. Customs (especially import) duties reigned supreme, with taxes on saltworks usually of secondary importance. Other taxes, including direct taxes and indirect excise taxes, were virtually nonexistent.[40] The fiscal properties of coffee did not drive tax policy or the government's stance toward coffee producers in general.

Colombia's geopolitical concerns were also peripheral to policymaking. Colombia did not fight a significant external war during the nineteenth century, its only conflict being a one-battle border skirmish with Ecuador in 1863. An absence of warfare may therefore account for Colombia's low state capacity. Yet three rivalries, with Ecuador (beginning in 1831), Peru (1824), and Venezuela (1831), left no imprint on state development.[41] European powers, including Britain, France, Germany, and Italy, periodically bullied Colombia through economic blockades but did not provoke military strengthening. Colombia likewise did little to counter the rising American regional influence at the end of the century.[42] Despite plain encroachments on Colombia's sovereignty in Panama, "the Bogotá government did not govern Panama well—sometimes it did not govern Panama at all."[43] Through it all, the army remained small, always below 4,000 men until the late 1880s.[44] Meanwhile, Colombia's seven civil wars between 1839 and 1902 were state breakers, not state makers—as they were in Chile and Argentina.

[38] Delpar (1981: x). See Smith (2007) on political parties as adjuncts to state building.

[39] Palacios (1980: 129–140).

[40] Bustamente (1974: 631); Deas (1982); and Soifer (2013: ch. 5).

[41] Thies (2005: 457). Colombia had a border dispute with Venezuela in the 1890s; the parties dealt with it through arbitration by the Spanish Crown, rather than preparing for conflict (e.g., Martínez Delgado 1970a: 410–414; Rausch 1993: 96–97, 139–140).

[42] Molina (1970: 208–217).

[43] Deas (2008: 185).

[44] López-Alves (2000: 138).

Colombia's Coffee Boom

Colombia's worst civil war—the War of the Thousand Days—was the catastrophic culmination of the coalitional politics that surrounded the coffee boom. All of Colombia's prior exports—cinchona bark (quinine), cotton, gold, indigo, and tobacco—paled in comparison to coffee, the first Colombian export to feature a lasting secular price boom and production growth. The coffee boom began when prices paid in New York rose 40 percent between 1887 and 1888, which translated to more than a 50 percent rise in prices in Colombia when adjusting for ongoing currency depreciation.[45] By 1893, world coffee prices were 77 percent higher than their 1887 level.[46] Colombians responded by planting coffee trees (or bushes, as they are known locally). The "rate of expansion of the industry was phenomenal and had no precedent."[47] Coffee exports tripled from 111,000 60-kg bags (1887) to around 340,000 bags (1894). This growth represented the "immediate" response to the 1887 price surge, as coffee trees take about six years to reach productive maturity. By 1898, Colombia exported 577,600 bags worth $9.4 million pesos ($oro), more than twice the height of quinine exports and vastly more than the apogee in gold or tobacco.[48]

Landed elites in Santander and Cundinamarca departments were the direct beneficiaries of the coffee boom. Santander's production rose from approximately 133,300 bags in 1890 to 270,000 by 1904. The boom was felt even more strongly in Cundinamarca, which received approximately 80 percent of investment in coffee production between 1870 and 1895. Cundinamarca's production rose from just 38,000 bags in 1888 to an annual average of 150,000 bags from 1895 to 1900. The boom came later to Antioquia, which would eventually become Colombia's coffee heartland but in 1900 accounted for less than 10 percent of overall production.[49] In the 1890s, Colombia's coffee boom mostly enriched the merchant-speculators in Santander and Cundinamarca, who formed the core of the Liberal Party.

The state and the political elites who controlled it were the indirect beneficiaries of the boom, due to surging revenue. From the late 1870s until the boom, state revenues were usually $5–6 million pesos per year. But in 1893–94, the year coffee production spurted, tax receipts exploded to $30.6 million,

[45] Palacios (1980: 130–131).
[46] Bergquist (1978: 21–23).
[47] López-Alves (2000: 238 n. 53).
[48] Ocampo (1984: 100–101, 316–317).
[49] Jiménez (1985: 132); Palacios (1980: 21); and Ocampo (1984: 321–322).

$20 million of which came from customs duties.[50] The state had never been so inundated with tax revenue. The boom at once created unmatched private wealth among coffee elites in Liberal strongholds and unprecedented revenue inflows to state coffers, which eliminated any fiscal rationale for state building. The boom did create state building possibilities, however, as coffee producers turned to the state to assist their economic goals.

Ostracized Coffee Exporters Fail to Obtain New Public Goods

Colombian export producers, like their counterparts in the other cases, sought state-supplied public goods to reduce transport costs and facilitate credit accessibility. High transport costs were "one of the major bottlenecks of the Colombian economy."[51] In fact, lowering transport costs was the best way to promote coffee producers' profitability, as labor costs were already low and there was no good mechanical substitute for traditional cultivation and processing techniques.[52] Coffee producers also sought easier credit, as coffee requires fairly sizable initial capital outlays compared to other agricultural commodities. Unfortunately, interest rates on agricultural loans often topped 100 percent in small towns.[53] A number of banks had been established in Colombia after 1850, particularly to serve tobacco producers, and the Liberal government had provided them "unconditional" "official protection and encouragement." The state accepted private banknotes for tax payments in the 1870s and used them to pay its creditors, which helped the credit worthiness of these banks. But most of these banks went bust along with tobacco, with the Banco de Bogotá being the lone permanent survivor.[54] Unlike the prior cases, however, the Colombian government refused to facilitate credit accessibility or improve transportation infrastructure because coffee producers stood outside the ruling political coalition.

[50] Bustamente (1974: 631) and Park (1985: 192).

[51] Palacios (1980: quote from 4, 150). See also Molina (1970: 103–107).

[52] Beyer (1948: 22–23) and Horna (1992: 129). However, Jiménez (1985: 181–191, quote from 191) notes that coffee estate owners in Cundinamarca sometimes had difficulty securing adequate labor. They did not appeal to the state for help, however, because they "tended in fact to distrust the Conservative authorities who would often undertake forced draft of hacienda laborers during political disturbances."

[53] Beyer (1947: 165–166) and Williams (1994: 147). Interest rates were 10–15 percent near larger cities.

[54] Palacios (1980: quote from 28) and Safford and Palacios (2002: 232–233, 256–257). The banks of the 1870s generally did not make loans to *cafeteros* (Jiménez 1985: 192–193).

RAILROAD POLICY DURING *LA REGENERACIÓN*

Coalitional politics explains why state railroad policy underserved coffee zones. Policymakers ignored Santander's desire for a state-supported railroad connecting its capital (Bucaramanga) to the Magdalena River. *Cafeteros* had sought a railroad as early as the 1870s, when Santander produced around 100,000 bags of coffee annually (then 90 percent of coffee exports).[55] Santander's production rose to 270,000 bags by 1904, still the majority of Colombian exports. But Santander was a Liberal bastion, did not receive government assistance, and consequently lost ground to areas that received railroads, such as Antioquia. The coffee zone around Bucaramanga relied instead on inadequate mule trails to move coffee to the Magdalena River.[56] The government likewise ignored other coffee areas, including Rionegro (Santander), Sumapaz and Tequendama (Cundinamarca department), and Chaparral (Tolima).[57] The lone railroad built in Santander was a 55 km feeder route from Cúcuta to the Zulia River near the Venezuelan border. The Cúcuta Railroad was built without central state assistance, relying instead on private capital and financial support from the local Santander government.[58]

The absence of railroads in major coffee zones in Santander and Cundinamarca was not for a lack of plans. In the 1870s, officials in the then-Liberal government developed extensive plans for the Northern Railroad, intended to service Boyacá, Cundinamarca, and Santander departments. The Northern Railroad would have been a watershed moment for the central *cordillera* region. But the railroad became a flashpoint for regional tensions because it would have been a substantial financial burden for the state while providing benefits to only three departments, and it was never built.[59] During *la Regeneración*, Núñez paid lip service to building an integrated railroad network, but never ardently pursued a national transportation plan. Instead, railroads were built here and there. Coffee producers felt exploited because they provided the bulk of foreign exchange. The *Diario de Cundinamarca* observed in 1882 that the government's fiscal reliance on customs duties meant that export-oriented provinces were effectively subsidizing railroad construction elsewhere in the country.[60]

[55] Park (1985: 32).

[56] Bergquist (1978: 107).

[57] Palacios (1980: 148).

[58] Bergquist (1978: 23) and Ortega Díaz (1923: 454–459). During the 1885 civil war, the central state expropriated the railroad.

[59] Park (1985: 66–69, 92–93); Delpar (1981: 112–114); and Ortega Díaz (1923: 418–429). Radical Liberals were the main proponents of the Northern Railroad, even though it conflicted with their espoused economic ideology (Ospina Vásquez 1955: 251).

[60] Park (1985: 200).

State-supported railroads were not entirely absent from coffee-producing areas, however. The Girardot Railroad was a 49 km spur that linked the town of Girardot on the Magdalena River to Tocaima in Cundinamarca department. In 1878, in the aftermath of the failed Northern Railroad, Congress authorized a feasibility study for a railroad project linking the Magdalena to Bogotá. The Girardot Railway was the first step in this process (though Bogotá would not be linked to the Magdalena River until 1915). Núñez supported the Girardot Railroad in principle, but delayed the project until Independents allied with him gained control of Cundinamarca's provincial government in 1881.[61] Núñez then employed Francisco Javier Cisneros, a Cuban who played an integral role in developing Colombia's railroads, to build the railroad. Unlike the Cúcuta Railroad, however, the Girardot Railroad was "almost entirely executed with government funds." The state promised a $600,000 peso subsidy, with Cundinamarca chipping in $100,000 more. Núñez also committed 50 percent of the Banco Nacional's profits and a tenth of the country's customs revenue to the project.[62]

Political imperatives were behind the Girardot Railroad. The railway was routed near the property of Salvador Camacho Roldán, a major landowner who was then director of the Banco Nacional. Camacho Roldán was a Liberal but had supported Núñez since 1875 and was thus a prominent example of Núñez's alliance with moderate, Independent Liberals. (The two would later split over Núñez's free-wheeling paper money emissions.)[63] The political rationale for the Girardot Railroad was not lost on Cisneros. In 1884, Ricardo Núñez, the president's younger brother, ran for deputy in the Cundinamarca provincial assembly. Cisneros wrote, in personal correspondence to Carlos Sáenz, the administrator of the Girardot project, "You very well know how useful it would be for the Girardot project if don Ricardo could be a member of the assembly, for in his presence there he could serve to exert his influence directly on the President in favor of the Girardot railway."[64] But construction was slow. By 1898, the Girardot Railroad had only pressed as far as Anapoima, at the edge of the Tequendama coffee zone in southwestern Cundinamarca. Overall, what was perhaps Colombia's richest area for coffee production largely lacked railway transport.[65]

A political logic also guided Núñez's stance toward the Antioquia Railroad, which *antioqueños* had sought since the 1870s. Cisneros signed a contract in

[61] Ortega Díaz (1923: 389–390) and Park (1985: 205).
[62] Horna (1992: 129–131).
[63] Horna (1992: 129–131) and Park (1985).
[64] Quoted in Horna (1973: 81).
[65] Palacios (1980: 148) makes this assessment.

1874 with the Liberal government to build one, and the *antioqueño* regional government promised a $2 million peso subsidy in exchange for a one-third ownership stake. But chronic labor problems, land clearing difficulties, and tardy subsidies left the project in disarray by 1880. Under Núñez, the central state assumed the leading financial role to expedite construction. Núñez sought to enliven Antioquia's internal market, which would aid artisans and traditional agriculturalists. (Recall that textile artisans around Antioquia's capital, Medellín, were a chief beneficiary of Núñez's tariffs.) In 1885, when the first 38 km of the railroad were inaugurated, minerals, lumber, and cattle were its principal freight items.[66] The Antioquia Railroad was not a forward-looking attempt to spur coffee production, as coffee had not yet boomed, but rather a side-payment to coalition members.

The two railroads with the heaviest financial toll likewise had little relevance to coffee. The first was the Cauca Railroad, which connected Cali to the Buenaventura port on the Pacific Ocean. Little coffee was produced in Cauca (just 3 percent of coffee exports circa 1900). Cisneros was again contracted to build the railroad, though he would complete only 26 km of the 138 km of promised track. The project hinged on a $3 million peso subsidy from the Cauca government, but payments were chronically late. When Núñez came to power, the state overtook this financial obligation and hastened completion of a 20 km link between Buenaventura and Córdoba in June 1882.[67] Núñez was motivated by a political debt to Cauca's Independent Governor, Ezequiel Hurtado. Hurtado had helped deliver Cauca, a department with acrimonious relations between Liberals and Conservatives, for Núñez in the 1880 presidential election. Underwriting the railroad both rewarded Hurtado and bolstered Núñez's support in Cauca.[68] Over the next twenty years, numerous contracts were signed but construction was sluggish. In 1907, after twenty-nine years of construction, the railroad stretched just 55 km—at an astounding cost of $4.7 million pesos.[69]

The second costly project was a set of three railroads emanating from Bogotá, collectively known as the Sabana de Bogotá railroads. The most important of them was the Ferrocarril de la Sabana, which stretched 40 km westward from Bogotá to Facatativá, where it would eventually link with the Girardot Railroad in 1915 and give Bogotá rail access to the Magdalena River. Less important lines went from Bogotá north to Zipaquirá (47 km) and south

[66] Coffee only became the leading freight item on the railroad in 1898 (Horna 1992: 55–74). Nevertheless, Antioquia's high transport costs were not "substantially reduced" until 1930 (Palacios 1980: 149).

[67] Horna (1992: 85–96). Export estimate from Ocampo (1984: 325).

[68] Park (1985: 175–180).

[69] Ortega Díaz (1923: 499).

to Soacha (18 km). Together these railroads represented about one-sixth of the track laid in Colombia up to 1904. But Facatativá, Soacha, and Zipaquirá were not noteworthy coffee-producing zones. Rather, they were the "stronghold of traditional agriculture and Nationalist [i.e., Núñez's] political support."[70] The Ferrocarril de la Sabana began as a joint venture between a private firm and the Cundinamarca government but, by the 1890s, the central state had assumed virtually all of its outstanding liabilities.[71]

Overall, railroad building barely aided the coffee sector. Transport costs rose steadily between 1886 and 1900, as most producers continued to rely on mule transport to river ports.[72] Still, the leaders of *la Regeneración* did not substantially alter railroad policy once coffee boomed. The Ferrocarril del Tolima seemed to be an exception when it was conceived in the 1890s. The state initially guaranteed the railway's bonds but later reneged, claiming technical violations of the contract, and only 17 km was built by 1904.[73] Despite Núñez's stated aims, Colombia did not create a national railway network, something that cannot be explained away by the country's challenging topography. Had Núñez provided export-oriented actors the integrated Northern Railway, state capacity would have expanded like it did from the construction of the FCSV and FCS in Chile. Variance in these countries' political coalitions explains why they differed so markedly in their transportation policies.

PAPER MONEY AND CONFLICT OVER BANKING AND CREDIT

The same political dynamic typified credit policy. Rafael Núñez came to power in 1880 on a protectionist platform and raised tariffs to 25 percent on a number of products competing with artisan crafts. Núñez sought a national bank to complement his import substitution strategy, believing that expanding the credit supply would aid national economic development. His Liberal opponents disagreed. They believed a national bank would wrongly move economic policy away from its laissez-faire orientation and create inflation.[74] In addition, export-oriented Liberals had little need for credit as of 1880: tobacco had gone bust, and cinchona bark (quinine) production, which peaked in 1880, required little capital. Speculators simply plundered cinchona bark trees on public lands (*tierras baldías*), removing sizable forests at relatively little cost.[75] Export-oriented actors had no desire for a national bank.

[70] Bergquist (1978: 52).
[71] Ortega Díaz (1923: 569–586).
[72] Palacios (1980: 130–131).
[73] Ortega Díaz (1923: 625–633).
[74] Park (1985: 196–203).
[75] Ocampo (1984: 289–300).

When Núñez proposed the Banco Nacional, merchants and bankers refused to purchase its shares. The government turned to financiers in New York to obtain a $3 million loan, secured with a pledge of income from the Panama Railroad Company until 1908. Núñez's legislative support enabled the bank's easy approval in 1880. But merchants and private banks refused to accept notes emitted by the Banco Nacional, spurring the government to compel them to do so under the threat of revoking their right to issue private banknotes. In its first year, Núñez used the bank to run a budget deficit twice that of government income.[76]

Even so, the bank's inflationary policies had the potential to benefit exporters by making exports relatively cheaper. Currency depreciation played little role in coffee's expansion, however, as the costs of coffee production rose faster than depreciation. The deteriorating monetary situation is why coffee producers exhibited such disdain toward Núñez. Most *hacendados cafeteros* were chronic debtors, in part because of coffee's startup costs. But their debts were typically denominated in gold, not Colombian pesos, giving them little benefit from peso depreciation. And inflation was pushing up wages that coffee producers paid at harvest time, something Rafael Uribe Uribe, a leading advocate for coffee interests and member of the Sociedad de Agricultores de Colombia, lamented.[77] Moreover, the projects funded by Banco Nacional emissions did not benefit coffee areas. The bank initially financed public works projects in areas far removed from coffee production, such as the Cauca railroad or an ironworks in Samacá (Boyacá department). The purpose of these projects was "securing political control over the (departments)," to Liberals' dismay.[78]

When coffee boomed in 1887, coffee producers sought greater public lending because private banks did not have dedicated mortgage loan sections (and would not form them until the 1910s). But the state did not form a mortgage bank. (Colombia's mortgage bank, the Banco Agrícola Hipotecario, was not founded until 1924.[79]) Many *hacendados* resorted to employing human capital. They would sign agreements with landless peasants, who would clear land and manage coffee trees until they began producing sellable beans. These deals were profitable for landed elites, though profit sharing with peasants occurred sometimes. Nevertheless, such arrangements were less advantageous than the symbiotic relationship between Chile's landed elites and their mortgage bank.[80] And as the Banco Nacional's paper money emissions spiraled out of

[76] Park (1985: 197–203, 272) and Safford and Palacios (2002: 241, 256).

[77] Palacios (1980: 125–129). See also Molina (1970: 189–190).

[78] Park (1985: 204).

[79] Romero (1994). Two private mortgage banks, the Banco de Crédito Hipotecario and the Banco Hipotecario, were founded in the early 1880s but went bust before coffee boomed.

[80] Bergquist (1978: 29–32).

control over time, it became impossible to establish a government-backed mortgage bank without retiring much of the country's outstanding paper money, a congressional committee concluded in 1909.[81]

Paper money emissions were rampant during the era's two civil wars. During the 1885 civil war, the government declared that only Banco Nacional paper could be used for contracts.[82] Núñez was undermining private banks, a pillar of Liberal power. The state further impinged on private banks' prerogatives in 1887 by decreeing that private banks had to recall their bills, maintain a one-third deposit reserve, and limit their interest rates. These requirements constrained lending and forced private banks to shore up deposits with government notes. By 1892, only twelve of the forty-two banks that existed in 1881 were still in business.[83] The leaders of *la Regeneración* deliberately limited credit accessibility to export-oriented actors because of their Liberal partisanship. Meanwhile, the government surreptitiously exceeded its agreed-upon $12 million note issuance ceiling, a bulwark against inflation. The Banco Nacional had emitted $21 million by 1894 and $31 million by the War of the Thousand Days in 1899.[84] (Some Liberals even offered the government a $4 million peso loan in exchange for a moratorium on new emissions.[85]) During the war, generals printed money, unsupervised, in the field. At one point Bogotá ran out of paper, and the government began printing money on chocolate bar wrappers.[86]

Monetary policy strained the ruling political coalition over time. As coffee production expanded in Antioquia, nascent export-oriented Conservatives increasingly gravitated to a dissident faction known as the Historical Conservatives, or *Históricos*. The *Históricos* accentuated their opposition with a political treatise entitled "Motives of Dissidence," published in 1896 and signed by twenty-one prominent former Conservatives, many of whom were *antioqueños*. The treatise railed against the system of inconvertible money, arguing it inhibited the development of credit and threatened the country's business climate. Motives of Dissidence also attacked customs taxes and the lack of a national railroad plan.[87] The government's refusal to provide new public goods

[81] Ibid., 250.

[82] Park (1985: 272). The civil war began in Santander, home to cinchona bark (quinine) production; a precipitous international price decline in 1882–83 plunged Santander's fortunes and triggered a revolt against Núñéz's government (Safford and Palacios 2002: 253).

[83] Bustamente (1974: 589–591).

[84] Safford and Palacios (2002: 257).

[85] Bergquist (1978: 90–91).

[86] Deas (1982: 325).

[87] Bergquist (1978: 57–59) and Delpar (1981: 158–163). The treatise is reprinted in Martínez Delgado (1958: 15–36).

was a central political flashpoint during *la Regeneración*, a rancorous era that culminated in civil war in 1899.

A Non-Elemental Threat Obviates Institution Building

Export-oriented actors encapsulated within the Liberal Party, who were politically marginalized despite their rising economic power, led two armed conflicts against the government in the 1890s. Their first confrontation was a short-lived uprising in Cundinamarca and Santander in 1895; the second episode was the protracted and devastating War of the Thousand Days, 1899–1902. The civil wars neither toppled the ruling political coalition nor induced the movement toward unmediated institutions. Unlike in Chile and Argentina, ruling coalition members confronted a serious political challenge, but not an elemental threat. The rising strength of export-oriented actors did not inherently imperil ruling coalition members' generative aim and thus did not trigger state building. Existing power holders instead gave Liberals a minority voice in the legislative branch,[88] which relieved their antipathy toward the government.

The first significant challenge to Núñez's ruling coalition came in 1884–85 from Santander, which had been suffering from a collapse in quinine prices since 1882. Santander's Governor, Solón Wilches, was a political oddity: he was an Independent allied with Núñez but also supported by Santander's Radical Liberals, due to his promotion of quinine exports. As quinine prices dropped, however, Wilches increased taxes in 1883 to make up the budgetary shortfall—and Santander's Radical Liberals retracted their support of him. Yet Wilches was re-elected in 1884 via widespread fraud. The Radical Liberals revolted against the government, and rebellions spread throughout the country. The revolts were easily suppressed due to internal divisions, as many, if not most, Liberal leaders did not actively support the insurrections.[89]

Núñez used the civil war as a pretext to replace the 1863 Constitution, which thoroughly delegated power to regional governments, with one that concentrated power in the central state. The 1886 Constitution empowered the president to appoint all departmental governors and thereby indirectly control all subnational appointments.[90] In theory, the new constitution functioned like Chile's 1854 Law of the Municipalities. In actuality, Colombia's

[88] Mazzuca and Robinson (2009).

[89] Delpar (1981: 129–131) and Park (1985: 170–174, 215–220, 254–263).

[90] Mazzuca and Robinson (2009: 292–293).

1886 Constitution did not produce unmediated institutions. Governors neither designated nor controlled electoral board members, unlike in Chile, where the state dominated electoral boards. The exercise of power in Colombia "followed more closely the vagaries of local politics." Power-sharing at the local level was common, despite the conservative "hegemony" over politics at the national level.[91] (Only two Liberals were elected to Congress between 1886 and 1899.[92]) A subsequent 1888 law, the so-called Law of the Horses, gave the president unprecedented authority to intervene in local affairs, but he lacked the institutional resources to do so.[93] The army was of little help, either: it did not monopolize violence, was small, and "had too many generals and too few soldiers."[94] In short, the 1886 Constitution did not significantly alter Colombian state institutions.

Liberals' political frustration grew with the coffee boom. Coffee production doubled in Santander and quadrupled in Cundinamarca. These regions accounted for 90 percent of coffee exports between 1895 and 1900.[95] Mortgage lending was meager; new railroads were not being built in coffee-producing areas; the country was awash with paper money; and the government imposed a coffee export tax in 1895. The following year, world coffee prices temporary declined due to Brazil's entry as a major global producer. Many Colombian producers began having trouble operating profitably due to debt service obligations and rising transport costs—problems they believed could be addressed by policy changes.[96]

Radical Liberals isolated the paper money regime as their paramount grievance, even more so than their lack of political representation at the national level. Yet reining in paper money emissions was unlikely because they were fundamental to the ruling coalition's side-payment strategy. Loose monetary policy helped bloat the government payroll in Bogotá[97] and shore up support within the military, which had recently received a large emission for the ostensible purpose of "modernization."[98] Radical Liberals and ruling coalition members were at loggerheads over paper money, and their positions were obstinate.[99] Loose monetary policy inhibited *cafeteros*' generative aim but was

[91] Posada-Carbó (1997: 265–266).

[92] Liberals frequently abstained from elections, partially accounting for their poor representation (Posada-Carbó 1997).

[93] Delpar (1981: 144).

[94] López-Alves (2000: 139).

[95] Ocampo (1984: 321).

[96] Delpar (1981: 162).

[97] Bergquist (1978: 70–71, 93, 117).

[98] Martínez Delgado (1958: 46).

[99] Bustamente (1974).

vital to sustaining the ruling coalition; tightening policy "would have gravely compromised the (ruling coalition's) hold on political power."[100]

Liberals were nonetheless divided over how best to confront the ruling coalition. The hardcore of the Liberal opposition became known as the War Liberals due to their bellicose posture. War Liberals believed "that their opportunities for social and economic mobility were unacceptably limited under the political exclusivism of the Regeneration governments." War Liberals regarded the state as their route of upward mobility, in other words. By contrast, a group of Peace Liberals tended to have direct stakes in the export economy and were comparatively compromising toward the government, which seems paradoxical at first blush. Many Peace Liberals found common cause with the *Históricos*, the moderate group of budding coffee producers from Antioquia.[101]

Peace Liberals were neither intrinsically pacific nor less aggrieved by economic policy than War Liberals. On the contrary, they were harmed more by the economic policies of *la Regeneración* than were War Liberals. Peace Liberals opposed war because they were pragmatic. They did not think that the Liberals, even if united, could defeat the government in armed conflict. In fact, Rafael Uribe Uribe, the leading War Liberal, worried that the "government does not have the power to halt the revolution; but the revolution does not have the power to defeat the government."[102] This belief was consonant with recent experience. In 1895, Eustacio de la Torre Narváez, one of Colombia's wealthiest coffee producers, helped organize anti-government revolts in Cundinamarca and Santander. As with the 1884–85 civil war, the state easily suppressed the rebellions because of divisions among the Liberals, many of whom refrained from participating.[103] The episode fortified the belief among many export-oriented actors that armed resistance to the state was futile. Peace Liberals concluded that war would merely cause economic calamity—without much hope for political gain.[104]

Peace Liberals tried to weaken support for the War Liberals' maximalist position by extracting political concessions from the ruling coalition. Peace Liberals' key demand was for electoral reform, specifically power-sharing arrangements that would guarantee Liberals representation at the national level. (Issues of economic policy were pushed down the line, given that War Liberals were centrally concerned with political representation, whereas Peace Liberals

[100] Bergquist (1978: 110).

[101] Bergquist (1978: 87–95, quote from 95) and Molina (1970: 188).

[102] Quoted in Palacios (1980: 146).

[103] Bergquist (1978: 48–50). Martínez Delgado (1970a: 337–350) details the run-up to the 1895 uprisings.

[104] Delpar (1981: 176) and Mazzuca and Robinson (2009: 296).

worried most about economic policy.) The government made a number of concessions, including a repeal of the Law of the Horses, a relaxation on press restrictions, and a suspension of the coffee export tax. But the government balked at electoral reform.[105] Ruling coalition members did not feel fundamentally threatened by the Liberal opposition, and many government officials believed (wrongly, as it turned out) that they could quickly defeat the bickering Liberal factions in war.[106]

The failure to secure electoral reform strengthened the hand of War Liberals, who in October 1899 initiated what became the War of the Thousand Days. A direct cause of the war was "the uncompromising position of the radical Conservatives and Nationalists towards a reinvigorated Liberal Party in the last half of the 1890s." Liberal leaders "rapidly recruited thousands of men in [Cundinamarca's] smallholder municipalities and from the haciendas of Liberal planters."[107] Although some government officials expected the war would be over in three months, it lasted three years and was Colombia's bloodiest civil war.[108] The state eliminated Liberals' conventional military threat in just eight months, at the Battle of Palonegro. But an ensuring guerrilla war wreaked havoc on the countryside and economy until November 1902. Coffee exports halted; *cafeteros* in Cundinamarca and Santander were particularly hard hit, while their counterparts in Antioquia were spared endemic violence.[109] Economic dislocation cost the state revenue, of course, but the ruling coalition could sustain itself through paper money emissions. The country became awash with paper money, which led to rampant inflation. The Colombian peso deteriorated from four pesos to 100 pesos per US dollar during the war, with the worst inflation coming in the guerrilla phase. A lack of army discipline also prolonged the war, as many soldiers took to plundering the countryside.[110]

A new president, José Manuel Marroquín, came to power in a military coup in July 1900, just as the war's conventional phase ended. Although Marroquín might have offered a conditional peace to the Liberals, he did not. Marroquín continued fighting "to inflict an irreversible defeat on the Liberals" and destroy their military capabilities.[111] The government zealously pursued Liberals in the countryside. Some guerrilla leaders tried to broker peace agreements, but the government rejected the proposals. In June 1902, Marroquín offered

[105] See Delpar (1981: 176) and Bergquist (1978: 121–122).
[106] Mazzuca and Robinson (2009: 298).
[107] Jiménez (1985: 229, 220, respectively).
[108] Mazzuca and Robinson (2009: 298).
[109] Bergquist (1978: 158, 158 n. 2).
[110] Bergquist (1978: 145, 164–165) and Bushnell (1993: 148–152).
[111] Mazzuca and Robinson (2009: 296–297).

Liberals amnesty, though the rebels felt the offer lacked sufficient protections or political guarantees. In late 1902, the government defeated Liberal forces along the Caribbean coast, which induced surrender by the remaining Liberal forces in Panama a month later.[112]

The War of the Thousand Days was enormously destructive. By its end, the "war had ensconced men in power from among the most authoritarian and Catholic elements of the Conservative party, the military, and the government bureaucracy."[113] Rafael Uribe Uribe, the most vocal War Liberal, reflected in 1903 that the "remedy (was), as it turned out, worse than the disease." He called on all Liberals to issue an "absolute renunciation of war as an ordinary means to obtain reforms, acquire rights, and gain power." Leaders who equivocated on this issue should lose "all credibility," Uribe Uribe believed.[114] In January 1904, Uribe Uribe got key Liberal leaders (Manuel Carvajal, Nicolás Esguerra, Juan Evangelista Manrique, and Diego Mendoza Pérez) to reconcile their differences and join him in publically issuing such a disavowal. They stated that the "views of the Liberal Party are essentially peaceful," recognized the "ineffectiveness" of extra-legal avenues to exact political change, and pledged that "the Liberal Party would not opt, then, for violent means to subdue those opposed to reform."[115]

Conservative leaders also assuaged the Liberals by adopting the "incomplete vote," an electoral system that gave the opposition a minority voice in government. The incomplete vote allocated two-thirds of a district's seats to the winning party and one-third to the runners-up. Sebastián Mazzuca and James Robinson maintain that this electoral rule was fundamental to Columbia's political stability in the early decades of the twentieth century. They conclude that electoral reform succeeded in 1905 (whereas it failed in 1898) because leaders from both parties had underestimated how prolonged and destructive the civil war would be.[116] The incomplete vote dissuaded Liberals from rebelling, and Colombia did not experience another civil war until *la Violencia* (1948–1962).

The incomplete vote may have been efficacious, but it did not alter the country's mediated institutions. Electoral reform provided the state some new legal prerogatives—the central Gran Consejo Electoral was given legal

[112] Bergquist (1978: 176–188) and Martínez Delgado (1970b: 139–141). During this period, the Liberals' remaining conventional military forces retreated to Panama, regrouped, and succeeded mostly in creating enough consternation that US diplomats began encouraging Panamanian secession (which occurred in 1903).

[113] Bergquist (1978: 195). See also López-Alves (2000: 129).

[114] *El Porvenir*, February 7, 1903 (Vol. 1, No. 62).

[115] *El Porvenir*, January 8, 1904 (Vol. 2, No. 132). See also Delpar (1981: 187).

[116] Mazzuca and Robinson (2009: 298–299). See also Martínez Delgado (1970b: 301–305).

control of local electoral boards, for instance. But governors, who worked in conjunction with local elected assemblies, "were far from omnipotent in their departments . . . [and] had no official role in setting up the electoral boards." In practice the central state could often do little to stop chicanery by electoral boards. Local power bosses, known as *gamonales*, controlled municipal elections despite the "Conservative Hegemony" in national politics until 1930.[117] Electoral reform may have contributed to newfound political stability, but it did not substantially enhance the government's ability to control local affairs. The incomplete vote was not, in other words, a state building project. Such state building was unnecessary, and not simply because Liberals had been defeated militarily, renounced violence, and been given the incomplete vote. Those developments mattered, but so too did the lack of an exigent and diametrical threat to ruling coalition members. Colombia thus limped into the twentieth-century with feeble institutions that were "virtually the same as (they) had been since the 1830s."[118]

Persistent State Weakness in Colombia

The Colombian state emerged from the War of the Thousand Days much as it had been twenty-five years prior. Colombia's ruling coalition of political elites disabled the country from realizing some of the state building gains that occurred during the prior three cases' first major commodity booms. Colombia's stagnating state capacity is consistent with other possible explanations as well, although these rival factors were not central to *Regeneración* politics. Bellicist pressures were of minor importance. The country's extractive capabilities were static (customs duties normally accounted for 60–65 percent of revenue), even though the resource curse literature expects policymakers to strengthen fiscal institutions to promote export commodities like coffee.[119] Insubstantial local state institutions had prevailed since colonial times, but they were formally changed multiple times in the nineteenth century; there was no persistent colonial institutional legacy in Colombia, in other words.[120] Finally, Colombia's ethnic fractionalization is today above the global mean, though it is on par with levels of ethnic diversity in Mauritius, which expanded state capacity during its first major commodity boom.[121] What is more, ethnicity is

[117] Posada-Carbó (1997: 257–258, 265–266).

[118] López-Alves (2000: 114).

[119] Cf. Centeno (2002: 123–125) and Soifer (2013: ch. 5).

[120] Cf. Mahoney (2010: 156).

[121] Fearon (2003).

not highly politicized in Colombia,[122] which suggests that other factors were responsible for the country's lack of state building.

On all measures, Colombian state capacity stagnated during *la Regeneración*. Although the government defeated the guerrillas in the War of the Thousand Days, it did not pacify the national territory. There remained frequent clashes between Indians and *llaneros* on Colombia's eastern frontier, an area of perennial government neglect.[123] The railroad building that occurred was piecemeal and slow, and the lack of an integrated transportation network hampered the deployment of state power. In fact, it would still be ten years until Bogotá was linked by rail to the Magdalena River. What transportation infrastructure existed was fragmented and localized; new railroads splintered, rather than solidified, the country.[124] Colombia's topography may be challenging, but coalitional jockeying was what ultimately scuttled plans for a more integrated network. As of 1905, Colombia's railway density measure was 0.0006, but a tenth of levels at the time in Chile (0.0064), Argentina (0.0072), and Mauritius (0.1137).[125] Colombia also spent nearly the entire case study period with its foreign debt in default (save January 1897 to August 1899). Its average bond yield spread versus British Consols during 1880–1905 was 11.2 percent, compared to 2.0 percent in Chile and 2.5 percent in Argentina.[126] Investors perceived Colombia's business climate to be frightful in part, I believe, because of the nature of its ruling political coalition.

The country's mediated institutions limited the influence of the central state. Presidents often had trouble finding people to serve as mayors, an administrative defect that has been chronicled for the Caribbean coast and the *Llaneros* grasslands in the east. The port city of Barranquilla, for example, had fifty-five different mayors in seventy-nine different administrations between 1890 and 1940. Municipalities relied fiscally on local liquor and slaughter taxes and central state subsidies, though these grants were spent according to local prerogatives.[127] Colombia's judicial system was also highly localized and lacked the burgeoning national development that characterized the prior three cases. In Santander, for instance, the justice system was partisan, underfunded, and ineffective, particularly at the municipal level, where local power bosses held sway. Indeed, "to a certain extent, the first decade of the twentieth century was a period without justice in the department of Santander."[128] On

[122] Lieberman (2009: 291).
[123] Rausch (1993: 209–210).
[124] Ospina Vásquez (1955: 282–283).
[125] Calculations based on data in Mitchell (1998a, 1998b).
[126] Calculations based on data from Mauro, Sussman, and Yafeh (2006).
[127] Posada-Carbó (1996a: 215–226) and Rausch (1993: 123–127).
[128] Melo Flórez (2012: 167–173, 219–232, quote from 228–229).

no measurement proxy did Colombia register a noteworthy increase in state capacity between 1880 and 1905 (see table 2.5), in spite of the 1886 Constitution, which supposedly "centralized" the polity. The coalitional basis of this arrested state building is supported by strikingly similar experiences in Ghana and Nigeria, despite being half a century and an ocean apart from Colombia.

CHAPTER 7

Nationalist Politicians Squander State Building Opportunities while Fleecing Cocoa Exporters in Ghana, 1945–1966

Two postwar African countries—Ghana and Nigeria—further bolster confidence in the relationships between commodity booms, coalitional politics, and state building, despite their temporal and spatial distance from the book's prior four case studies. The end of the Second World War marked the beginning of a massive and prolonged secular boom in primary commodity prices, and it was the first such boom to thoroughly affect most African countries.[1] However, political elites led ruling coalitions in Ghana and Nigeria, as in Colombia a half-century earlier. In Ghana, the ruling coalition refused to aid cocoa producers by creating an integrated transportation network, facilitating credit accessibility, or paying market prices through the country's marketing board. Not only did cocoa producers find their economic goals stymied, but Ghanaian state capacity stagnated as well.

Yet some scholars consider this period of Ghanaian history to be one of momentous institutional change. They judge that Kwame Nkrumah, Ghana's iconoclastic ruler, substantially strengthened state institutions as he sought to extend his Convention People's Party (CPP) and government agencies throughout the cocoa belt. This institutional assessment runs counter to my theoretical expectation for resource booms, like Ghana's, which exclusively benefit actors outside of the ruling coalition (i.e., when political elites lead the ruling coalition; see table 2.4). This chapter details that, although Nkrumah implemented a flurry of institutional modifications, they did not amount to a movement toward unmediated rule or institutional fortification in general. Most of Ghana's institutional invigoration was illusory. Nkrumah's main

[1] Williamson (2012). Ghana was known as the Gold Coast until independence in 1957, but I refer to the country as Ghana throughout the chapter for ease of reading.

institutional success was the Cocoa Marketing Board, which captured cocoa farmers' economic surplus and redirected it as side-payments to urban constituencies. The marketing board was efficacious not because it was institutionally vigorous but rather because cocoa farmers lacked alternative marketing outlets. None of Nkrumah's other institutional modifications substantially enhanced the state's ability to implement its decrees at the local level. This generalized institutional debility was permissible because cocoa farmers did not constitute a diametrical threat to the ruling political coalition, which could sustain itself via cocoa receipts even as discontent percolated in the cocoa heartland. Overall, Ghana's first major commodity boom yielded scant growth in state capacity.

Ghana at Mid-Century

The coalitional jockeying that contributed to the stagnation of Ghanaian state capacity involved five main social actors: colonial administrators, British merchants, emerging nationalist politicians, and tribal chiefs and peasants in Asante (a.k.a. Ashanti), the center of Ghana's cocoa production. Up through the Second World War, a coalition of colonial administrators, British merchants, and tribal chiefs ruled Ghana. This coalition was strained by a burgeoning urban nationalist movement after 1945. The British therefore displaced their existing coalitional partners in lieu of an alliance with indigenous nationalist politicians, who effectively became the leaders of Ghana's ruling political coalition.

Colonial officials had little choice to do otherwise because of the meager resources at their disposal. There were only a few hundred British colonial officials in Ghana: "for many Ghanaians a glimpse of a white man was no more than an occasional experience." British officials, who knew "the frailty of their position," had to administer the colony with "extreme caution."[2] The actual administration of the colony depended on local chiefs, and colonial rule in Ghana was an "almost purely Western façade of administration."[3] Native Authorities heavily influenced governance in Ghana up until 1945, both in the countryside and through advisory institutions like the colonial Legislative Council.[4]

The Asante chiefs were the most important of these chieftain groups. Asante is located in central Ghana and coterminous with some of the country's

[2] Kay (1972: 9).
[3] Apter (1963: 163).
[4] Apter (1963: 131–141) and Rathbone (2000: 9–19).

richest cocoa-producing areas, which made the Asante chiefs vital allies for the British. Asante's chieftain structure is hierarchical, and chiefs traditionally had jurisdiction over communal lands, the judiciary, and tax collection. These prerogatives positioned chiefs to capture cocoa producers' economic surplus, and some chiefs became involved in cocoa marketing as well. Chiefs also controlled credit in rural areas, which enabled them to effectively consolidate communal landholdings from indebted peasants and develop into a stratum of "planter-chiefs."[5] Planter-chiefs were directly engaged in cocoa farming, representing about 5 percent of cocoa farmers and producing about one-third of cocoa exports.[6] As a sign of their power, in 1937–38 the Asante chiefs organized a cocoa "hold-up" to protest collusion, or "pooling," by European merchants. The hold-up was "the most successful episode of collective action waged against European trading houses in all of colonial Africa."[7] Given the chiefs' social power, the British found them to be key allies.

The other main ruling coalition member through 1945 was European merchant firms, who were heavily involved in Ghana's commodity trade. The United Africa Company, for instance, controlled as much as half of the Ghanaian cocoa trade and was a weighty political force, as they were organized through the Association of West African Merchants and enjoyed representation on the Legislative Council.[8] Yet although British merchants had been traditionally influential, their sway waned with the growth of the nationalist movement after 1945.

Nationalist pressures grew throughout Africa after the Second World War. In Ghana, the movement crystallized under the leadership of Kwame Nkrumah and his CPP. Nkrumah became General Secretary of the United Gold Coast Convention in 1947, then the main group pressing for independence. Urban middle classes formed its backbone, and Nkrumah toiled to cultivate alliances with Youth Associations and rural producers as well. In 1948, Ghanaian nationalism boiled over into riots in Accra, triggered by rising import prices and anger toward foreign merchants. After the riots, Nkrumah distanced himself from the urban middle classes. He began building his CPP as a youth movement and made overtures to cocoa producers by echoing their frustrations with the Cocoa Marketing Board.[9] Nkrumah and other CPP leaders principally harnessed ideological power to attract a following. Indeed, "it

[5] Boone (2003).

[6] Beckman (1976: 39–40).

[7] Boone (2003: 146–159, quote from 157).

[8] Austin (1964: 68–69) and Beckman (1976: 43). Lebanese traders, who had a strong presence in the budding system of motorized lorry transport, were not a vibrant political force.

[9] Austin (1964: 116–117) and Beckman (1976: 51–57).

was not easy (even by 1960) to see the CPP as the vanguard of a clearly defined social class."[10]

Certainly the CPP did not represent cocoa producers. Roughly two-thirds of Ghanaian cocoa production occurred on small- and medium-sized farms. In Asante, nearly 70 percent of cocoa farmers were locals, or "citizens," who enjoyed usufruct land rights. Migrant laborers from the northern savannah, or "strangers," also farmed cocoa. Chiefs granted them land use though the so-called *abusa* system, and others worked as wage laborers. Small-scale producers constituted 60 percent of Ghana's cocoa farmers but produced just 20 percent of its cocoa. Middle-sized farmers, about 30 percent of the country's total farmers, produced half of its cocoa. Overall, about 500,000 people were involved in cocoa production, roughly 20 percent of the "employed" population.[11] But they were politically marginalized. Despite Nkrumah's rhetoric, "farmers' organisations . . . were not closely linked" to the CPP during the late 1940s, and the gulf widened in the 1950s.[12]

Although cocoa producers were perennially excluded from political power, Ghana's ruling political coalition changed substantially after the 1948 riots in Accra. The British effectively sidelined chiefs and merchants by holding the colony's first noteworthy elections in 1951, as a means to stave off independence. The CPP dominated the election, winning all five municipal slots and twenty-nine of thirty-three rural seats.[13] Nkrumah and the CPP appealed to cocoa farmers during the campaign by railing against the marketing board and what farmers regarded as a poor governmental response to swollen shoot disease. But following their 1951 victory, "CPP leaders showed no desire to discontinue the policy of using Marketing Board funds for general development expenditure."[14] In other words, Nkrumah's side-payment strategy hinged on exploiting cocoa.

Early in the postwar period, the colonial Ghanaian state exhibited low levels of state capacity. The government relied heavily on easy forms of revenue: import and export duties supplied half of its revenue. The British had also recently implemented a tax on income and profits, which constituted another 20 percent of revenue. But Britain's Office of the Government Statistician noted that "wide sections of the public are untouched by income tax," and personal income taxes accounted for a scant 0.26 percent of personal income earned.[15]

[10] Austin (1964: 12).
[11] Beckman (1976: 35–40) and Boone (2003: 149–155).
[12] Beckman (1976: 54).
[13] Austin (1964: 49–152).
[14] Beckman (1976: 51–59, quote from 57).
[15] Kay (1972: 87, 348–357).

Like its fiscal institutions, the country's transportation infrastructure was embryonic. Ghana had 805 km of railway in 1945, with two main lines: one linked Accra and Kumasi, the capital of the Asante region, and the other line connected Kumasi to the port city of Sekondi-Takoradi. (Sekondi-Takoradi handled about 94 percent of exports by weight in 1949.) The British government considered the railway network unsatisfactory because it did not touch sizable portions of the colony and could not cope with rising usage. They concluded that "roads do not make up for the limitations of the rail system . . . [because] all roads are in a poor state of repair."[16]

Ghana's institutions were correspondingly weak. The British "ruled through indigenous tribal groupings" via the Native Administration system.[17] Tribal chiefs ruled at the local level (i.e., they were the country's "mayors") but were not appointed by the central state. Mediated rule prevailed. Chiefs also principally controlled coercive power in colonial Ghana, something indicated by the colloquial names of police forces, such as the *Asantehene's* or *Omanhene's* police. The police were "instruments of personal arbitrary rule . . . of chiefly rulers," as were local courts and prisons.[18] I thus do not consider Ghana to have achieved territorial pacification as of 1945. Ghana's court system had been thoroughly decentralized to chiefs circa 1945 and "in every sense embodied the high point of Indirect Rule."[19] The British reviewed just 0.24 percent of Native Court decisions in 1946–47 (and 0.15 percent in 1948–49).[20] Moreover, only 0.4 percent of Native Court decisions were appealed to Magistrates' Courts in 1947–48 (253 appeals from 57,054 cases).[21] Chiefly decisions were almost always final. The Ghanaian state did not exert authority through the Native Courts system.

Ghanaian localities were also largely fiscally autonomous from the center. Native Authorities relied on annual rates (i.e., head taxes) for the biggest portion of their income (about 28 percent in 1947–48). Federal grants made up about 13 percent of revenues, but these grants were themselves a form of matching funds based on the local rates collected. Even at the local level, the collection of rates did not indicate institutional vigor, as it was akin to tax farming, as tax collectors received 7.5 percent of what they collected.[22] Overall, "so long as a colony could balance its books, its [fiscal] administration

[16] Kay (1972: 83–84).

[17] Apter (1963: 119). See also Mamdani (1996: 52–61) and Phillips (1989: 39–43).

[18] Killingray (1986: 428). The *Asantehene* is the highest chief in the Asante kingdom. A divisional chief within this hierarchy is known as an *omanhene*.

[19] Crook (1986: 84).

[20] Rathbone (2000: 48 n. 3).

[21] Hailey (1951: 214).

[22] Ibid., 208–209.

remained a highly decentralized affair."[23] The central government did not wield its influence through electoral manipulation, either, as local chiefs were not elected, or at least not "elected" in ways that the central state influenced.[24] There were, however, three elected municipal councils in Ghana as of the late 1940s, in Accra, Cape Coast, and Sekondi-Takoradi; but it appears their elections were not heavily influenced by the government.[25] In 1945, Ghana shared with the other case studies a low level of state capacity, including institutional debility and limited logistical resources at the government's disposal.

The Revenue Imperative and Ghanaian State Building

The revenue imperative was not responsible for Ghana's state building vicissitudes after 1945. For instance, Ghana's structure of tax revenue confounds the orthodox logic of the resource curse, which anticipates that policymakers will shift the tax burden away from non-rent-generating export commodities in order to preserve their international competitiveness. But, as of 1945, when cocoa accounted for half of exports, export duties made up 20 percent of government revenue. During the first decade of Ghana's Cocoa Marketing Board (1939–51), the marketing board purchase price (i.e., tax) cost cocoa producers 34 percent of their potential incomes, and export duties consumed another 9 percent.[26] British officials relied heavily on cocoa for revenue because the state was weak and could not have implemented a diverse revenue mix.[27] At least in this case, the theoretical logic of the resource curse is backward: the prevailing level of state capacity was not an outgrowth of the country's revenue-raising strategy but rather a cause of it.

Postwar Africa was a region with little inter-state war, however,[28] and Ghana did not fight one, which may account for its low state capacity. At the same time, there is an emergent belief that external rivalries can trigger state building as rulers prepare for war. Ghana is perhaps best situated among African countries to experience these purported benefits, as its rivalries were fairly intense.[29] Moreover, its rivalries developed quickly—between 1960 and 1961,

[23] Mamdani (1996: 56–57).
[24] Ibid., 53.
[25] Hailey (1951: 218).
[26] Bauer (1954: 291).
[27] See the official report reprinted in Kay (1972: 87–88).
[28] Herbst (2000: 103–126).
[29] See Kacowicz (1998: 126–127).

rivalries began with Ivory Coast, Nigeria, and Togo—which should have elicited a noticeable response from policymakers.[30] But, as I discuss more when I measure Ghanaian state capacity at the end of the chapter, Ghana continued to rely on cocoa receipts for its revenue during the 1960s, and revenues fluctuated with the world price for cocoa. Policymakers made no significant effort to diversify or deepen the state's revenue mix. Simply put, the idea that rivalries lead to more thoroughgoing revenue extraction is not evinced in the Ghanaian case.

Ghana's Postwar Cocoa Boom

Beginning in 1945, world cocoa prices began a stunning upward secular trend, jumping more than tenfold between 1945 and 1954, before eventually declining in the 1960s.[31] Although Ghana's Cocoa Marketing Board paid producers below-market prices (on average, around half of the prevailing world price), the boom still "made it possible for the marketing authorities to raise the producer price in real terms two or three times . . . during the first few years after the war."[32] Whereas cocoa producers were paid £23 per ton of cocoa in 1944–45, producers received £84.0 per ton in 1949–50 and £135.6 per ton, on average, in the 1950s, with little yearly variability.[33] Cocoa production rose 30 percent between 1944 and 1949.[34] The full impact of the boom on production was not felt until the 1960s, however, because Ghanaian farmers favored trees that took about ten years to reach full productivity.[35] By the 1960s, cocoa production averaged 444,000 tons annually, up from 235,000 tons annually in the late 1940s.[36] During the case study period, cocoa accounted for roughly two-thirds of Ghana's exports, and Ghanaian cocoa usually constituted 30 to 40 percent of world production. The value of cocoa exports in 1965 was roughly ten times what it had been twenty years prior.[37]

Cocoa producers were the direct beneficiaries of the boom, especially during the bountiful 1950s. The aggregate payments from the marketing

[30] Thies (2007: 722). Kacowicz (1998: 145) also notes a border dispute with Upper Volta (Burkina Faso) in 1963–1966 and an ideological rivalry with Guinea in 1966 that are not included in Thies' counting.

[31] Kay (1972: 338–340).

[32] Beckman (1976: 191).

[33] Bauer (1954: 347) and Beckman (1976: 282).

[34] Kay (1972: 336–337).

[35] Beckman (1976: 38).

[36] Ibid., 279.

[37] Ibid., 36; Kay (1972: 334–335); and Rimmer (1992: 76–77).

board increased from £20.8 million in 1949–50 to a yearly average of £34.9 million from 1950 to 1965 (including an average of £46.4 million from 1960 to 1965).[38] These payments benefitted cocoa producers of every size, including the Asante chiefs involved in cocoa production and marketing.[39]

Nkrumah and the political elites at the helm of the CPP were the indirect beneficiaries of the cocoa boom. Government cocoa income spiked from the boom, from £0.1 million (1947–48) to £15.5 million (1950–51)—or, from 1 percent to 74 percent of government revenue.[40] Before 1951, the Cocoa Marketing Board had accumulated £71 million in reserve, a fortuitous outcome due mostly to rising world prices. When the nationalists gained power in the 1951 elections, they stopped holding surplus earnings in reserve and began to transfer them to the state to fund government operations. These transfers equaled 80 percent of government expenditures on average in the first half of the 1950s. In effect, the CPP was overtly fleecing the cocoa sector. Marketing board funds remained important after independence in 1957 and funded about one-third of public expenditures.[41] In short, export-oriented actors and political elites were locked in a zero-sum battle over the economic surplus generated in the cocoa sector.

The CPP Frustrates Exporters' Efforts to Obtain New Public Goods

As in Colombia, Ghanaian export producers' political marginalization disabled them from obtaining their desired public goods. First, cocoa farmers wanted to eliminate the Cocoa Marketing Board, which extracted much of their potential income. Second, they wanted new road construction and maintenance, as Ghana's roads were in poor shape. Third, cocoa producers sought greater credit accessibility, as indebtedness to the planter-chiefs and merchant firms was common. Farmers also wanted credit to hire laborers, buy fertilizer, and purchase insecticide spraying equipment. But, rather than fulfill these public goods requests, nationalist elites used cocoa wealth to build a patronage network, which kept Ghana from receiving the positive state building byproducts associated with public goods provision.

[38] Rimmer (1992: 54, 76).

[39] Mikell (1989: 153–154).

[40] Beckman (1976: 281). Cf. Kay (1972: 345).

[41] Beckman (1976: 184–185, 281–282).

THE COCOA MARKETING BOARD RETAINED

Cocoa farmers hated the marketing board, for obvious reasons.[42] In September 1945, a delegation of cocoa farmers went to London to protest the board's pricing policies, which had paid farmers around 4 shillings per 60 lb. load (in real terms) throughout the Second World War. Booming world prices made it easy for the Cocoa Marketing Board (CMB) to raise prices (in real terms) to 13 shillings per load in 1946–47 and then to over 26 shillings by 1948–49. (As it turned out, 1948–49 marked the apogee of real prices paid by the marketing board from 1945 to 1966.)[43] Opposition to the marketing board "subsided."[44] In addition, the CPP appealed to cocoa farmers in the lead up to the 1951 election and tried to wedge itself between cocoa farmers and the Asante chiefs, which undermined a unified "cocoa voice" against the CMB. The CPP also co-opted leaders of the farmers' movement, such as Ashie Nikoi.[45] Above all, the CPP's manifesto promised that "farmers will be given control of the vast funds with the Cocoa Marketing Board to use for the benefit of the farmers primarily, and the country in general."[46]

The rhetoric was mere lip service, and after 1951, prices paid to farmers declined in nominal and real terms.[47] The CPP began directing CMB reserves into government coffers. Whereas, in 1947–48, the CMB placed just £0.4 million into the state treasury, it funneled £16 million there in 1952–53. Two years later, the CPP channeled over £38 million in cocoa proceeds to the state. In some years, such contributions were nearly 100 percent of state expenditures. Throughout the 1950s, cocoa producers typically surrendered 43 percent of their potential incomes to the marketing board.[48] Ultimately, Nkrumah and the CPP retained the marketing board to help them build a political coalition that preyed on cocoa exporters.[49]

[42] On the origins monopsony purchasing in West Africa, see Bauer (1954: 257–259) and Southall (1978).

[43] The nominal prices paid were 27 shillings 6 dinars in 1946–1947 and 65 shillings in 1948–1949 (IBRD 1969: table 5).

[44] Beckman (1976: 191).

[45] See Austin (1964: 65–66, 116–117) and Beckman (1976: 52–56).

[46] Beckman (1976: 57).

[47] Beckman (1976: 195) and IBRD (1969: table 5).

[48] Beckman (1976: 280–281). Prices were so lousy that smuggling cocoa into neighboring countries became "lucrative" (IBRD 1969: 7).

[49] Cf. the favorable pricing policies in colonial Zimbabwe, where a settler agrarian elite dominated politics (Herbst 1990a: 82–85).

TRANSPORTATION POLICY AS SIDE-PAYMENT TO CPP MEMBERS

Cocoa producers also failed to get the government to improve the country's roads. By the end of the Second World War, Ghana's "roads had deteriorated greatly, and the railway was in an exhausted state owing to lack of replacements."[50] The cocoa boom added reasons to enhance transportation infrastructure, and over the next two decades, things appeared to improve. The amount of paved or graveled roads managed by the Public Works Department more than doubled, from 2,388 miles (1945) to 5,490 miles (late 1960s).[51] However, the quantitative growth in Ghana's roadway system was deceptive. Transportation policy was not attuned to reducing transport costs but rather formulated road building contracts as side-payments for CPP allies. The CPP cared little if an integrated road network developed.

Railroads were the centerpiece of Ghana's transportation infrastructure before 1945, but an integrated road network had never developed. The country's railroads had been built to service the gold industry, and most cocoa producers relied on lorries and road transport to market their crop. (Lorries functioned reasonably well on Ghana's roadways, most of which were built with communal labor.[52]) Over time, a stratum of rural middlemen came to dominate lorry transport. Most of these middlemen had chiefly links; once a chiefly lineage acquired significant wealth, it would branch out and finance a startup middleman from its ranks. Middlemen often helped chiefs identify cocoa farmers who might want to "pledge" their farms (a form of traditional mortgage lending that I discuss below). Many lorry transporters thereby helped chiefs solidify their economic and political clout.[53]

Middlemen brokers also engaged in arbitrage, especially with farmers in isolated areas. Statutory export marketing diminished arbitrage opportunities, however. For example, the marketing board paid a uniform price for cocoa at railheads, regardless of the distance from the port, which theoretically subsidized producers' transportation costs. The pricing policy increased demand for railway transport, to the detriment of lorry owners. When lorries trucked imports into Kumasi, the capital of Asante, they were prohibited from reloading with cocoa and returned to the coast empty (thus limiting aggregate hauling capacity). Another rule made it illegal to transport cocoa on roads which ran alongside coastal railway lines, even though road transport was more cost-effective for short-haul coastal runs. Finally, despite the ostensible

[50] Gould (1960: 77).

[51] Kay (1972: 396) and IBRD (1970: 40).

[52] Bates (1983: 67–69).

[53] Mikell (1989: 97).

subsidization of transport, in fact cocoa paid a railway rate that was "comparatively high" to other commodities, according to the World Bank. Overall, government policy raised transportation costs for cocoa producers.[54]

The British were aware of the problems in the transportation sector. In 1952, the colonial government reported that railway facilities were insufficient to meet the demands of cocoa producers, particularly in areas of expanding production, such as Western Asante. Existing roads could not make up for the shortfall, either.[55] But the government allocated just £8 million for new road construction in the 1951 Development Plan, even though this level of funding "was totally inadequate for the basic minimum requirements" of a decent road network.[56] CPP leaders did not redesign policy to help cocoa producers once they gained control of the Cocoa Marketing Board. Instead, they brought lorry operators under the purview of the United Ghana Farmers' Council (UGFC), a government-run organization that oversaw cocoa buying for the CMB. The government also imposed new licensing regulations on lorry operators, and officials at buying stations levied various unauthorized fees on them. Sometimes UGFC officials became directly involved in transportation by surreptitiously using Council funds to purchase their own lorries and then crowd out established private haulers. In short, the CPP used transportation policy to injure the Asante-affiliated lorry operators and replace them with "a new class of bureaucratic middlemen."[57]

Funding allocations for the transport sector further underscores the CPP's distributional agenda. Party leaders awarded road-building contracts to myriad contractors—many of whom did not possess the equipment needed to build roads—instead of employing few contractors capable of achieving economies of scale.[58] The CPP saw road contracts as patronage. Roads were poorly built, barely maintained, and progressively ignored in the 1960s.[59] By decade's end, there had been a "severe deterioration" of the roadway system; it was "in serious disrepair." Although the amount of roadway managed by the Public Works Department had grown, more than one-third of roadway mileage needed "complete restoration."[60] Transportation

[54] Bates (1983: 66–69); Beckman (1976: 47–48); Gould (1960: 78); and IBRD (1957: 44–45). Despite the regulations, Beckman (1976: 129) notes that much cocoa continued to move to the port by road.

[55] See Kay (1972: 83–84).

[56] Gould (1960: 80–84). Plans were also made for a new railway spur to link Kumasi with Sunyani in Western Asante, though by 1960 construction on this line had not begun.

[57] Beckman (1976: quote from 109, 129–130).

[58] IBRD (1970: 5).

[59] Killick (1978: 189, 209 n. 15). Railway maintenance did not keep pace with usage, either (IBRD 1970: 12).

[60] IBRD (1970: 1–3).

policy was not attuned to assisting cocoa producers but was rather part of the CPP's side-payment strategy.

FUNDED BY COCOA EXPORTS, CREDIT FUNNELED TO CPP ALLIES VIA IMPORT SUBSTITUTION INDUSTRIALIZATION

Cocoa producers were similarly foiled in their quest for greater credit accessibility. Without credit, cocoa farmers could not hire wage laborers to clear and establish new farms, so they instead used collaborative arrangements with laborers who were entitled to sell a portion of the land they cleared.[61] Farmers also wanted credit for insecticide spraying equipment to combat a capsid infestation and for fertilizer to improve the productivity of their cocoa trees.[62] When farmers needed liquid capital, they would "pledge" their land to an area chief, in a traditional form of mortgage lending. Chiefs, in turn, used debt to sustain their power vis-à-vis peasants.[63] Consequently, "long-term indebtedness (was) the problem that (was) uppermost in farmers' minds."[64]

Concerns over indebtedness increased with the cocoa boom, as farmers sought to expand production. At the same time, they were frustrated by a compulsory policy to "cut out" cocoa trees infected with the swollen shoot virus. Farmers objected to the practice because untrained former military servicemen were responsible for cutting out infected trees and did so indiscriminately. In addition, infected trees could still produce fruit for a couple years, while new trees required seven to ten years for maturation. "Cutting out" cost cash-starved cocoa farmers revenue in the short-term, and farmers considered their compensation for replanting to be inadequate. Most important, without good trees as collateral, pledging one's farm became difficult. Indebtedness and credit sector reform were key issues which spurred peasants' involvement in the 1948 Accra riots.[65]

Early on, Nkrumah seemed to make good on his promise in the CPP's 1951 election manifesto to address peasants' indebtedness. First, he suspended compulsory cutting out in April 1951 (though he re-implemented the policy in October 1952). Second, Nkrumah directed the new Cocoa Purchasing Company (CPC) to make loans to indebted farmers. By 1955, the CPC had made approximately 15,000 loans of up to £1,500 (nearly three times an average farmer's income). Yet these loans were mostly "one-off" and simply used

[61] Hill (1956: 40–47).
[62] IBRD (1957: 26–27).
[63] Boone (2003: 152–153) and Mikell (1989: 95–97).
[64] Hill (1956: 72 n. 1).
[65] Austin (1964: 59–66); Danquah (2003); Hill (1956: 75); and Owusu (1970: 256 n. 30).

to undercut the creditor power of the Asante chiefs. These loans, although noteworthy, would have directly reached less than 10 percent of the estimated 200,000 Ghanaians employed by cocoa, so they were not a thoroughgoing remedy. In fact, lending was used for electoral mobilization, particularly leading up to the 1956 election, when the CPP faced a burgeoning challenge from the Asante-based National Liberation Movement (NLM). (I discuss the NLM in the section on institutional change below.) The CPP discontinued the loan program after winning the election; it also reduced compensatory payments for cutting out in 1957 and later eliminated them.[66] Things got worse after 1960, which the World Bank characterized as "a period of deliberate neglect" toward cocoa.[67]

Rather than assisting cocoa producers, Ghana's political elites funneled expenditures to state-owned agricultural plantations and industrial enterprises, which the World Bank noted at the time would effectively starve the cocoa sector of funds.[68] State-owned agricultural plantations failed. The government began supporting the State Farms Corporation to mechanize and diversify agriculture in the east near Lake Volta in 1963. By 1965, only 10 percent of the land allocated for state farms had been planted, and functioning farms had low yields and only about one-fifth of the labor productivity of the typical Ghanaian peasant farm. Meanwhile, private farmers who wanted to engage in commercial agriculture had trouble obtaining the appropriate permits, and the government frequently retook their lands after permission had been granted. Many of these agricultural entrepreneurs marketed or transported cocoa, rendering them doubly aggrieved by agricultural policy. State farms were a dismal failure and accounted for the vast majority of the overall losses realized by state-owned enterprises in the mid-1960s. Poor performance resulted from farm "managers [who] were often political appointees knowing little of agriculture."[69]

State farms were part of an import substitution industrialization (ISI) strategy pursued by Nkrumah and the CPP. The push began with the Second Development Plan in 1959 and was financed by cocoa. The CMB transferred an astonishing £127.8 million to the government during the plan's existence. An estimated £25 million of this funding came from a euphemistically termed "voluntary contribution" by cocoa farmers—in actuality, a compulsory 17

[66] Austin (1964: 159–173); Beckman (1976: 62–63); Boone (2003: 161–168); and Owusu (1970: 255–261). Beckman notes that loan records, when kept, were usually fabricated after the fact. Thus, the loan program did not promote bureaucratization or render cocoa farmers more "legible" to state agents or party apparatchiks (see Slater 2008).

[67] IBRD (1969: quote from 6) and Killick (1978: 119).

[68] IBRD (1957: 52).

[69] Killick (1978: 192–194, 219, quote from 194) and Mikell (1989: 184).

percent reduction in the marketing board's purchase price.[70] The development plan foundered. Many initiatives "had a weak economic rationale. Some appear to have had no economic rationale at all."[71] The associated government contracts usually included a 5 to 10 percent kickback, to be shared by the pertinent government minister and the CPP.[72] In addition, Ghana's Industrial Development Corporation "suffered greatly from outside interference, in the shape of members of Parliament and other influential persons expecting staff appointments to be made irrespective of merit, redundant staff be kept on the pay-roll . . . businesses to be purchased at inflated prices, loans to be made irrespective of security" and so on.[73]

The ongoing lack of attention to cocoa producers' public goods preferences became disastrous when global prices fell in 1964. Prices paid by the CMB declined from 50 to 40 shillings per load the following year. In real terms, producers were receiving less than 6 shillings per load—the lowest price paid in twenty years.[74] Because the government had never seriously addressed high transportation costs, cocoa cultivation became unprofitable for many peasants. Migrant laborers from the north left for Ivory Coast and its brighter economic prospects.[75] Absentee owners of moderately sized farms returned to find them "deserted and turned into bush."[76] Cocoa production plummeted 28 percent in one year: from 568,032 tons in 1964–65 to 409,172 tons the next year.[77] Had the government addressed transportation costs earlier, or offered a higher marketing board price (the board continued to offer below-market prices in the 1960s), cocoa may have better weathered the storm. But it entered a period of crisis.[78] There was a "collapse" of public income derived from cocoa, which precipitated Nkrumah's overthrow in 1966.[79] Meanwhile, Nkrumah's state-owned enterprises were "scattered all over the place" and had created "an administrative jungle," over which there was little coherent bureaucratized control.[80] The lack of new public goods forestalled a route to new state capacity.

[70] Beckman (1976: 202, 280). On cocoa farmers' opposition to the "contribution," see Beckman (1976: 202–205). Cocoa funds more than covered the £82 million spent on state-owned enterprises up to 1966 (Rimmer 1992: 91).

[71] Rimmer (1992: 90).

[72] Killick (1978: 242–243).

[73] Ibid., 245, quoting a report by W. Arthur Lewis.

[74] IBRD (1969: table 5).

[75] Mikell (1989: 187).

[76] Beckman (1976: 219).

[77] IBRD (1969: table 2).

[78] Mikell (1989: 193–231).

[79] Beckman (1976: 218–222).

[80] Berg (1971: 211), quoted in Rimmer (1992: 91).

The Persistence of Mediated Institutions in Postwar Ghana

When Nkrumah and the CPP gained power in 1951, they were intent on curtailing the political power of Asante chiefs and subsequently modified local institutions to do so. Catherine Boone, for instance, considers Nkrumah's strategy to be one of "usurpation," whereby the state deployed its agents to rule at the village level, a characterization redolent of unmediated institutions. My analysis differs. Although the formal design of Ghanaian institutions changed after 1951, the Nkrumah government did not create unmediated institutions, even though it impaired the chiefs. I maintain that institutional weakness persisted because Ghana's ruling coalition was not diametrically threatened by rising exporters. Nkrumah and the CPP used non-institutional methods to frustrate their opponents, such as occasionally raising the cocoa price paid through the CMB or co-opting some opposition leaders, rather than moving toward mediated institutions.

THE CPP UNDERMINES CHIEFTAIN POWER

Nkrumah's most noteworthy initiative against the chiefs was the elimination of the Native Authorities (NA) structure, the backbone of indirect rule. The CPP replaced NA administration with new "Local Councils" through the Local Government Ordinance of 1951. The new councils were two-thirds "elected members" (typically CPP party men) and one-third traditional members. The ordinance also gave government officials control over communal "stool" lands. Revenue derived from stool lands, a cornerstone of chieftain power, was now sent to the Local Council. The CPP began threatening "destoolment" of chiefs who opposed the party.[81] In 1958, the CPP eliminated traditional members from Local Councils,[82] and in 1962, Nkrumah's party passed legislation that granted the state the right to acquire stool lands without compensatory payments to destooled chiefs.[83]

The CPP also impinged on chiefs' roles as judges and tax collectors. The Native Court system was substantial, as 300 courts nationwide had dealt with 83,000 cases in 1950–51. The CPP wanted to complement the new Local Councils with a set of "Local Courts." The Korsah Commission of 1951 envisioned a major overhaul of the country's judicial system, though a radical change in the judiciary did not occur, even with the Local Courts Act of

[81] Apter (1963: 195, 241–251); Boone (2003: 164–169); and Firmin-Sellers (1996: 138–143).

[82] Boone (2003: 166) and Rathbone (2000: 65–66, 85).

[83] Berry (2001: 80).

1958. Instead, the CPP placed its members into existing judicial positions, or expanded the size of judicial panels, in order to marginalize chiefs.[84] And, as noted, taxes and tributary payments based on land use became the purview of the Local Councils and were no longer considered chiefly stool revenues.[85] The CPP was assaulting the cornerstones of chieftain power.

The final institutional changes intended to weaken the Asante chiefs were the creation of the CPC in 1951 and the UGFC in 1953.[86] The creation of these organizations followed a rift between Nkrumah and Ashie Nikoi, who was charged with cultivating rural CPP support through the Ghana Farmers' Congress but later defected from the CPP.[87] The CPC bypassed the Ghana Farmers' Congress and "was staffed and managed by CPP businessmen and clerks, recruited from the primarily urban cadres of the party."[88] The CPC cultivated support by extending loans to indebted cocoa producers, as discussed above. By swaying peasants' selling preferences toward the CPC, Nkrumah's party challenged the existing commercial links controlled by Asante chiefs and merchant firms like the United Africa Company.[89] The CPC was essentially a CPP outpost in rural areas.

The UGFC functioned as an adjunct to the CPC and ostensibly acted as the advocacy organization for cocoa farmers. Its true aims were to displace cooperative societies, sideline cocoa buyers other than the CPC, and heighten the CPP's political influence.[90] The UGFC established buying centers throughout cocoa-producing areas, which created the opportunity for CPP officials to contact the rural masses, at least in Asante and surrounding cocoa areas.[91] At independence, the UGFC became the only officially recognized farmers group in Ghana. Catherine Boone judges that the organization was a "sprawling bureaucratic apparatus" with "a commanding presence in every village in the cocoa belt."[92] The UGFC, CPC, and Local Councils collectively amounted to a major assault by the CPP on the prevailing power structure in cocoa areas.

[84] Rathbone (2000: 48–58).

[85] Rathbone (2000: 31–32, 43–46).

[86] The CPC was liquidated amid scandal in 1957 but later reappeared as the Ghana Farmers' Marketing Association, a subsidiary of the UGFC. The UGFC became the United Ghana Farmers' Council Cooperatives (UGFCC) in 1961. For ease of reading, I simply refer to them as the CPC and UGFC.

[87] Beckman (1976: 53, 193).

[88] Ibid., 234.

[89] Beckman (1976: 58–59) and Boone (2003: 167).

[90] Beckman (1976: 60–63); Boone (2003: 168–169); and Mikell (1989: 176–179).

[91] Beckman (1976: 231–236).

[92] Boone (2003: 168–170).

OPPOSITION TO THE CPP'S INITIATIVES

The CPP's actions naturally engendered opposition. The marketing board, now under CPP control, continued to frustrate cocoa producers. In 1954, the government proposed freezing cocoa prices at 72 shillings per load, roughly 40 percent of world prices. In response, a group of Asante chiefs and disaffected former CPP members formed the NLM, whose slogan was "Vote for Cocoa."[93] The *Asantehene*'s treasury, as well as European merchant firms, funded the NLM. Among their first initiatives was to funnel loans to cocoa farmers to dampen the burgeoning influence of the CPC.[94] The NLM proposed a federal structure for Ghana, which would have given cocoa interests greater control of marketing board pricing and accumulated reserves.[95] Early on, the NLM looked promising due to some high-profile CPP defections. The group also "maintained a steady stream of violent political protests," while its paramilitary wing "organized street riots, beat CPP sympathizers, and bombed CPP leaders' homes and offices."[96] The UGFC disintegrated, and CPP apparatchiks fled Asante as the party "began to fall apart."[97] Meanwhile, the NLM cultivated a nationwide movement by forging alliances with opposition groups in the north, southern coastal areas, and east (Togoland).[98] Cocoa interests were mounting a formidable challenge to the CPP.

Yet despite a violent and growing opposition, Nkrumah ignored the NLM for months, and "the CPP was strangely slow in taking anything like the proper measure of the NLM."[99] I maintain that one reason for this indifference was that the NLM did not fundamentally threaten Nkrumah's basic interests, which, as an intellectual and nationalist politician, were not grounded in cocoa. Of course, the CPP's side-payment strategy hinged on cocoa receipts, but cocoa farmers had little choice but to sell to the government, as I discuss below. Rather than strengthen institutions, the CPP employed various non-institutional measures to frustrate the NLM in the lead-up to an important election in 1956.

[93] See Allman (1993: 26–28); Austin (1964: 253–265); and Boone (2003: 161–162).

[94] Boone (2003: 161, 168 n. 54).

[95] Beckman (1976: 196) and Mikell (1989: 179).

[96] Austin (1964: 267–268); Beckman (1976: 67, 196); and Firmin-Sellers (1996: 127, 130, quote from 127). The NLM was also succeeding electorally, as it won a majority on the Kumasi municipal council in 1955 and a special election in the rural Asante constituency in mid-1955 (Austin 1964: 274–276; Rathbone 2000: 84).

[97] Austin (1964: 258).

[98] Beckman (1976: 196) and Boone (2003: 162).

[99] Austin (1964: 282).

First, the government raised the cocoa purchasing price from 72 to 80 shillings per load in 1955–56, which dampened enthusiasm for the NLM.[100] Second, the CPP assailed the NLM's hodgepodge alliances. For example, it promised the cocoa-producing Brong states, historically dominated by their Asante neighbors, a separate administrative unit in return for their support. The Brong sided with Nkrumah, diluted NLM support in the 1956 election, and were rewarded with their own regional state in 1959.[101] The CPP likewise supported dissident chiefs in cocoa zones to undermine the chiefly hierarchy. Third, and perhaps most important, the NLM had difficulty garnering durable support outside of Asante. CPP alliances proved resilient in northern and coastal areas, in part because the NLM's fiscal aim was to redistribute cocoa wealth back into Asante.[102] The NLM did not dissipate but captured just twelve of 104 legislative seats in the nationwide 1956 election. This poor showing was a consequence of the NLM's limited appeal, not institutional subjugation. In fact, the CPP received just 36 percent of the vote in Asante, indicating the limited influence of the government's party in opposition areas.[103] Overall, however, the Asante threat was not diametrical and exigent, but rather circumscribed and permeable.

ASSESSING INSTITUTIONAL CHANGE IN POSTWAR GHANA

A close inspection reveals the limited efficaciousness of Nkrumah's institutional modifications. In the first years after the 1951 Local Government Ordinance, there was a "widespread breakdown in the local administration in many areas" due to conflict between chiefs and CPP officials.[104] Local Councils were also fairly ephemeral. Between 1959 and 1960, the government reduced the number of Local Councils from 252 to sixty-nine, but the "new amalgamated councils suffered from a 'loss of contact' with the people." The government reversed course two years later, increasing the number of councils to 155. These new councils were mostly patronage outlets and commonly "did little more than pay some staff salaries."[105] In short, the state exerted

[100] Beckman (1976: 197). The price hike marked an increase from 38 to 65 percent of world prices (Beckman 1976: 282), or a 10 percent increase in real terms (IBRD 1969: table 5).

[101] Mikell (1989: 159–165, 180).

[102] Boone (2003: 162–166).

[103] Austin (1964: 316–362).

[104] Rathbone (2000: 46–47, 68, quote from 81) and Austin (1964: 158).

[105] Schiffer (1970: 72–73). Ayee (1994: 56–57) suggests that the fragmentation of Local Councils in the mid-1960s resulted from increasing political strains on the CPP, which viewed new Local Councils as means to co-opt traditional elites and defuse political opposition.

tenuous influence over local affairs, despite the country's ostensible institutional centralization.[106]

The palpability of Local Councils declined further in the 1960s. The enervation of Local Councils was evinced in the Brong-Ahafo region, where cocoa production flourished. By the 1960s, its Local Councils were becoming increasingly dysfunctional, and the local Town Development Committees were much more palpable. There were over 600 community development officers spread throughout Ghana's "wards," administrative conglomerations of about ten villages, as of the mid-1960s. However, unlike the Local Councils, development committees were largely grassroots organizations and had "a marked lack of formal control" from Accra. In the Ahafo region, Town Development Committees "acquired considerably greater significance to the Ahafo citizens than the Local Councils."[107]

Moreover, although the new Local Courts implanted government appointees over questions of customary law, traditional chiefs remained the de facto judicial system in some areas.[108] Indeed, despite the legal infringements on chiefly prerogatives, Sara Berry concludes that "if anything, chiefs in Asante have extended their authority over land" since independence.[109] And Local Councils had trouble collecting taxes and remained financially dependent on the Cocoa Marketing Board. By the mid-1950s, "a large number of local councils were close to bankruptcy."[110] In 1954–55, for example, the state collected £181,391 in "stool land" revenue—a mere 0.28 percent of overall taxation. The taxpayer rolls used by Local Councils "were old and inaccurate . . . [and] *many councils had no idea of the total number of those who should have paid rates.*"[111] When government officials tried to energetically collect taxes, peasants would often riot and occasionally kill them.[112] The financial health of Local Councils continued to deteriorate, despite "vigorous 'Pay-Your-Rates' campaigns." By the time of Nkrumah's overthrow in 1966, Local Councils were insolvent.[113]

Feebleness characterized the institutions associated with export marketing, too, even though they spread throughout the cocoa belt. Statutory marketing in cocoa areas served two ends. First, the marketing board was the lifeblood of the CPP's side-payments. Second, the marketing board interfered

[106] Ayee (1994: 63–64) and Wunsch (1990: 62–64).

[107] Dunn and Robertson (1973: 305–306) and Schiffer (1970: 72).

[108] Rathbone (2000: 89–92).

[109] Berry (2001: 80).

[110] Rathbone (2000: 80–81).

[111] Rathbone (2000: 134 n. 40, emphasis added). The individual taxes collected by Local Councils were known as "rates." Calculation of relative taxation based on Kay (1972: 349).

[112] Austin (1964: 158, 158 n. 11).

[113] Dunn and Robertson (1973: 294–295).

with Asante chiefs' interests in cocoa marketing. The CPP did not need unmediated institutions to achieve these objectives. Bjorn Beckman, in the most detailed assessment of the CPP's rural efforts, concludes that the party had a "weak rural political organisation" and that the "broad mass of agricultural producers were only marginally touched by (the UGFC's) mobilising activities." The CPP featured an "absence of any effective channels for supervision" within its hierarchy, particularly when it came to overseeing farmers.[114] Joseph Ayee likewise concludes that local governments proved "incapable of bringing together the areas and people under their administration" and were an ineffective "means of linking local areas with the CPP regime directly."[115] Ghana's institutions were neither unmediated nor stout.

Yet the CPC and UGFC did not need to establish robust links with the rural peasantry to achieve their aims. Cocoa production in Ghana was almost entirely oriented to external trade (aside from some cocoa that was processed domestically as part of Nkrumah's ISI scheme). Cocoa was a captured market, so local marketing agencies could be at once effective in monopolizing trade but ineffective in exerting influence over rural inhabitants. Consider the options facing the Ghanaian cocoa farmer. Farmers could, theoretically, smuggle their crop into Togo or Ivory Coast, which paid higher prices. And some farmers did. But smuggling cocoa is not as easy as smuggling, say, diamonds. Cocoa is a low value-added bulk crop, making transportation costs a consequential determinant of profit or loss. Cost considerations, combined with police checkpoints in borderlands, dissuaded smuggling.[116] The World Bank estimated that just 5,000 to 10,000 tons—about 1–2 percent of cocoa production—were smuggled annually in the 1960s, when marketing board prices were at their nadir.[117] The state's exclusive purchasing arrangement obviated the need to build strong institutions in cocoa areas.

By contrast, Nkrumah's other efforts to implement monopsony purchasing arrangements failed miserably. When Nkrumah established the Food Marketing Board, ostensibly to help farmers expand food production, he expected it would function like the Cocoa Marketing Board and gave the UGFC oversight of it. But the marketing arrangement led to a decline in food production, and the UGFC succeeded mostly in antagonizing farmers. The Food Marketing Corporation operated at a loss.[118] For unlike the marketing of exports, which are usually cultivated in specialized areas and ultimately move through ports, food production is spatially diffuse, and farmers have ample

[114] Beckman (1976: 241, 159).

[115] Ayee (1994: 58).

[116] Dunn and Robertson (1973: 41–42).

[117] IBRD (1969: 43).

[118] Killick (1978: 186–192, 219).

opportunities to avoid marketing boards.[119] Nkrumah's failure to regulate the domestic food market suggests that his success with the CMB was due to the fact that cocoa was an exported commodity, rather than due to the prowess of state agencies.

And the CPP's supposedly robust institutional presence in Asante is difficult to reconcile with its extremely poor electoral showing there in 1956. The importance of the election "could hardly be exaggerated" due to the NLM, yet the CPP captured just 36 percent of the vote in the Asante heartland.[120] This tepid support was not for lack of effort on Nkrumah's part. The UGFC "ordered its members to vote CPP. Council officials at all levels were engaged in campaign work."[121] The CPP's loss in Asante indicated the inability of new institutions to constrain NLM partisans. By contrast, the unmediated institutions built a century earlier in Chile regularly delivered electoral victories for the ruling coalition in opposition strongholds. Electoral mobilization was similarly ineffective to challenge power holders in Argentina. Ghanaian institutions could not match such effectiveness because they were qualitatively different than those in Chile and Argentina.

Finally, it is worth remembering that, even if the state had established robust, unmediated institutions in cocoa areas, they would have incorporated only about one-third of Ghana's agricultural workforce.[122] In contrast to efforts in the cocoa belt, the CPP did little to alter the prevailing institutional arrangements in northern Ghana. The traditional hierarchies utilized for indirect colonial rule persisted and, in some areas, the "transformation of Native Authority into Local Council happened without much upset or discernible change."[123] In sum, the CPP accomplished some impressive political feats in the 1950s and 1960s. The party injured Asante chiefs and consolidated the state's grip over cocoa wealth. Ultimately, however, these developments did not entail the creation of unmediated institutions.

Ghana in 1966: Illusory State Building and Low State Capacity

Decolonization and the early independence era were heady times in Ghana, but they did not lead to a remarkable growth in state capacity. It is tempting

[119] Bates (1981: 39–40).
[120] Austin (1964: 316–362, quote from 316).
[121] Beckman (1976: 68).
[122] Ibid., 242.
[123] Boone (2003: 175).

to attribute Ghana's underwhelming state building to colonial legacies.[124] Yet although the British did little to build a robust Ghanaian state, the CPP was at the helm of policymaking from 1951 until independence in 1957 and helped craft the country's institutional inheritance. Like colonial legacies, ethnic diversity is often cited to account for Africa's state building woes. And Ghana scores very high on measures of ethnic fractionalization and features politically salient ethnic boundaries.[125] But cocoa producers and CPP members mainly hailed from Akan ethnic groups, and some of Nkrumah's staunchest allies were in the northern savannah region, where non-Akan groups predominate. Ethnic difference did not animate politics.

Bellicist pressures were likewise inconsequential to the period's politics, even though Ghana developed three external rivalries in the early 1960s, which arguably should have spurred deeper revenue extraction as leaders prepared for war.[126] Indeed, Ghana featured steadily rising "tax ratios" (tax revenue ÷ GDP) between 1961 and 1966 (from 0.128 to 0.158).[127] This change did not reflect deeper revenue extraction, however, but rather growing cocoa production, as trees planted during the early boom years reached productive maturity.[128] The government continued to rely on export taxes and import duties for about half of its revenue, plus revenue from the Cocoa Marketing Board and "voluntary" contributions paid by cocoa farmers.[129] The country's structure of tax revenue suggested its low levels of state capacity. Ghana's fiscal policies thoroughly confound the expectations in the resource curse literature for agricultural exporters.

On only one indicator—territorial pacification—did Ghana register a noteworthy increase in state capacity. I consider Ghana to have achieved territorial pacification following the defeat of the NLM in 1956. Since then, the country has not succumbed to the widespread regional or secessionist violence that characterizes an "unpacified" country, even though Ghana has experienced low-level ethnic strife and military coups, some of which had regionalist dimensions.[130] My other measurement proxies do not record growth in state capacity. The country's logistical infrastructure did not substantially improve. In 1970, the World Bank inventoried Ghana's 2,747 miles of tarred

[124] E.g., Lange (2003: 173–174).

[125] Fearon (2003: 218) and Lieberman (2009: 291), respectively.

[126] Thies (2007).

[127] From the replication data set for Thies (2010), available at http://www.prio.no/Data/. Thies (2010) operationalizes the tax ratio as total revenue minus non-tax revenue and social security contributions ÷ GDP.

[128] Rimmer (1992: 76–79).

[129] IBRD (1967: 89).

[130] Boone (2003: 170–172) and Mikell (1989: 241–247).

and graveled roads and found just 20 percent in good working order; nearly twice that amount—37 percent—needed restoration above and beyond normal maintenance.[131] The state provided few public goods.

State institutions remained mediated as well, despite Nkrumah's flurry of institutional changes. While it is true that the CPP inserted its apparatchiks as regional commissioners, the idea "that the local authorities (were) in fact agents of the central government . . . (was) only partly true."[132] Before Ghana became a one-party state in the 1960s, the CPP did not politically control many localities and could not compel Local Councils in those areas to implement its dictates.[133] Nkrumah's envisioned judicial transformation was arrested as well,[134] and local governance was effectively decentralized as of 1966.[135] By then, the central government had been moving away from giving localities "percentage grants," which gave it spending oversight, and toward "block grants" that were not attached to specific projects and therefore "spent more at the discretion of the local councils."[136] In Accra, administration became increasingly personalistic, haphazard, and inept throughout the 1960s.[137] Senior civil servant posts often went unfilled, as qualified administrators feared Nkrumah's personalistic and unpredictable management style.[138] In sum, Ghana's state building in the two decades after 1945 was largely illusory.

131 IBRD (1970: 40).
132 Wraith (1964: quote from 61, 106). See also Owusu (1970: 286).
133 Wraith (1964: 29–30, 60–65).
134 E.g., Rathbone (2000: 48–58, 124–125).
135 Olowu (1990: 83).
136 Wraith (1964: 98, 108–113, quote from 112). See also Schiffer (1970: 73).
137 Ryan (1970: 154–155).
138 Killick (1978: 337–338).

CHAPTER 8

Exporters' Marginalization and the Persistence of Nigeria's Weak State, 1945–1966

Today, ethnic and religious conflict plagues Nigeria. Anti-government guerrillas run amok in the oil-rich Niger Delta region, and the country's bureaucracy is notoriously corrupt and ineffectual. Observers commonly attribute these pathologies to the country's oil wealth. But Nigeria's state weakness pre-dates its emergence as a substantial oil producer in the 1970s. A generation before the rise of oil, the country's first major commodity boom in cocoa, groundnuts, and palm oil created state building opportunities, which were wasted. Export producers sought better transportation infrastructure and easier credit access to promote their economic goals. However, a ruling coalition of political elites elected not to provide new public goods. Exporters were aggrieved but did not constitute an exigent, diametrical threat, so the ruling coalition was content to govern through mediated institutions. In fact, a ruling group of nationalist politicians, similar to the CPP in Ghana, pressed British colonial administrators to devolve power to regional governments. The British did so in 1954 as a means to stave off independence and thus sapped the central state of what little capacity then existed. The ruling coalition during Nigeria's first major commodity boom inaugurated a wanting state building trajectory.

My analysis of Nigerian state building challenges two leading interpretations of this period of Nigerian politics. First, I do not attribute state weakness to ethnic enmity. Although ethnicity is a key basis of political mobilization in contemporary Nigeria, the salience of ethnicity was itself magnified by the decentralization of power in 1954. Regional political parties came to define themselves in ethnic terms, which stoked inter-ethnic conflict at the national level. But what is particularly perplexing for ethnic-based theories of state building is that, during this time, political party leaders in Nigeria's three main regions refused to provide public goods to area export producers, who were their ethnic brethren. I instead emphasize how public goods requests asked political elites to, in effect, direct resources to coalitional outsiders.

A second leading explanation emphasizes the frail institutions Nigeria inherited at independence in 1960 to account for its lasting state weakness.[1] While I do not dispute the deficiency of these institutions, the country's coalitional politics during decolonization sheds light on why British administrators and nationalist politicians progressively enfeebled them between 1945 and 1960. The British regarded institutional devolution as a stopgap strategy to placate nationalist politicians. Nationalists, for their part, believed that a decentralization of power would enable them to more thoroughly fleece exports in their respective regions and thereby build patronage networks. Nigeria's institutional debility and low state capacity more generally stemmed from coalitional politics.

Nigeria at Mid-Century

Around 1945, most Nigerians were subsistence farmers but, increasingly, cultivated export crops on communal land plots, the rights to which village chiefs controlled. Export-oriented agriculture was segmented by product and region: cocoa was produced in western Yoruba lands, palm products in the Igbo east, and groundnuts in the Hausa-Fulani north. Nigeria's exports were roughly balanced between these three regional economies: cocoa accounted for 16 percent of export receipts, palm products, 26 percent, and groundnuts, 24 percent. The volume of external trade would rise sharply after 1945 as Nigeria experienced its first major commodity boom.[2]

Up until 1945, the British governed colonial Nigeria based on political alliances with indigenous tribal chiefs and British merchant firms. Tribal chiefs were the principal means of administration in Nigeria.[3] Some areas featured relatively well-developed chieftain hierarchies at the outset of colonial rule, as in the Hausa-Fulani north and Yoruban southwest. In other areas, such as southeastern Nigeria, where chiefly hierarchies did not exist, the British foisted a new class of "chiefs" to serve as their local agents. Overall, chieftain figures throughout Nigeria gained income-generating opportunities as colonial tax collectors, which some chiefs parlayed into bureaucratic posts for themselves and their kin.[4]

[1] E.g., Kohli (2004).

[2] Helleiner (1966: 1–23, 530–531) and Kohli (2004: 291–332).

[3] Herbst (2000: 58–89). See also Gerring et al. (2011).

[4] Tignor (1971); Vaughan (2000); and Watts (1983).

British merchants were the other coalition member in colonial Nigeria. Three merchant firms (the United African Trade Company, the River Niger Company, and the African Eastern Trade Corporation) controlled the West African export trade, were organized through the Association of West African Merchants, and enjoyed statutory representation on the colonial Legislative Council.[5] Merchants colluded to fix prices paid to peasant producers and local middlemen and were also the main source of rural credit, which they used to indebt middlemen.[6] As a sign of their political influence, when merchants faced new competition in the cocoa trade in the late 1930s, they compelled the British to implement statutory export marketing (a.k.a. marketing boards). New rules thwarted upstart competitors by allocating a firm's share of the regional commodity trade based on 1939 levels.[7] The episode underscored merchants' power.

Nigeria's export-producing peasants stood outside this ruling coalition and remained politically marginalized throughout the case study period. In the southwest, Yoruban peasants engaged in small-scale cocoa farming, while, in the southeast, Igbo peasants harvested the fruit of wild and semi-wild palm trees for the export market. A typical peasant in the Hausa-Fulani north allocated about an acre of land to groundnut production. Like the other export-oriented actors profiled herein, Nigerian peasants sought better transportation infrastructure and easier credit.[8] They also wanted to end statutory export marketing because it chronically paid them below-market prices.[9] These policy preferences would go unfulfilled due to peasants' exclusion from the ruling political coalition.

Following the Second World War, a new political actor—indigenous nationalist elites—developed. Nigeria experienced urbanization during the Second World War, especially in southern Nigerian cities like Ibadan and Lagos, as the number of wage earners rose from 183,000 (1939) to 300,000 (1946). The core of the nationalist movement included educated elites, students, professionals, and the budding working class. Many of the movement's intellectual leaders had studied abroad in London during the war and associated through the West African Students' Union. Nationalist leaders lacked a noteworthy basis of power in the economic realm, much like Kwame Nkrumah and the CPP in Ghana. The leading nationalist organization was the National Council of Nigeria and Cameroons (NCNC), which became Nigeria's first modern political

[5] Olukoju (1995: 26–29).

[6] Bauer (1954: 120–121, 202–204); Mou (1986: 181–189); and Watts (1983: 164–176).

[7] Bauer (1954: 246–259) and Fieldhouse (1994: 229–239).

[8] Olakolu (1979: 19–25).

[9] Tignor (1998: 212–220).

party.[10] Nationalists demanded a "Nigerianization" of the colonial state and the import-export trade and wanted to promote industrialization.[11]

The ascent of urban nationalism in Nigeria triggered coalitional change. During the Second World War, many British administrators were recalled to London, and more Nigerians became part of the colonial bureaucracy.[12] In 1945, the NCNC and affiliated trade unions launched a general strike, which demonstrated to British officials that Nigerian nationalists, "when organized, had great power, that they could divide the white bureaucracy, that they could virtually control strategic centers throughout the country, and that through force or the threat of force they could compel the government to grant concessions."[13] Nationalist elites effectively forced the British to refashion the ruling coalition, at the expense of tribal chiefs and merchants, and became the coalition leader.

The low level of state capacity in colonial Nigeria encouraged coalitional change. Britain dispatched few officials to Nigeria—in 1939, a mere 1,315 colonial officials oversaw 373,000 square miles and 20 million inhabitants.[14] All of my measurement indicators suggest limited state capacity (see table 2.5). Nigeria featured mediated rule through the Native Authority structure. In practice,

> British District Officers (assumed) the role of adviser to chiefs rather than (giving) them direct orders. Thus the British administration usually did not summon chiefs from outlying districts to his office for orders . . . but visited them in their parishes. . . . This temperamental disposition to assume the role of adviser was fortified by the pressure of shortage of funds and staff. . . . Essentially public works and administration at the local level was left in (chiefs') hands . . . even the task of keeping of the peace devolved on native authorities.[15]

Given the reliance on chieftain power to maintain law and order, colonial Nigeria did not qualify as territorially pacified.[16]

The central state exerted limited influence over its chieftain allies. For instance, village chiefs carried out the collection of direct taxes, which

[10] Coleman (1958: 239–267, 291–295) and Sklar (1963: 41–64).

[11] Fieldhouse (1994: 375).

[12] Crowder (1968: 504).

[13] Coleman (1958: 259).

[14] Mamdani (1996: 73). See also Kirk-Greene (1980).

[15] Crowder (1968: 211–213). See also Coleman (1958: 50–54); Mamdani (1996: 52–61); Phillips (1989: 39–43); and Tignor (1993: 177–180).

[16] Cf. Centeno (2002: 108–109).

contributed about 15 percent to the colonial budget, but embezzlement and tax evasion were rampant. (Customs duties typically accounted for about half of government revenue.)[17] Native Authorities ran the judicial system, with little oversight from the British. Of the half million cases before the Native Courts in 1947, British officials reviewed less than 4 percent of decisions. Of those decisions reviewed, less than half were overturned.[18] And, as in Ghana, there was no electoral system that afforded the government an opportunity to extend its power into localities. Before 1946, a restricted franchise (of those earning at least £100 annually) elected four members of the Legislative Council (three seats for Lagos and one for Calabar, in Eastern Nigeria).[19] Perhaps the lone bright spot was Nigeria's logistical infrastructure, particularly 1,900 miles of railway formed mostly by two trunk lines emanating from Lagos and Port Harcourt. But the railroads had few inland connections to rail or road, and during the Second World War, the quality of the railroads deteriorated from personnel and equipment shortages.[20] Overall, little state capacity radiated beyond Lagos as of 1945.

The Revenue Imperative and Nigerian State Building

Theories predicated on the revenue imperative do not seem central to Nigeria's state building experience after 1945. The conventional wisdom on the resource curse, for instance, would expect Nigeria to have had a relatively diversified and capable taxing apparatus, so as to aid the international competitiveness of cocoa, palm fruit, and groundnut exports. Yet Nigerian governments hurt export producers through statutory export marketing, which extracted a sizable percentage of the potential producer income and thereby decreased incentives for export production. During the 1940s, cocoa producers lost 66 percent of their potential income to the marketing board, and producers of palm products and groundnuts respectively lost 30 and 40 percent of their potential incomes. These taxes constituted as much as 30 percent of state revenue in some years. Export duties tacked another 3–4 percent of taxes on producers.[21] Nigeria's taxing strategy confounds the expectations of resource curse theories.

Bellicist theories of Nigerian state building fare no better. Although Nigeria did not fight an inter-state war between 1945 and 1966, it featured external

[17] Ekundare (1973: 106–117).

[18] Calculations based on data in Hailey (1951: 33, 86, 139, 175–176).

[19] Sklar (1963: 28).

[20] Tignor (1998: 199).

[21] Bauer (1954: 292) and Helleiner (1966: 211).

rivalries with Ghana and Ivory Coast,[22] though they did not spur the deepening of extractive capacity. Trade duties, excise taxes, and marketing board revenues remained the core of state income.[23] The military was small (10,500 soldiers), poorly trained, and increasingly a patronage outlet, with officer recruitment determined by an ethnic quota system. Until 1965, British expatriates staffed many of the highest military posts, preserving a degree of political neutrality that quickly dissolved with two military coups in 1966.[24] Nigeria's bellicist pressures yielded no discernible impact on revenue extraction or state building.

The Agricultural Commodity Boom

However, Nigeria had state building opportunities that were connected to the major secular boom in commodity prices beginning around 1945.[25] In fact, even with the marketing board price distortions, Nigerian exporters had incentives to expand their production. The prices paid to cocoa producers rose 125 percent between 1945 and 1948 and, by 1955–56, were seven times higher than in 1945. Cocoa exports grew from 77,004 tons in 1945 to 154,176 tons in 1960 and 255,000 tons by 1965. Their worth increased from £2 million in 1945 to £42 million by 1965. Prices paid to groundnut producers rose by 33 percent from 1945 to 1947 and by three times by 1960–61. Groundnut exports rose from 176,242 tons in 1945 to 512,000 tons by 1965, or from £2.7 million (1945) to £37.8 million (1965). Lastly, in the decade after 1945, prices paid for palm kernels and palm oil rose by three and five times, respectively. Palm product exports grew from 406,787 tons in 1945 to 588,916 tons in 1950. Their value rose from £5.4 million (1945) to £28.8 million (1950) and eventually £40 million (1965).[26] All segments of Nigeria's agricultural export economy were enjoying unprecedented booms.

Nigeria's commodity booms enriched two social actors in particular. First, export-oriented peasants' incomes rose substantially. Between 1945 and 1954, cocoa producers' real income increased fivefold, groundnut producers' income more than quadrupled, and palm oil producers' income grew by sixfold.[27] The postwar commodity booms enriched Nigerian peasants, in spite of the marketing board tax. Second, these booms indirectly bolstered nationalist

[22] Thies (2007: 722) and Kacowicz (1998: 127, 144–145), respectively.
[23] Adedeji (1969: 157–161).
[24] Luckham (1971: 238–246).
[25] See Deaton (1999) and Williamson (2012).
[26] Bonat (1989: 50); Helleiner (1966: 461–471, 501–507, 590–591); and Wells (1974: 62).
[27] Helleiner (1966: 461–471).

politicians, who were enhancing their control of the state. In the late 1940s, Britain broke up the West African Produce Control Board into country- and commodity-specific marketing boards. Nigeria inherited about £25 million for its new cocoa, groundnut, and palm oil marketing boards. By 1954, these commodity boards accumulated about £77 million more, which lubricated nationalists' side-payments to urbanites. The Nigerian government derived about £250 million from these boards, export taxes, and a produce purchase tax between 1947 and 1961.[28] In sum, nationalist politicians' side-payments hinged on fleecing export producers via the country's marketing boards.

Politically Marginalized Exporters Fail to Obtain New Public Goods

PREFERENCES FOR NEW PUBLIC GOODS

Nigeria's commodity booms induced export-oriented peasants to seek three public goods. First, the booms intensified peasants' opposition to the marketing boards, which typically captured one-third to two-thirds of their potential income. Groups such as the Nigerian Farmers Union (NFU) and the Maiyegun Society called for the elimination of statutory export marketing.[29] Second, export-oriented peasants wanted improved transportation infrastructure. Northern groundnut producers had few tarred roads to railroads, their primary means of groundnut transportation. High transport costs disadvantaged them vis-à-vis producers in Niger and Senegal. Booming groundnut production strained the capacity of Nigerian railways[30] and crowded out cocoa from them. Groups like the NFU began to press the government for new tarred roads in Yorubaland, as roads built with communal labor could not sustain motorized traffic and deteriorated quickly.[31] Most villages in the Eastern Region were untouched by anything resembling a modern road, which hindered palm oil exports.[32] There were widespread desires for better roads.

Third, export-oriented peasants sought greater capital accessibility. They wanted to end merchants' control over a "highly usurious credit system" in the countryside.[33] Many peasants were chronically in debt and unable to obtain sufficient credit to enlarge export production. Peasants in northern Nigeria

[28] Ibid., 161–163.
[29] Beer (1976: 41–69) and Tignor (1998: 212–220).
[30] Helleiner (1966: 107–113) and Osayimwese (1971: 7–10).
[31] Beer (1976: 53) and Galletti, Baldwin, and Dina (1972: 26–28, 51).
[32] See Helleiner (1964a: 101) and Usoro (1974: 92).
[33] Ekundare (1973: 218–219) and Watts (1983: quote from 175–176).

sought credit to transition into "mixed farming," purchase fertilizer, and pay taxes. As of 1956, 68 percent of northerners were in debt and paid 80 percent interest on average. Grassroots solutions like cooperative societies helped little, and peasants wanted state assistance.[34] In western Nigeria, peasants needed capital to purchase cattle, plows, and carts for mixed farming. Cocoa producers also needed cash to hire seasonal labor and for insecticide spraying equipment to fight a capsid infestation.[35] Igbo peasants in the east wanted credit to purchase hand presses for palm oil extraction, but the presses cost between £25 and £50, far more than their cash on hand. Solutions such as rotating credit and savings associations had proven ineffective, too, as elsewhere in Nigeria.[36]

THE MARKETING BOARD RETAINED

In addition to their exclusion from the ruling political coalition, Nigerian export producers faced significant barriers to collective mobilization, given that commodity-producing peasants were a large group, physically segmented, and ethnically and linguistically diverse. Collective action, when it occurred, was difficult to sustain. During the 1945 general strike, for example, leaders of the Nigerian Farmers Union found that translating their aims "into terms relevant to the peasant farmer by organizing 'hold-ups' in the marketing of export produce were ineffective due to the immense problems of enforcing any degree of solidarity" among peasants. Still, peasant mobilization did occur and could be effectual. After cocoa producers received just 32 percent of world prices in 1948, the NFU and the Maiyegun Society organized a selling boycott and cajoled the government to pay 98 percent of world prices in 1949.[37]

Moreover, government officials knew that peasants opposed the marketing boards. But statutory export marketing was profitable for Britain, and the debt-ridden British state wanted to continue purchasing commodities at discounted rates.[38] When colonial officials affirmed their commitment to statutory export marketing,[39] peasant groups like the NFU began pushing for the "Nigerianization" of export marketing. Nationalist politicians echoed this demand, and colonial administrators gradually devolved the oversight of export marketing to them, which I discuss in the following section on institutional change. Arthur Richards, the Governor of Nigeria, believed the concession to the nationalists

[34] Watts (1983: 247–249, 324–325).

[35] Galletti, Baldwin, and Dina (1972: 206–215) and Oluwasanmi and Alao (1965: 36–42).

[36] Kilby (1967: 186) and Austin (1993: 102–103).

[37] Beer (1976: 49–53, quote from 53) and Tignor (1998: 218).

[38] Fieldhouse (1994: 251).

[39] Tignor (1998: 213).

was an important sign of good faith. More tangibly, the deal fostered cooperation among the British and nationalists by giving the latter an ability to disburse material side-payments. Over the next twenty years, the marketing boards paid export producers just 54 to 65 percent on average of world prices for their commodities.[40] Nationalists used the accumulated surplus to elaborate a patronage network, particularly through new regional development corporations.

TRANSPORTATION POLICY FRUSTRATES EXPORT PRODUCERS

Export producers in each region were likewise unable to secure a significant improvement in the transportation network. In the north, the Northern Region Development Corporation (NRDC)[41] allocated just 1 percent of its expenditures for transportation infrastructure between 1949 and 1955, despite high world groundnut prices and an overwhelmed railway system.[42] World Bank observers noted "the backlog of 185,000 tons of groundnuts piled up in tarpaulin-covered pyramids at northern [railway] stations in November 1953."[43] This spending pattern "radically reversed" in 1955, as the NRDC began constructing feeder roads.[44] The northern government spent approximately £10 million on road development, especially to purchase heavy mechanical equipment, between 1955 and 1960.[45] But there was not enough qualified staff to use and repair the heavy machinery,[46] and new roads were built without enough input from qualified engineers, especially as expatriates gradually left Nigeria. In 1964, for instance, nearly 50 percent of the Ministry of Works positions were vacant. Newly-built roads drained improperly, had other design shortcomings, and deteriorated quickly. The regional government could not effectively maintain both regional and federal roadways (i.e., the Trunk A and B roads), as stipulated. Costs soared, from £95 per mile in 1958–59 to £223 per mile by 1963–64.[47] There was considerable spending on transportation from the mid-1950s on, but it was of little aid to groundnut producers.

[40] Mou (1986: 214, 233–235) and Tignor (1998: 212–220).

[41] Nigeria's regional development institutions went through many name changes between 1946 and 1966 (see Helleiner 1966: 247). I refer to a single institution throughout the case studies for ease of reading.

[42] Helleiner (1964b: 243).

[43] IBRD (1955: 60).

[44] Helleiner (1964b: 245–250).

[45] Ekundare (1973: 265).

[46] Falola (2004: 149–150).

[47] IBRD (1964).

Where roads were built, peasants quickly moved into export-oriented farming. But too few roads were constructed: as of the late 1950s, only 13 percent of northerners lived within one mile of a road, the proximity needed to viably undertake export-oriented groundnut production.[48] The lack of adequate transport was so pressing that in 1964 the World Bank concluded that in order for groundnut producers "to remain competitive in the world market . . . it is of great importance that the land transport system of Nigeria be improved." Nonetheless, many roads were built with little regard for their potential economic impact, as World Bank consultants concluded in 1963.[49] The northern regional government initially spent too little on transportation infrastructure and, later, allocated funds haphazardly. The experiences of other commodity-producing peasants in Nigeria reveal that transportation spending was intended to distribute largesse, not sensibly reduce transport costs.

The western regional government built roads with Western Region Marketing Board funds to compensate for the north's monopolization of railway transport. By 1965, western Nigeria had nearly 3,000 miles of paved roads, which seems to signal responsiveness to export interests. However, many "paved" roads were one-lane former footpaths, about the width of two people, which had been graveled and sometimes paved later. Only about one-fifth of the 3,000 miles of paved roads (the Trunk A roads) could handle motorized shipping. Roads in western Nigeria were poorly built and received little maintenance; by the mid-1960s, many of them could not be fixed with routine maintenance and required reconstruction. Yet the Ministry of Works of Transport was understaffed and unqualified to fix them. The World Bank concluded in 1965 that, if not rectified, transportation costs could rise 15–20 percent. And the stakes were high: the Bank suspected that Nigerian cocoa could not remain internationally competitive without a reduction of transport costs.[50]

The leaders of the Action Group (AG), western Nigeria's dominant political party, compounded the problem though its allocation of commodity-purchasing rights. Cocoa was transported from the point of sale to the port by Licensed Buying Agents (LBAs), most of whom were small-scale operators who lacked the capital resources to purchase large vehicles capable of achieving economies of scale in produce transport. Rather than try to reduce transport costs, the AG saw LBA licenses as a useful side-payment, and the number of LBAs in western Nigeria rose from 25 in 1948 to 336 by 1966. Moreover, the Western Region Marketing Board paid LBAs above-market rates to transport cocoa, between 6.5 and 8 pence per ton-mile, even though transporters

[48] Hawkins (1958: 16).
[49] IBRD (1964: 13).
[50] IBRD (1965).

incurred around 4 pence in costs per ton-mile. LBAs did not to pass these savings along to peasants.[51] Statutory marketing served the AG's political ends, at the expense of the cocoa sector.

Even so, the regional government claimed to the World Bank in the early 1960s that it lacked sufficient funds to improve the region's transportation infrastructure. In actuality, the Western Region Marketing Board had then accumulated over £62 million in trading surplus.[52] Consequently, peasants tried to remedy their transportation bottlenecks with non-governmental solutions. At times, they built roads with communal labor. Other times, they appealed to municipal or village-level authorities. But the roads built by local authorities or "hometown" associations were of the poorest quality—unpaved, narrow, and dangerous—yet they constituted the vast majority of the region's road network. These roads were usually last-ditch efforts by communities to supply local public goods "because the relevant central ministry or parastatal agency did not first provide the desired service."[53] As of the early 1970s, many parts of the region were "still waiting for the advantages of fast, cheap transport."[54]

The story was much the same in eastern Nigeria. During the postwar commodity boom, the Eastern Region government embarked on an ill-fated scheme—the "Pioneer" oil mills—to transform palm oil production from small-scale peasant operations toward modern factory processing. As I discuss later in the chapter, for the Pioneer oil mills to succeed, the regional government needed to reduce transport costs, because pressed palm oil is about half the weight of unpressed, harvested palm fruit. Therefore, to convince peasants to transport the bulky fruit to the new oil mills, rather than use traditional hand presses near the point of harvest, transportation costs needed to be low (or the price paid at the mill had to be sufficiently high, which it was not).[55] In the late 1940s, the Eastern Region Development Corporation (ERDC) devoted substantial funds to road construction. But, as elsewhere, new roads deteriorated quickly, to the point that motorized lorries could not transport palm oil drums on them.[56] In 1954, the Eastern Regional Production Development Board reported that "bad roads, weak bridges, [and] inadequate ferry facilities" were preventing Pioneer oil mills from operating at full capacity.[57]

Yet when nationalist politicians gained firm control over regional development spending in 1954, they spent little on road construction and

[51] Ogundana (1971: 366–369) and Hay (1970: 175).

[52] Helleiner (1966: 245–250).

[53] Barkan, McNulty, and Ayeni (1991: 469).

[54] Galletti, Baldwin, and Dina (1972: 618).

[55] Kilby (1967: 195).

[56] Falola (2004: 138).

[57] Quoted in Usoro (1974: 92).

maintenance. Whereas the ERDC had disbursed £449,300 on road development between 1949 and 1955, it spent just £79,800 from 1955–57 and nothing from 1958–62.[58] Paradoxically, however, government officials recognized the need for better infrastructure. Official reports characterized the region's transportation infrastructure as insufficient for the needs of the palm industry. Nevertheless, voluntary local labor took the lead in road building after 1955.[59] Overall, Nigeria's regional governments displayed an undeniable pattern: as political elites progressively gained power during decolonization, attention to road building waned in lieu of divisible side-payments, such as purchasing licenses, that could firmly entrench a patronage network.[60]

CREDIT DIVERTED TO POLITICAL ELITES, NOT EXPORTERS

A lack of accessible credit was the other major economic bottleneck facing Nigeria's export producers, who sought credit to relieve debt burdens, hasten the transition into mixed farming, and improve their productivity. The responses by regional governments starkly reveal ruling coalition members' indifference toward commodity producers. Initially, nationalist politicians latched onto the issue of credit accessibility and blamed what they argued were racist colonial officials for peasants' plight.[61] Ultimately, however, nationalists' lip service was a ploy to press for control over marketing board surpluses.[62] When nationalists gained control over the accumulated reserves, they established banking institutions but used the new credit outlets to funnel money to political allies, not peasant commodity producers, who remained credit starved up to 1966.

Political elites ruling through the Northern People's Congress (NPC), the north's dominant political party, allocated groundnut surpluses through the NRDC. When colonial administrators decentralized governance in 1954 (which I discuss in the next section), northern leaders gained control over the NRDC and shifted public spending away from agriculture and toward large-scale manufacturing. NPC officials hid many of these allocations in the "Miscellaneous Projects and Investigations" sections of the budget to obfuscate the redistribution of wealth from groundnut producers to budding industrialists. In fact, the NRDC sent just 1 percent of its expenditures to agriculture, even though the institution was explicitly charged with extending credit to

[58] Helleiner (1964a: 111–113).

[59] Ekundare (1973: 265).

[60] Cf. Bates (2008: 42–52).

[61] Coleman (1958: 85–86).

[62] Bauer (1954: 265–266) notes that marketing boards exacerbated peasants' credit needs, as producers were paid below-market prices while prices for imported goods (e.g., fertilizer, spraying equipment) appreciated.

farmers.[63] There was little formalized bureaucratic control over lending, and the NRDC staff "found it impossible to withstand pressures from high levels." Similar loan proposals received varying interest rates without justification. The Provincial Loans Board Secretary, who was charged with vetting loan applications, was a single part-time employee. Many Native Authorities also played a prime role in determining loan recipients, as northern Nigeria featured the country's most entrenched chiefly hierarchy.[64] Because peasant commodity producers were rarely politically well-connected, they received little relief from the NRDC.

With government policy failing them, local communities began organizing cooperative savings and thrift societies to address credit shortages. Such initiatives faced two daunting obstacles: the limited deposit potential of area inhabitants and a shortage of qualified managerial staff. The Northern Region government stepped in to supplement deposits with marketing board surpluses. But the inadequacy of managerial staff gave Native Authorities an opportunity to take charge of the thrift societies. As appendages of the NPC, they infected lending. By the early 1960s, "the cooperative movement had been completely politicized and, in a sense, made illegitimate. The largest loans ended up in the coffers of the powerful NPC supporters, embezzlement flourished, and outstanding loans were never redeemed." Most cooperative societies had depleted their capital by 1970, having failed to address the peasants' credit demand. As with transportation policy, peasants' political marginalization frustrated their desires to fully participate in the groundnut boom.[65]

Peasants in the Western Region were similarly unable to significantly increase credit accessibility. The first powerful regional bank in colonial Nigeria, the National Bank of Nigeria, emerged in the Western Region and could have conceivably filled peasants' credit void. But the National Bank received a substantial amount of its funds from the Western Region marketing board and became beholden to AG politicians. The National Bank subsidized the party and its media outlets and "virtually constituted itself into a banking asylum for the Action Group."[66] Virtually every loan recipient was associated with the AG, and AG officials nearly destroyed the bank in 1960 with a £675,000 overdraft. The bank behaved according to a political logic, with little regard for the small-scale cocoa producers that indirectly funded it.[67]

[63] Helleiner (1964b: 246–253).

[64] Schatz (1970: 51–55).

[65] Adeyeye (1978) and Watts (1983: quote from 325–326, 339).

[66] As detailed by the Coker Commission, which illuminated these practices (quoted in Mackintosh 1966: 435 n. 1).

[67] Mackintosh (1966: 434–439) and Sklar (1963: 455–456).

The region's development corporation, the Western Region Finance Corporation (WRFC), was also funded by cocoa surpluses and controlled by the AG. To obtain a loan, one had to be a staunch AG supporter, and the WRFC systematically denied loans to communities that elected non-AG politicians. One also had to bribe government officials, though bribes did not guarantee loan approval. Bribes were relatively sizable, usually £10–15 for loans that were almost always less than £40. In fact, the WRFC's politicized lending aided only about 4 percent of the region's farmers. The primary beneficiaries were "councilors . . . members of the Local Loan Boards, Parliamentarians, judges and members of customary courts . . . and civil servants and members of their families."[68] Local Loan Boards, which were subsidiaries of the WRFC, commonly recorded loans to nonexistent or deceased persons.[69] And WRFC officials frequently directed loans to manufacturing and large-scale plantation agriculture.[70] They fleeced the cocoa sector so thoroughly that when world prices fell in 1961, the marketing board could not subsidize producer prices because its reserves were nearly exhausted.[71] Overall, the Western Region government did little to address the credit or transportation bottlenecks facing cocoa producers.[72]

In eastern Nigeria, officials from the NCNC, the region's dominant political party, established the Eastern Regional Development Corporation (ERDC) to serve as the conduit between the marketing board and the party. In 1955, the ERDC began transferring sizable sums into the then-insolvent African Continental Bank, which was owned and controlled by Nnamdi Azikiwe, the head of the NCNC. The bank became the financial arm of the NCNC, making "soft loans" to party members, businessmen, and LBAs. Bureaucrats were forced to resign if they did not extend politically motivated loans. Default rates were high: 57 percent of loans to incipient manufacturers were in default by the 1950s. The NCNC also used the ERDC to create affiliated boards and corporations as patronage outlets. The party deliberately kept these relationships opaque to hide the astounding levels of corruption.[73] As for export-oriented peasants, "no channels of public investment or credit provision were created by which producers could benefit." Simply put, government policy "did not promote [palm export] production increases."[74]

[68] Oluwasanmi and Alao (1965: 38–46).

[69] Schatz (1970: 6–7).

[70] Falola (2004: 114–115).

[71] Mackintosh (1966: 441).

[72] Cooperative societies were unsuccessful, too, as they usually lacked capital at harvest, when peasants wanted to hire wage laborers (Galletti, Baldwin, and Dina 1972: 506, 525–526, 531–533).

[73] Helleiner (1964a: 104); Nnoli (1978: 184–186); Post (1963: 59–60); Schatz (1970: 61–62); and Sklar (1963: 178).

[74] Usoro (1974: 100, 103).

Government policy failed to help export-oriented peasants purchase hand presses for palm oil production. Yet the colonial government had encouraged peasants for years to purchase hand presses because they improved extractive efficiency of palm oil. The presses cost £25–50, beyond what most peasants had at their disposal, so a government loan program helped them purchase hand presses. The program managed to increase the number of presses in use from 1,300 (1945) to 4,481 (1951). Demand was robust, with over 3,500 loan applications submitted in 1950–51. But nationalist politicians terminated the loan program as they gained control over eastern Nigeria's development institutions. The ERDC instead channeled marketing board surpluses into the mechanized Pioneer palm oil mills.[75] These mills epitomized the side-payments extended to budding manufacturers and other urbanite NCNC members.

Not only did Pioneer palm oil mills consume money that could have been used as loans to peasants, but they fundamentally threatened the relationships upon which peasant commodity production rested in the east. Households in eastern Nigeria tended to feature a gendered division of labor: men collected palm fruit, and women extracted the oil. Women actually bought the palm fruit from their husbands, pressed out the palm oil, and sold it for cash. Large-scale mills would eliminate women from this economic chain because the mills offered to buy uncracked nuts directly from male fruit collectors. But, as noted above, the Eastern Region government could not persuade men to use the mills because of high transport costs, given the weight differential between harvested palm fruit and its pressed oil. Many Pioneer mills had shut down by the late 1960s, and those remaining operated at just 40 percent capacity. This colossal failure consumed 71 percent of ERDC agricultural spending during 1955–65, even though mill-processed oil constituted just 5 percent of marketing board purchases.[76] In each region, coalitions led by nationalist political elites repeatedly ignored export-oriented actors' public goods requests and instead preyed upon export wealth. The lack of new public goods contributed to the stagnation of Nigerian state capacity between 1945 and 1966.

Institutional Decentralization to Placate Nationalist Elites

Nigeria did not undergo remarkable institutional strengthening during its postwar commodity booms. Although the booms enriched political outsiders, Nigerian peasants only generated sporadic collective action against power

[75] Falola (2004: 125–128); Kilby (1967: 184); and Usoro (1974: 94, 100).

[76] Falola (2004: 125–128); Hinds (1997: 473–476); Kilby (1967: 191–195); and Usoro (1974: 102–129).

holders and, more important, did not constitute a diametrical threat to them. Policymakers did, however, alter institutions during this era, but without any noteworthy movement toward unmediated rule. If anything, institutional capacity enervated. Nigeria's institutional adjustments reflected the rising strength of nationalist politicians, who pressed for political and fiscal autonomy. The British acceded to nationalists' demands in order to preserve political stability.[77] Yet the British tried to yield as little formal power as possible. In the Richards Constitution (1947), colonial administrators tried to keep power vested in their traditional chieftain allies. Nationalists balked and forced the British to sideline the chiefs in the Macpherson Constitution (1951), which gave nationalists more power—but without say over how accumulated export surpluses would be spent. Nationalists pressed on, to be satisfied only when power was decentralized to regional governments and they gained control over the marketing boards, under the Lyttleton Constitution (1954). These incremental developments underscore how institutions tend to reflect prevailing power balances. With nationalists' rising strength came institutional modification, which continued until nationalists consolidated control over the marketing boards, their main source of side-payments.

RICHARDS CONSTITUTION, 1947

Through the Richards Constitution in 1947, the British hoped to preemptively placate nationalists by offering them formal representation on the Legislative Council, the key formal institution in colonial Nigeria. Colonial administrators also created new regional councils (one each for the East, West, and North Regions), ostensibly to give Nigerians more say in political affairs. Their real rationale, however, was to divert nationalist attention away from Lagos and toward regional capitals and hopefully segment and fracture the nationalist movement. Crucially, the British stipulated that the new regional councils would be filled via indirect elections, which would enable village chiefs to capture many of the new posts.[78] Nationalists thus regarded the Richards Constitution as a dead letter.

Britain also sought to dilute nationalist opposition by changing the way in which revenue was allocated. The Legislative Council in Lagos was responsible for allocating revenue to the new regional councils, and much of this revenue came from the marketing boards. In 1947, Britain broke up the West African

[77] Lynn (2006: 245). In 1944, the Governor of Nigeria, Sir Arthur Richards, wrote that the "problem of Nigeria to-day is how to create a political system which is itself a present advance and contains the living possibility of further orderly advance" (cited in Wheare 1950: 168–170).

[78] Coleman (1958: 273–275) and Crowder (1966: 273–274).

Produce Control Board into country-specific marketing boards. Two years later, the British divided Nigeria's marketing board into multiple commodity-specific marketing boards, with boards for cocoa, palm oil, and groundnut exports. Yet the choice to split Nigeria's marketing board into commodity-specific, rather than region-specific, boards fomented regional tensions. No single region monopolized any one export commodity (e.g., some palm oil was produced in western Nigeria, even though most was produced in the east), which begot contention over revenue allocation. Moreover, leaders from western and northern Nigeria charged (accurately) that the Eastern Region—home to the NCNC, then Nigeria's most powerful nationalist organization—received a disproportionate share of revenue.[79] Battles over revenue allocation stoked inter-regional enmity.

Nationalists also lamented that they had little say over how export surpluses were spent. The British created development corporations in each region to spend monies allocated from the marketing boards.[80] But since, under the Richards Constitution, tribal chiefs controlled the regional councils, they principally determined development corporations' expenditures. Nationalists called for greater influence over spending and further decried the slow pace of "Nigerianization" in the central state bureaucracy.[81] The NCNC, which was trying to establish itself as a countrywide nationalist political party, embarked on a national fundraising campaign against the Richards Constitution to eighty-one eastern, twenty-four northern, and forty-eight western communities in 1946. The campaign "stimulated hundreds of thousands of Nigerians in the interior to an awareness of the nationalist ideal. [Party head Nnamdi] Azikiwe and the NCNC were at the peak of their power and prestige, atop the crest of the highest wave of postwar nationalism." NCNC candidates subsequently won the three seats allotted for nationalists on the Legislative Council and argued for the repeal of the Richards Constitution. The British, lacking the resources to inhibit the nationalists, capitulated and announced in 1948 that the Richards Constitution would be replaced long before its expected termination date in 1956.[82]

MACPHERSON CONSTITUTION, 1951

The Macpherson Constitution of 1951 eliminated tribal chiefs as a vibrant political force and gave more formal power to the nationalists, though the

[79] Helleiner (1966: 156–159) and Nicolson (1969: 252–255).

[80] Helleiner (1966: 244–248).

[81] Nicolson (1969: 251–253).

[82] Coleman (1958: 291–295, 310–312, quote from 292).

British retained control over marketing board reserves and revenue allocation. Regional elections became direct, and nationalists quickly created regionally based political parties to capitalize on electoral opportunities. The NCNC dominated eastern Nigeria's elections, but lacked a strong social base elsewhere and ultimately could not develop into a nationwide party.[83] Parties with deeper social roots captured elections in the west and north. The AG won in western Nigeria, and the Northern Peoples' Congress (NPC) captured the Hausa-Fulani areas. Each party became the dominant political force within its region.[84] (Regionalization thus provided electoral incentives for parties to emphasize their regional and ethnic credentials.[85]) The new parties dramatically changed the composition of regional legislatures, as young nationalist politicians displaced the older tribal elites who held power in regional assemblies before 1948.[86]

Burgeoning regionalization also encouraged centrifugal tendencies. For instance, the British created a central House of Representatives, whose members would be elected indirectly by regional legislatures. The policy consequently "made power at the centre dependent on power in the regions."[87] Regional elites haggled over the distribution of seats, with northerners agreeing to the Macpherson Constitution only when they received half of the seats in the House of Representatives.[88] Inter-regional competition infected the Nigerianization of the bureaucracy as well. Southern Nigeria was the comparatively educated half of the country, which meant meritocratic recruitment would favor southerners. Northern fear of a "southernized" state led to ethnic quotas for bureaucratic staffing.[89] But even with some bureaucratic Nigerianization, nationalist politicians lamented British control of key policy decisions, which undercut support for the Macpherson Constitution.

The paramount failing of the Macpherson Constitution was that it did not give nationalists a say over revenue allocation, which was bound together with their calls for greater self-government. Many nationalists thought that revenue should not be accumulated by commodity-specific marketing boards or allocated by the Legislative Council in Lagos. They wanted to devolve revenue accumulation and allocation to regional governments. The AG was particularly vocal in this regard, since it controlled western Nigeria, which possessed

[83] The NCNC's nationwide appeal was dampened by a corruption scandal over how it used funds raised from its protest campaign against the Richards Constitution (Falola 2004: 34).

[84] Nnoli (1978: 154–157) and Sklar (1963: 87–140).

[85] Lynn (2006) and Nnoli (1978).

[86] Coleman (1958: 378–384).

[87] Lynn (2006: 251).

[88] Ezera (1960: 105–131).

[89] Nicolson (1969: 274–279, 295–299).

Nigeria's greatest export wealth. (Revenue allocation formulas consistently punished the west and favored the NCNC in the east.[90]) The AG pressed for "strict derivation" in revenue allocation, ideally coupled with new region-specific marketing boards. Strict derivation would enable the AG to control virtually all cocoa surplus (then Nigeria's most lucrative export) as well as the area's palm wealth (then about one-third of all palm exports). AG leaders recognized that regional control over export wealth could be used to create unassailable patronage machines. Creating a patronage network was a pressing concern because the NCNC fared reasonably well in western urban centers like Ibadan and Lagos, even if the party was not a nationwide force.[91] Nationalists further pressed the British to relax spending restrictions and allow regional governments to spend accumulated export reserves on broad "developmental" efforts, not just agriculture. In the face of growing opposition, the British agreed to draft a new constitution.

LYTTLETON CONSTITUTION, 1954

Nationalists were contented with the Lyttleton Constitution of 1954, which created region-specific marketing boards, gave nationalists discretion in spending accumulated reserves, and established regional bureaucracies that became patronage outlets. But the new regional bureaucracies sapped power from the central state in Lagos, as regional party leaders enticed bureaucrats back to their regional homelands with attractive compensation packages.[92] Party leaders staffed their regional bureaucracies with locals, even if more qualified "strangers" from elsewhere in Nigeria applied. This predilection was pronounced in the north, which featured lower levels of education. Administration was also politicized. In the northern judicial system, many judges "were said to take dictations from the politicians as to how to decide cases pending before them."[93] In the west, AG officials used bureaucratic control to fend off political rivals. When some NCNC candidates won seats in federal elections in western areas in 1954, the AG dissolved the local councils where the NCNC won and inserted AG apparatchiks to undermine the NCNC footholds.[94] In short, nationalist elites viewed the state as an appendage of their political parties.

Nationalists further solidified their power with their control over the revamped, region-specific marketing boards. The change from commodity- to

[90] Phillips (1971: 390–396).

[91] Lynn (2006: 250–252).

[92] Ezera (1960: 191–194) and Nicolson (1969: 283).

[93] Bolaji (1970: 77).

[94] Akpotor (1996: 104–105).

region-specific boards entailed an inter-regional reallocation of funds, with the Western, Northern, and Eastern Regions given £43 million, £33 million, and £11 million, respectively, in accumulated surpluses.[95] Regional governments gained "virtually unimpeded powers to fix producer prices and impose sales taxes."[96] They also obtained distribution rights for produce-buying licenses (i.e., the LBAs), which became valuable patronage tools. For example, when AG head Nnamdi Azikiwe faced a leadership challenge from dissident elements aligned with the NCNC in 1958, the regional government withdrew the produce buying license from one of the main financial supporters of the insurgent candidate. Other disaffected party members "recanted and scurried back to the party."[97] The Lyttleton Constitution fundamentally altered the resources at the disposal of nationalist elites.

Nationalist leaders also gained broad latitude in spending export surpluses, as regional governments obtained the right to allocate funds to general developmental initiatives, not just agricultural programs. This change allowed nationalists to entrench themselves with sturdy patronage networks via regional development corporations.[98] Rather than using the development institutions to provide public goods to exporters, political elites constructed bloated state agencies, extended low interest loans to political cronies, and funded private banks that became financial appendages of each region's dominant party.[99] These institutional features remained largely unchanged after independence in 1960, and independent Nigeria maintained a federal political structure. Marketing boards remained regionalized, and regional governments controlled their pricing policies and spending.

Nigeria's institutional modifications during decolonization reflected the era's coalitional politics. First, the prevailing weakness of the colonial Nigerian state constrained British officials. They could neither ignore nor curtail the rising power of nationalists and therefore placated them with institutional devolution as a means to forestall independence. This low cost strategy was politically expedient, though with little benefit to state capacity. Second, nationalist leaders fleeced export producers, who were politically marginalized. Even though exporters were being enriched by the good economic times, they did not pose a diametrical, exigent threat to ruling coalition members. Nationalist political elites could maintain their political advantage without moving

[95] Helleiner (1966: 165). The principle of derivation was applied more strictly in general as well, limiting the influence of central bodies like the Legislative Council (Adedeji 1969: 96–108).

[96] Suberu (2001: 50).

[97] Awa (1964: 230 n. 8).

[98] Helleiner (1966: 164–169); Nnoli (1978: 179–181); and Sklar (1963: 162–163).

[99] Mou (1986: 237–240) and Nnoli (1978: 146–147, 181).

toward more unmediated forms of rule. Nigerian state capacity enervated, or at best stagnated, in the two decades following the Second World War.

Nigeria in 1966: An Enervated State

My coalitional analysis suggests a reconsideration of two leading accounts of Nigeria's state weakness as of 1966. First, ethnic enmity in Nigeria was very much a product of colonial rule. Larry Diamond notes that "in creating Nigeria, the British also fostered large-scale ethnic consciousness and conflict."[100] The devolution of power in 1954 heightened ethnic identity, and much of the ensuing inter-ethnic and inter-regional jockeying revolved around how the central state would allocate revenue to the regional governments.[101] Thus, the salience of ethnicity was bound together with the political jockeying between nationalist politicians and British officials. Second, Nigeria's colonial legacies were likewise fashioned by coalitional politics and not simply implanted by British administrators, fit to do as they pleased.

The approaches predicated on the revenue imperative fare little better. Although Nigeria's lack of geopolitical competition may accord with its prevailing low level of state capacity, bellicist factors have difficulty accounting for the way in which the state grew weaker in this era. When external rivalries developed in the early 1960s, the Nigerian military nevertheless remained small and poorly trained and increasingly beset by ethnic rivalry.[102] Policymakers did not deepen revenue extraction, either. In fact, two-thirds of federal and regional government revenue came from customs duties in 1965–66. And the exploitation of export producers—marketing board revenue roughly equaled 80 percent of total tax revenue collected in 1964–65—thoroughly confounds the expectations of the resource curse literature. If one combines marketing board income with government taxes, trade flows and commodity marketing provided about 85 percent of total government revenue.[103]

The fact that political elites led Nigeria's ruling coalition helps to explain why the government relied so heavily on foreign trade for revenues and failed to provide public goods to exporters. Many of the roads built after 1945

[100] Diamond (1988: 26). See Horowitz (1985: esp. 141–228) on the colonial roots of ethnic difference.

[101] Diamond (1988: 71–74).

[102] See Luckham (1971: 88–92, 232–246).

[103] Adedeji (1969: 158, 168). Nigerians pervasively evaded their direct tax obligations (Falola 2004: 91).

amounted to little more than wide footpaths, were not subsequently maintained, and did not substantially reduce transport costs.[104] The new roads were also segmented regionally with few interconnections throughout the country, posing obstacles to deploying state power.[105] The state did not pacify the national territory during this era, either, which the coming Biafran civil war (1967–70) painfully demonstrated. The state eventually defeated the secessionists in the east, though only after a long, tumultuous, and ghastly military campaign. Today, territorial pacification in the east remains elusive, as the Movement for the Emancipation of the Niger Delta operates with impunity, and vigilante justice is common.[106]

The lack of territorial pacification indicated the paucity of institutional control throughout the country. Nigeria's institutional devolution corroded central state capacity, as regional governments lured qualified bureaucrats back to their regional homelands.[107] The central state increasingly became an arena for inter-regional, inter-ethnic rivalry, and administration grew ineffective, haphazard, and incomprehensible.[108] Meanwhile, public sector employment exploded. By 1965, the federal bureaucracy employed 65,000 people, and regional institutions added 50,000 more.[109] The state grew weaker as it grew larger, with public sector employment used as a side-payment to entrench regional patronage networks.

The regionalization of power deepened the mediated nature of rule in Nigeria. One period observer judged that the 1960s central state did not have "the same control over the county, divisional or district councils that (it) used to have over the native authorities" in southern Nigeria.[110] As in Ghana, Nigerian localities gained discretion over how they spent central state grants during the period; although localities were subject to audits, in practice the auditors were "understaffed and overworked."[111] Local tax collection was also controlled by the regional governments, not the central state.[112] Nor did the state influence local elections, as in Chile or Argentina. Electoral oversight was the purview of

[104] Ekundare (1973: 266) and Olaloku (1979: 85).

[105] Taafee, Morrill, and Gould (1963: 513). There was no new railway construction during this period, either. The mismanagement of the railroads was "so scandalous" that, after the 1966 coup, the ruling junta established an investigatory tribunal in an attempt to improve the railroad (Usman 1989: 140).

[106] Ukiwo (2007) and International Crisis Group (2009).

[107] Cf. Kirk-Greene (1980: 42–44).

[108] Diamond (1988: 298–299) and Nicolson (1969: 298–299).

[109] Kohli (2004: 335, 347).

[110] Wraith (1964: 103; see also 105–106).

[111] Ibid., 101.

[112] Diamond (1988: 40).

regional bureaucrats who, as the London-based magazine *West Africa* noted in 1965, "in the last analysis will obey the regional governments—which can also mean parties."[113] Furthermore, regionally dominant political parties exercised personalistic control over local judicial systems, which formally stood apart from the national, federal judiciary.[114] On all measures, Nigerian state capacity was paltry. Yet the country did have opportunities to expand its state capacity in the two decades following the Second World War. But its ruling coalition of political elites forestalled those possibilities.

[113] *West Africa*, October 23, 1965, as cited in Diamond (1988: 280). See also Diamond (1988: 86–87) and Wraith (1964: 60–65).

[114] See Diamond (1988: 84, 148, 285).

CHAPTER 9

Conclusion and Implications

Theoretical Implications

This book's findings have general theoretical pertinence for the study of state building in the developing world. First, my analysis indicates that the two leading theoretical worldviews on postcolonial state formation—bellicist theories and studies of the resource curse—place too much emphasis on state building as a top-down process driven by revenue-hungry rulers. The bellicist view is built upon Charles Tilly's analysis of European state formation, a bloody process whereby rulers either found ways to adeptly extract revenue to fight incessant wars or were extinguished.[1] Those rulers who prospered not only created standing bureaucracies to acquire revenue but also "seduced" the creation of taxable wealth by curtailing predatory behavior and providing public goods. Yet the comparatively pacific environment facing rulers outside of Europe has meant that their survival has demanded neither the erection of probing fiscal institutions nor the supply of plentiful public goods.[2] This variance in geopolitical environment means that rulers in the non-European world face a relatively tepid revenue imperative. This actuality suggests that perhaps one ought to find more state building similarity throughout the postcolonial world than is the case.[3]

Studies of the resource curse likewise maintain that state building is largely a top-down process propelled by fiscal exigencies. The conventional wisdom contends that immobile rent-generating commodities, like oil and minerals, yield revenue windfalls that obviate the need to build strong taxing

[1] Tilly (1975, 1992).

[2] Bates (2010: 34–64).

[3] See Evans (1995: 11) and Slater (2010: 3) on the variance in state capacity in the postcolonial world.

institutions. Conversely, agricultural commodities, which do not produce rents, arguably demand a diversified fiscal apparatus and should therefore yield greater state capacity.[4] There is certainly much veracity in this distinction. Without a doubt, rent-generating commodities disincline the creation of robust extractive capabilities.[5] And I do not dispute that the revenue imperative may be important to explain the development of extractive prowess, or the lack thereof. Yet most developing countries have historically employed revenue-raising strategies requiring little institutional power, regardless of their natural resource endowments. What is more, I note in chapter 2 that students of state building are usually interested in explaining "state capacity," the conceptual content of which is more far-reaching that extractive capacity. In short, the revenue imperative is a state building motive, but it is not the chief motive in the developing world, contrary to what is often implied in the extant literature.

This book emphasizes complementary "bottom-up" societal pressures that can induce state building. First, I look to the pursuit of profit as a key motive that indirectly stimulates state building by way of public goods provision. Adam Smith long ago observed that "it is not from the benevolence of the butcher, the brewer, or the baker that we expect our dinner, but from their regard to their own interest."[6] Smith pointed out how a country could collectively benefit from the pursuit of such narrow objectives. In much the same way, I find that resource booms often generate positive inducements for state building by revealing barriers to expanded export production. Export-oriented actors may lobby their governments to mitigate economic bottlenecks by supplying new (and often impure) public goods. Public goods provision is thus a byproduct of export-oriented actors' self-interested desire to maximize their economic wealth and power. State capacity tends to grow from the supply of public goods, because states regularly generate new power and accrue new capabilities while providing and later maintaining public goods.

Second, I highlight how the pursuit of distributional political advantage can spawn remarkable institutional strengthening and a growth in state capacity. Whereas I identify how positive inducements can stimulate the provision of new public goods, I argue that negative inducements may spark projects of momentous institutional change. Resource booms usually alter the balance of

[4] E.g., Karl (1997); Sala-i-Martin and Subramanian (2003); and Shafer (1994: 35–36). Isham et al. (2005) contend that "point source" agricultural commodities produced on plantations also obviate state building because they are spatially concentrated, like most fuel and mineral commodities.

[5] Dunning (2008: 39–52).

[6] Smith (1986: 119).

economic power and thereby create contingent possibilities for institutional change. Specifically, when booms enrich exporters both within and outside of the ruling coalition, ruling coalition members will perceive that they face a diametrical threat and initiate the movement toward unmediated institutions, in order to exert greater institutional control over their opponents. In such situations of "dual enrichment," ruling coalition members will calculate that the prospect of coalitional change would be catastrophic, for it would not only likely make them the fiscal target of the new coalition's side-payments, but it would also disable them from obtaining new public goods in support of their economic goals. Consequently, ruling coalition members will conclude that the potentially catastrophic costs of inaction outweigh the costs and uncertainty associated with institution building. Overall, I isolate two motives—the pursuits of profit and distributional political advantage—that propel social actors to press for policies with state building implications. These bottom-up motives complement the prevailing top-down emphasis on the revenue imperative and thereby enrich our understanding of state formation in the developing world.

These pathways to new state capacity hinge on coalitional politics, which is responsible for the contingent nature of these theoretical relationships. Export-oriented actors only successfully impel the public goods route to new state capacity when they are part of the ruling political coalition. When exporters are politically marginalized, they will be unable to obtain new public goods because their policy requests, in effect, ask the government to redirect scarce resources away from political insiders. This finding is commonsensical, of course, but it is an actuality that eludes much theorizing on natural resource wealth. Staples and dependency theorists, for instance, consider the linkage effects associated with primary commodity production to be more or less functional outgrowths of economic activity: agricultural commodities generate comparatively robust linkages, they maintain, whereas fuel and minerals yield scant linkages.[7] The resource curse literature echoes these expectations.[8] By contrast, the case studies in this book illustrate that there is a crucial political dimension to linkage effects, which often manifest themselves as public goods. Coalitional politics may matter as much as commodity type when it comes to the provision of new public goods and, by extension, state building.

In my case studies, export-oriented actors in Chile, Argentina, and Mauritius demanded and received new public goods because they led the ruling political coalition. Chilean landed elites impelled the state to establish an

[7] E.g., Hirschman (1977); Watkins (1963); Cardoso and Faletto (1979); and Gallo (1991).
[8] See, e.g., Karl (1997: 52–54) and Ross (2012: 44).

important mortgage bank and facilitate the construction of two railroads critical to wheat exports. Policymakers in Argentina, where export-oriented ranchers from Buenos Aires dominated politics, likewise underwrote railroads, curtailed rural workers' mobility, and created a mortgage bank in Buenos Aires, while obstructing credit accessibility where the opposition thrived. These states also pacified their national territories to advance the economic goals of ruling coalition members. In Mauritius, politically dominant sugar planters, the Franco-Mauritians, got the state to improve the island's transportation infrastructure, undertake research and development on their behalf, and "regulate" the island's labor force via coercion and harassment. State capacity grew from public goods provision in these countries. However, in Colombia, Ghana, and Nigeria, where exporters were politically marginalized, governments did not provide public goods. They instead fleeced exporters and distributed export wealth as divisible benefits to their coalitional followers, with few, if any, positive ramifications for state capacity.

The institutional pathway to new state capacity likewise pivots on coalitional politics. My finding on resource booms and institutional strengthening is perhaps the starkest departure from the conventional wisdom on the political economy of resource wealth. Existing studies anticipate that resource wealth will corrode already weak institutions.[9] Those countries fortunate enough to possess strong institutions when they discover resource wealth, like Norway, should be able to maintain them.[10] But virtually no one expects that resource booms will lead to institutional strengthening. Benjamin Smith is an exception here, as he argues that "rulers who come to power facing the dual challenges of political opposition and revenue scarcity [and therefore build strong institutions] are likely to use later windfall revenues to continue their state-building projects," in part by fortifying institutions. Yet Smith's empirical presentation of this relationship, in Indonesia, highlights administrative devolution and developmental patronage as the means through which Indonesia's rulers secured political quiescence during the oil boom.[11] This evidence implies a movement toward more mediated forms of rule, not a deepening of unmediated institutions, amid boom times. Nevertheless, what most differentiates my account from Smith's is that, whereas he points to prior path dependent "lock-in" to account for how resource booms affect institutions,[12] I locate the source of institutional change in the boom itself—specifically, in the coalitional threats that can emerge from shifting economic power.

[9] Karl (1997); Isham et al. (2005); Leite and Weidmann (1999); and Sala-i-Martin and Subramanian (2003).

[10] Karl (1997: 213–220).

[11] Smith (2007: 129–134, quote from 129).

[12] Smith (2007: 44–55).

My case studies of Chile and Argentina illustrate how situations of dual enrichment provoked the movement toward unmediated institutions. Burgeoning and diametrical threats boiled over into civil war in both countries, prompting subsequent institutional strengthening. The Chilean state fundamentally transformed its leverage over municipalities, among other things, and institutional change in Argentina was similar, if less profound. A first reason why I believe the existing literature has overlooked the relationship between resource booms, coalitional politics, and institutional strengthening is because of its contingency. Major violent episodes in two other cases—a ravaging civil war in Colombia and substantial regionalist violence in Ghana—did not precipitate institutional invigoration, even though the violence was spawned by rising exporters, as were civil wars in Chile and Argentina. Hence, the pertinent causal relationship—that the movement toward unmediated institutions depends on dual enrichment, not merely an enrichment of political outsiders—is subtle.

A second reason why the positive institutional byproducts of resource booms may have gone unnoticed is that the conventional wisdom is predicated upon a certain type of resource-exporting country. Many analyses of the resource curse begin with the "Big Oil Change" around 1970, when cartelization, rising demand, and nationalization altered the world oil market.[13] Governments began receiving hitherto unprecedented revenue windfalls, which obviated state building for the purposes of taxation, encouraged rent-seeking, and promoted institutional enervation. Without discounting these effects, I want to also note that the Big Oil Change marked a coalitional change, as oil wealth was transferred from the private to public sector. Consequently, the archetypical rentier state could not feature the sort of dual enrichment that led to institutional strengthening in Chile and Argentina, since there was no noteworthy group of politically marginalized exporters to be enriched by a boom. Contemporary fuel and mineral exporters—which epitomize the resource curse—therefore likely suffer institutional debility because of the lack of threat facing ruling coalitions, in addition to the fiscal disinclinations for institutional building. Not all is tranquil in oil economies, of course. Groups like the Movement for the Emancipation of the Niger Delta are exacting,[14] but they do not constitute the sort of exigent, diametrical threat I argue triggers thoroughgoing institutional change. My findings on resource booms, coalitional threat, and institutional strengthening offer a fresh reason why many contemporary fuel and mineral exporters feature frail institutions.

[13] Ross (2012: 37–43). For more on the Big Oil Change, see Andersen and Ross (forthcoming).
[14] On MEND, see Omeje (2006) and Ukiwo (2007).

In sum, this book makes three principal contributions to scholars of state building in the non-European world. First, I highlight the role that bottom-up, societal pressures play in state formation. These pressures were more responsible for the state building observed in the book's case studies than were rulers and their top-down quest for revenue. Second, I note that resource booms can lead to new state capacity in ways that are underappreciated in the existing literature on natural resource wealth. For instance, commodity booms can trigger institutional fortification, not just enfeeblement. Third, and most fundamentally, resource booms do not automatically translate into new state capacity. Rather, the state building possibilities encapsulated within commodity booms hinge on coalitional politics. So too may the "resource curse" pivot on coalitional politics.

What Is the Resource Curse?

Over the past generation, the notion of a resource curse has solidified within and beyond academia.[15] Like any research program, hypotheses linking natural resource wealth to various economic, political, and social outcomes have been advanced, refined, qualified, and sometimes imperiled. Following the publication of some seminal studies, many researchers regarded all natural resource wealth as problematic; at present, they increasingly believe that only certain types of primary commodities are perilous. Scholars now also consider the resource curse as something that is conditioned by context, particularly by the caliber of a country's institutions. I agree that the resource curse is conditional but diverge from the institutional orientation of this emerging conventional wisdom. Instead, I contend that the pathologies associated with natural resource wealth—especially with respect to state building—are largely a function of coalitional politics. Put differently, I believe that countries that appear to be cursed by the intrinsic properties of certain export commodities and weak institutions are actually victims of a certain type of coalitional politics.

The changing way in which scholars have operationalized resource abundance reflects their evolving understanding of how resource wealth influences economic and political outcomes. Two seminal studies of the resource curse, by Jeffrey Sachs and Andrew Warner and Paul Collier and Anke Hoeffler, conceived of resource abundance as the share of primary commodity exports

[15] Two seminal studies were Auty (1993) and Sachs and Warner (1995), and Frankel (2012) offers an excellent review. Thomas Friedman (2006) is one prominent, mainstream example of the resource curse's currency beyond academia.

of Gross Domestic Product, labeled as "*sxp*" in quantitative analysis.[16] The *sxp* variable is noteworthy, nearly twenty years on from Sachs and Warner's study, because it treats all primary commodities the same; no distinction is made between rent- and non-rent-generating commodities.[17] However, subsequent analyses of these studies have shown that rent-generating commodities were the more consequential part of the *sxp* variable, which suggests that resource exports are not uniformly worrisome. James Butkiewicz and Halit Yanikkaya, for example, interrogated Sachs and Warner's findings and concluded that mineral exports were more strongly correlated with poor economic growth rates than were agricultural or food exports.[18] James Fearon similarly found that the fuel exports component in Collier and Hoeffler's *sxp* variable was responsible for most of the predictive association between primary exports and civil war onset.[19] Consistent with these findings, the notion of a resource curse has become circumscribed to fuel and mineral, and especially oil, exports.[20]

Still, the relative importance of fuel and mineral exports coheres with Sachs and Warner's central premise: that Dutch Disease is probably why resource-abundant economies grew more slowly than their resource-scarce counterparts during the 1970s and 1980s. Dutch Disease refers to a situation when an explosion of primary exports causes currency appreciation, which renders traditional exports less internationally competitive and undermines domestic manufacturing by making substitute imports cheaper. Since commodities like oil tend to feature the largest revenue windfalls, they also place comparatively strong upward pressures on domestic currencies.[21] Therefore, limiting the scope of the resource curse to fuel and mineral exports, instead of all primary commodity exports, did not threaten the core theoretical logic accounting for the lower rates of economic growth observed in resource-rich countries.

Yet various critics maintain that there is nothing inherently perilous about fuel and mineral exports. Graham Davis, for instance, does not uncover strong evidence of Dutch Disease in mineral export economies, nor does he find that mineral exporters have performed considerably worse than other countries. He has recently argued that fuel and mineral production eventually becomes

[16] Sachs and Warner (1995) and Collier and Hoeffler (2002).

[17] Another seminal study, by Gylfason (2001: esp. 848 n. 2), uses a similarly inclusive operationalization ("natural capital") of resource wealth.

[18] Butkiewicz and Yanikkaya (2010).

[19] Fearon (2005: 487, 491–492, 500–501).

[20] Incidentally, Auty's (1993) seminal study was narrowly concerned with minerals, not primary exports in general.

[21] On Dutch Disease, see Auty (1993); Frankel (2012); Ross (2012: 48–49); and Sachs and Warner (1995).

static or declines and thus will not grow substantially over time; but this outcome is a characteristic of mineral production and not due to Dutch Disease or other pernicious factors.[22] Other scholars argue that the lower growth rates among oil exporters were because international capital markets lent recklessly to them after the first oil shock, thereby creating debt service burdens and constraining growth during the lean 1980s.[23] In fact, since the 1970s and 1980s (the period of analysis that gave rise to resource curse theories), oil exporters have grown faster than their non-oil counterparts—and on par with them from 1970 to 2006 overall.[24] These critiques are noteworthy because they move beyond fairly narrow objections over how resource abundance is operationalized for statistical analysis and instead challenge the core logic linking resource wealth to economic underperformance.

An emergent conventional wisdom serves as an even more thoroughgoing critique. Scholars increasingly believe that the resource curse flourishes only in weak institutional contexts. Researchers have therefore moved away from merely emphasizing the intrinsic properties of commodity exports and begun to examine the caliber of institutions in resource-exporting countries. One prominent study finds that the negative relationship between resource abundance and economic growth identified by Sachs and Warner hinges on institutional quality: countries with abundant natural resources (*sxp* of 10 percent or greater) and weak institutions do indeed feature poor economic growth; yet countries with stronger institutional profiles exhibit no significant association between *sxp* and growth.[25] A related study argues that strong institutions can moderate the predatory temptations facing rulers who oversee publically owned resources, like fuel and minerals (which, as I note above, are most responsible for the low rates of economic growth in resource-abundant countries). Rationalized, meritocratic bureaucracies can serve as a bulwark against plunder, patronage, and myopic policymaking.[26] This finding is consistent with Norway's judicious management of its oil and gas discoveries since the 1960s. In short, researchers now generally regard the resource curse as something that afflicts "weakly institutionalized polities."[27]

The solidifying belief that the resource curse pivots on institutions has profound implications. By maintaining that various "cursed" outcomes depend on institutional context, resource curse scholars are emphasizing problems that are widespread in the developing world, not problems of resource wealth

[22] Davis (1995, 2011).
[23] Manzano and Rigobón (2007) and Nooruddin (2008).
[24] Ross (2012: 190).
[25] Mehlum, Moene, and Torvik (2006).
[26] Robinson, Torvik, and Verdier (2006).
[27] See Acemoglu, Robinson, and Verdier (2004) on weakly institutionalized polities.

per se.[28] Andrew Schrank, for instance, points out that lots of developed countries, including Norway and the United States, produce oil without succumbing to economic or political pathologies. These countries differ, he argues, not merely because they have effective institutions but because of their broader sociopolitical environment. Developing countries export primary commodities because they are poor, but not simply because they are poor: their prevailing property rights regimes discourage long-term investment and thus disable them from utilizing their primary commodities to engender transformative economic development. Accordingly, specialization in resource exports does not cause obstacles to development; it is rather an outcome of them.[29] Marcus Kurtz similarly notes that so much of the resource curse literature focuses on how rent-generating commodities encourage rent-seeking and policy failures, which may indeed be the case. Yet such pathologies characterize many developing countries, regardless of their resource endowments.[30] These critics together suggest that the resource curse is, in a sense, a symptom of underdevelopment.

The changing understanding of the resource curse—as something that blossoms amid weak institutions and underdevelopment—suggests that my historical examinations of agricultural exporters are pertinent to a scholarly literature that oftentimes limits its scope to contemporary fuel and mineral exporters. As I note in chapter 2, my six case studies shared important features with many developing countries historically. Each country was oriented to primary commodity production during colonialism, as were virtually all colonial dependencies. There is a voluminous literature, epitomized by dependency theory, that details how colonialism implanted obstacles to development. Colonialism often created national boundaries in many countries that established small domestic markets, which limited the viability of import substitution industrialization and therefore encouraged former dependencies to retain their reliance on primary commodity exports. Moreover, European powers bequeathed notoriously weak institutions to most colonies, and generalized institutional weakness has been a hallmark of the postcolonial world. Overall, these features—a history of colonization, an agrarian economy, and weak institutions—are shared among my six case studies and many other countries

[28] Other researchers demonstrate how foreign aid and other types of non-tax revenue are like resource rents in that they obviate the need for strong fiscal institutions, sever a key means through which citizens hold rulers accountable, and enable despotic rule. Some pitfalls associated with resource rents are not unique to natural resource wealth but rather apply to various non-tax revenues. See Morrison (Forthcoming) for a synthetic analysis.

[29] Schrank (2011). See also Herb (2005: 303). See North (1989) on the relationship between institutions and economic growth.

[30] Kurtz (2009: 482–484).

in the developing world, both historically and in the contemporary era. All of them are arguably susceptible to a resource curse.

Yet, as my case studies suggest, which countries succumb to a curse does not appear to be stochastic. It hinges on coalitional politics. Colombia, Ghana, and Nigeria—where political elites led ruling coalitions—could easily be categorized as being "cursed" by their commodity booms. Chile, Argentina, and Mauritius—where export-oriented coalitions prevailed—could not. In fact, scholars commonly point to Chile and Mauritius as countries that have successfully averted the resource curse,[31] though few of them point to political coalitions as their key differentiating trait.[32] None of my case studies featured strong institutions at the start of their first major commodity booms, and all of them exported similar, non-rent-generating commodities. Their coalitional difference is why some of them provided public goods, while others did not, and why some developed threats that were deemed sufficiently exigent to provoke institution building. Coalitional politics was the cause of their state building divergences.

My findings indicate that the resource curse may arise from a type of coalitional politics, perhaps more so than from resource rents. After all, although fuels, minerals, and especially oil generate sizable revenue windfalls, I note in chapter 2 that all primary commodity exports are easy revenue targets.[33] Robert Bates's landmark study on African marketing boards shows how even the most spatially diffuse agricultural commodities can fiscally buoy a ruling coalition.[34] This actuality dissolves somewhat the theoretical distinction made between rent- and non-rent-generating commodities (or, if one prefers, the distinction between "point source" and spatially diffuse commodities[35]). Let me be clear that I am not arguing there are no significant distinctions to be made between rent- and non-rent-generating commodities. I am simply noting that the fiscal implications of primary export commodities are more alike than commonly acknowledged in the extant literature. The simplicity with which all primary export commodities can be taxed reminds us that resource rents accrue to the state only because of prior policy decisions that have either nationalized or imposed substantial taxes on them.[36]

[31] See, for example, Acemoglu, Robinson, and Verdier (2004: 166) and Frankel (2012) on Chile and Bräutigam (2008) and Frankel (2010) on Mauritius.

[32] Poteete (2009), however, emphasizes coalitional politics as the reason why Botswana has avoided the resource curse. See also Richardson (2009) for a coalitional analysis of contemporary soybean exports in Argentina.

[33] On the exceptional scale of oil rents, see Ross (2012: 27–33).

[34] Bates (1981).

[35] Isham et al. (2005).

[36] Karl (1997: 48–49) and Ross (2012: 4–5).

Recent research on apparent anomalies bolsters confidence in the political, rather than fiscal, source of the resource curse. Thad Dunning, for example, depicts how Bolivia's tin mines produced substantial economic rents in the era before 1952, but the state did not prey upon them because a narrow stratum of tin barons led the country's ruling political coalition and kept the tin rents for themselves.[37] Similarly, in contemporary oil-rich states, rentierism flourishes when oil firms are state-owned. But where private ownership prevails, governments extract less revenue from oil firms and feature less dysfunction in general.[38] This finding implies something about coalitional politics. When states nationalize oil, they eliminate private economic actors from control and replace them with managers who are more beholden to political imperatives.[39] In other words, state-owned oil firms have affinities with coalitions led by political elites, whereas countries with private ownership feature more influence of export-oriented actors.[40] Coalitional politics may lurk behind variation in ownership structure. What is certain, however, is that the resource curse literature developed many of its basic premises by analyzing oil producers over the 1970–1990 timeframe, when state ownership, rentierism, and rule by political elites were the norm.[41] In sum, as research on the resource curse matures, more scholars are challenging its core claims. Investigating the coalitional dimensions surrounding natural resource wealth may help elucidate why a resource curse seems to take hold in some countries but not others.

Policy Implications

The prospect that the resource curse hinges on coalitional politics has important implications for how countries ought to manage their natural resources. In a recent survey, Jeffrey Frankel identifies three broad ways in which countries have tried to ensure that resource wealth will not produce cursed outcomes.[42] First, he notes that governments can adeptly design contracts to mitigate their risk associated with volatile commodities markets.[43] They can index contract

[37] Dunning (2008: 231–238). See also Gallo (1991).

[38] Jones Luong and Weinthal (2010: esp. 331–335).

[39] Cf. Ross (2012: 43–43, 62).

[40] Jones Luong and Weinthal's (2010: 87–94, 134–138) description of fiscal regimes in the former Soviet Union supports this analogy. Turkmenistan and Uzbekistan, where the state controls oil production, heavily tax oil as well as cotton, the countries' traditional agricultural export. Russia, where domestic private ownership exists, has a diversified tax base with less fiscal reliance on oil.

[41] Cf. Jones Luong and Weinthal (2010: 6, 322–323).

[42] Frankel (2012). See also Humphreys, Sachs, and Stiglitz (2007) and Ross (2012: 234–250).

[43] E.g., Humphreys, Sachs, and Stiglitz (2007: 53–151).

prices to future market fluctuations of a given commodity, for instance. Or, if they are debtors, countries might denominate their debt in the world price of their leading commodity, so that their export fortunes and debt service obligations move in lockstep. A radical contract design option is the "barter contract," whereby a resource-rich country trades the rights of extraction for a public good, like infrastructure.[44] This approach is being tried in some African states, which feature notorious corruption and weak state capacity. Contract design options seek to extricate politicians as much as possible from the oversight and management of natural resource wealth, given the pathologies of many resource-rich countries.

Second, governments can implement judicious macroeconomic policy to temper Dutch Disease effects and smooth the intertemporal shocks associated with commodity price fluctuations. Chile has adroitly managed its recent copper boom through budgetary rules intended to foster countercyclical fiscal policy, for example. There are similar options for exchange rate management and monetary policy as well.[45] There is some encouraging news on this front: during the commodity booms of the 2000s, about one-third of developing countries employed countercyclical policy, whereas virtually none of them had from 1960 to 2000. This policy shift has been associated with improvements in institutional quality, which may have enabled developing countries such as Chile, Botswana, and Brazil to commit to countercyclical policy.[46] Along with countercyclical policies, scholars note that governments should spend wisely, ideally curtailing consumption spending and focusing on investment, which better promotes long-term growth and development.[47]

Natural resource funds are a third way policymakers might manage resource wealth and possibly avoid the curse.[48] Botswana has a professionally managed reserve fund that intends to offset the eventual depletion of its diamonds, and the fund is run by financial professionals unencumbered from political dictates.[49] A radical version of the natural resource fund directly transfers resource proceeds to citizens, as does the Alaska Permanent Fund; some analysts believe such arrangements, though imperfect, are the best hope for limiting the impact of predatory governments.[50] These advocates

[44] Ross (2012: 236–237).

[45] Frankel (2012) and Humphreys, Sachs, and Stiglitz (2007: 155–193).

[46] Frankel, Végh, and Vuletin (2013).

[47] Ross (2012: 247–249). See Easterly (2003) for a related statement on how developing countries tend to impede economic growth by using foreign aid for consumption, rather than investment.

[48] See especially Humphreys and Sandbu (2007).

[49] Frankel (2012).

[50] Ross (2012: 237–239) and Sala-i-Martin and Subramanian (2003).

are justifiably wary of government management of natural resource wealth. Other researchers believe that decentralizing resource revenues to provincial governments may curb corruption and rent-seeking,[51] though federalism in Nigeria has arguably heightened local dependence on the central state, rather than providing a check against it.[52] In varying degrees, these solutions seek to "remove politics" from the management of resource booms and enhance transparency, the lack of which is ever more seen as a crucial link between resource wealth and cursed developments.[53] Many of these strategies underwhelm in practice, however, motivating some researchers to call for greater private ownership of natural resources as a better defense against the resource curse.[54]

Much of the literature surrounding resource wealth management eventually invokes institutional quality to differentiate successes from failures. After all, governments might renege on well-designed contracts, and barter contracts are not immune from corruption.[55] Rules intended to induce countercyclical fiscal policy presume that institutions are sufficiently vigorous to restrain politicians' temptations to raid accumulating surpluses, especially during hard political times. Such institutional vigor is routinely absent, of course. For instance, the World Bank went to excruciating lengths to implement rules to help Chad avoid deleterious outcomes when it built an oil pipeline to the Gulf of Guinea; yet the Bank's efforts have done little to curtail corruption or foment cooperation with Chadian officials.[56] And while some natural resource funds have worked well (e.g., Alaska, Norway), others have not (e.g., Chad). The variation in fund performance is not a matter of particular institutional rules but rather the broader institutional context. In short, successfully managing natural resource wealth "goes to the heart of state-building."[57]

Policy advocates who recognize the value of effective institutions usually stress "capacity building" as a necessary remedy.[58] Yet not all contexts are equally ripe for enhancing public administration. Some configurations of coalitional politics in primary commodity exporters seem to be more conducive to bureaucratic improvement than others. The export-oriented coalitions

[51] Ross (2012: 239–240).

[52] Suberu (2001).

[53] Karl (2007) and Ross (2012: 244–247).

[54] Jones Luong and Weinthal (2010); Ross (2012: 240–242); and Weinthal and Jones Luong (2006).

[55] Ross (2012: 237).

[56] Pegg (2006).

[57] Humphreys and Sandbu (2007: 196).

[58] E.g., Stiglitz (2007).

that ruled Chile, Argentina, and Mauritius reflexively provided exporters new public goods, and it seems reasonable that such coalitions would be more willing to facilitate sound export development via administrative overhaul than would the political elites who preyed upon export wealth in Colombia, Ghana, and Nigeria. Indeed, Amy Poteete maintains that Botswana's export-oriented coalition is why the country has featured "good governance" and smart technocratic management of its diamonds.[59] On a related note, Erika Weinthal and Pauline Jones Luong advocate private ownership of resource wealth because they expect it to create new bargaining dynamics between asset owners and the state—and perhaps yield stronger institutions as well.[60] Privatization may create a new form of coalitional politics, in other words.

Throughout the book I have drawn attention to private export-oriented actors as being more likely to spur state building projects amid commodity booms. This finding animates the entire book. I would like to close with two caveats, in order to remind the reader that I am ultimately interested in explaining state building processes, not uncovering policy remedies for weak states. First, my findings indicate that countries with export-oriented actors at the helm of policymaking build stronger states, at least during resource booms. This conclusion seems to have an affinity with the "Washington Consensus" of the 1980s and 1990s, which prescribed to developing countries an outward economic orientation, privatization, and state retrenchment as the route to economic development.[61] Yet there exists plenty of evidence that the most thoroughgoing developmental successes, both historically and in the contemporary era, were forged through heavy (and judicious) state direction.[62] The World Bank's ensuing embrace of "good governance" as a necessary ingredient for economic development reflects the demise of the "stateless" Washington Consensus.[63] Accordingly, one should not glean from my explanatory conclusions that export-oriented coalitions necessarily portend developmental success. After all, even if commodity exporters press the state to provide public goods to help them achieve their economic goals, they may very well balk at industrial development, since it implies a relative decline of the primary sector. Overall, I simply find that export-oriented coalitions better harness the state

[59] Poteete (2009).

[60] Weinthal and Jones Luong (2006: 46).

[61] Williamson (1990).

[62] See, e.g., Chaudhry (1993) and Rodrik (1997) for critiques of the Washington Consensus in this vein. On the cruciality of the state in fostering economic development, see Evans (1995); Schwartz (2010); Smith (1979); and Weiss and Hobson (1995).

[63] Kaufmann, Kraay, and Mastruzzi (2010). See also Herbst (1990b) on the overlooked political dimensions of structural adjustment in Africa.

building opportunities encapsulated within commodity booms than do coalitions led by political elites.

This clarification dovetails with a second caveat: that one should not confuse the gains in state capacity brought about by export-oriented coalitions in the book's case studies with righteousness. The export-oriented coalitions profiled herein did propel gains in state capacity and thereby indirectly facilitated good things, such as economic growth. But ruling coalition members did so by harnessing their disproportionate power for narrow gain. When they strengthened institutions, ruling coalitions expressly designed them to subjugate and repress the weak. They similarly impelled the state to provide new public goods tailored to their private enrichment, insofar as possible. And some of their behavior was downright reprehensible. Mauritian sugar planters compelled the government to ignore mistreatment on sugar estates, implement unreasonable fines and annual passport fees in the name of preventing "vagrancy," and harass workers who sought a better life in urban professions. Chile's northern central valley *hacendados* behaved likewise. When plebs migrated south of the Bío Bío River to establish family farms during the wheat boom, power holders got the state to designate them as "squatters," forcibly remove them if need be, and then permit existing elites to consolidate haciendas, many of which laid fallow for fifty years. Even so, export-oriented coalitions do not always resort to exploitation to achieve their ends, and coalitions led by political elites are not necessarily altruistic and benevolent. I merely want to note that my explanatory findings should not be construed as prescriptive remedies for countries featuring little state capacity.

What is clear is that commodity booms can spur state building, depending on coalitional politics. State building is not a narrow technical or administrative endeavor but, rather, a deeply political process. My findings are noteworthy not just because they illustrate how resource booms can promote the growth of state capacity. They are significant because they suggest that the "good" and "bad" outcomes associated with resource wealth do not simply hinge on pre-existing institutions, as the scholarly literature increasingly suggests. Coalitional politics seems to play an underappreciated role in the growth of state capacity in primary export economies and probably influences how those countries manage their resource wealth as well. Indeed, Macartan Humphreys and Martin Sandbu suggest that coalitional instability may be why political leaders act myopically with resource wealth—using it for short-term distributional payoffs rather than long-term collective goals.[64] These choices seem to have much to do with the types of side-payments leaders use to forge coalitions. Viewed in this way, the conundrum of resource wealth

[64] Humphreys and Sandbu (2007). See also Poteete (2009).

management—and perhaps the broader notion of the resource curse—has much to do with why politicians have been so reluctant to shed their commitment to narrow and divisible side-payments (e.g., government contracts, soft loans) in lieu of broader and more indivisible ones (e.g., providing public goods). If such coalition-building strategies may indeed reside at the core of why a resource curse takes hold, then placing more attention on coalitional politics may enrich our understanding of the political economy of resource wealth.

REFERENCES

Aagesen, David. 2000. "Crisis and Conservation at the End of the World: Sheep Ranching in Argentine Patagonia." *Environmental Conservation* 27(2): 208–215.

Accominotti, Olivier, Marc Flandreau, and Riad Rezzik. 2011. "The Spread of Empire: Clio and the Measurement of Colonial Borrowing Costs." *Economic History Review* 64(2): 385–407.

Acemoglu, Daron, and James Robinson. 2006. *Economic Origins of Dictatorship and Democracy.* New York: Cambridge University Press.

———. 2008. "Persistence of Power, Elites, and Institutions." *American Economic Review* 98(1): 267–293.

Acemoglu, Daron, Georgy Egorov, and Konstantin Sonin. 2008. "Coalition Formation in Non-Democracies." *Review of Economic Studies* 75: 987–1009.

Acemoglu, Daron, Simon Johnson, and James Robinson. 2001. "The Colonial Origins of Comparative Development: An Empirical Investigation." *American Economic Review* 91(5): 1369–1401.

Acemoglu, Daron, James Robinson, and Thierry Verdier. 2004. "Kleptocracy and Divide-and-Rule: A Model of Personal Rule." *Journal of the European Economic Association* 2(2–3): 162–192.

Adedeji, Adebayo. 1969. *Nigerian Federal Finance: Its Development, Problems and Prospects.* London: Hutchinson Educational.

Adelman, Jeremy. 1999. *Republic of Capital: Buenos Aires and the Legal Transformation of the Atlantic World.* Stanford, CA: Stanford University Press.

Adeyeye, Samuel. 1978. *The Co-operative Movement in Nigeria.* Göttingen, Germany: Vandenhoeck and Ruprecht.

Akpotor, S. A. 1996. "Constitutional Engineering from Richards to Macpherson." In *Nigerian Politics and Constitutional Development,* ed. P. Agbebaku. Lagos, Nigeria: Oshioke Yakubu.

Alesina, Alberto, Reza Baqir, and William Easterly. 1999. "Public Goods and Ethnic Divisions." *Quarterly Journal of Economics* 114(4): 1243–1284.

Allen, Richard. 1999. *Slaves, Freedmen, and Indentured Laborers in Colonial Mauritius.* Cambridge: Cambridge University Press.

———. 2008. "Vagrancy in Mauritius and the Nineteenth-Century Colonial Plantation World." In *Cast Out: Vagrancy and Homelessness in Global and Historical Perspective,* ed. A. Beier and Paul Ocobock. Athens: Ohio University Press.

———. 2011. "Creating Undiminished Confidence: The Free Population of Color and Identity Formation in Mauritius, 1767–1835." *Slavery & Abolition* 34(2): 519–533.

Alliende Edwards, María Piedad. 1993. *Historia del ferrocarril en Chile.* Santiago: Goethe-Institut.

Allman, Jean Marie. 1993. *The Quills of the Porcupine: Asante Nationalism in an Emergent Ghana.* Madison: University of Wisconsin Press.

Almeida, Paul. 2003. "Opportunity Organizations and Threat-Induced Contention: Protest Waves in Authoritarian Settings." *American Journal of Sociology* 109(2): 345–400.

Alonso, Paula. 1999. *Between Revolution and the Ballot Box: The Origins of the Argentine Radical Party in the 1890s*. Cambridge: Cambridge University Press.

Amaral, Samuel. 1998. *The Rise of Capitalism on the Pampas: The Estancias of Buenos Aires, 1785–1870*. Cambridge: Cambridge University Press.

Andersen, Jørgen, and Michael Ross. Forthcoming. "The Big Oil Change: A Closer Look at the Haber-Menaldo Analysis." *Comparative Political Studies* 47.

Apter, David. 1963. *Ghana in Transition*. Revised edition. New York: Atheneum.

Ardant, Gabriel. 1975. "Financial Policy and Economic Infrastructure of Modern States and Nations." In *The Formation of National States in Western Europe*, ed. Charles Tilly. Princeton: Princeton University Press.

Arteaga Alemparte, Domingo, Ricardo Claro, Pedro León Gallo, José Victorino Lastarria, and Manuel A. Matta. 1868. *A nuestros electores*. Santiago: Imprenta de la Libertad.

Austin, Dennis. 1964. *Politics in Ghana: 1946–1960*. London: Oxford University Press.

Austin, Gareth. 1993. "Indigenous Credit Institutions in West Africa, c. 1750–c. 1960." In *Local Suppliers of Credit in the Third World, 1750–1960*, ed. Gareth Austin and Kaoru Sugihara. New York: St. Martin's Press.

Auty, Richard. 1993. *Sustaining Development in Mineral Economies: The Resource Curse Thesis*. London: Routledge.

Awa, Eme. 1964. *Federal Government and Nigeria*. Berkeley and Los Angeles: University of California Press.

Ayee, Joseph. 1994. *An Anatomy of Public Policy Implementation: The Case of Decentralization Policies in Ghana*. Aldershot, UK: Avebury.

Baldwin, Kate, and John Huber. 2010. "Economic Versus Cultural Differences: Forms of Ethnic Diversity and Public Goods Provision." *American Political Science Review* 104(4): 644–662.

Barkan, Joel, Michael McNulty, and M. A. O. Ayeni. 1991. "'Hometown' Voluntary Associations, Local Development, and the Emergence of Civil Society in Western Nigeria." *Journal of Modern African Studies* 29(3): 457–480.

Barnett, Michael. 1992. *Confronting the Costs of War: Military Power, State, and Society in Egypt and Israel*. Princeton: Princeton University Press.

Barros Arana, Diego. 1906. *Un decenio de la historia de Chile (1841–1851)*, Tomo II. Santiago: Imprenta Universitaria.

Barros Arana, Diego, and Ramón Sotomayor Valdés. 1858. *Manifestó de la Oposición de Santiago a la República*. Santiago: Imprenta del País.

Barros Arana, Diego, Marcial González, José Victorino Lastarria, and Domingo Santa María. 1861. *Cuadro histórico de la Administración Montt, escrito según sus propios documentos*. Valparaíso, Chile: Imprenta i Librería del Mercurio.

Bates, Robert. 1981. *Markets and States in Tropical Africa: The Political Basis of Agricultural Policies*. Berkeley and Los Angeles: University of California Press.

———. 1983. *Essays on the Political Economy of Rural Africa*. Berkeley and Los Angeles: University of California Press.

———. 2008. *When Things Fell Apart: State Failure in Late-Century Africa*. Cambridge: Cambridge University Press.

———. 2010. *Prosperity and Violence: The Political Economy of Development*. 2nd edition. New York: W. W. Norton.

Bauer, Arnold. 1972. "The Hacienda El Huique in the Agrarian Structure of Nineteenth-Century Chile." *Agricultural History* 46(4): 455–470.

———. 1975. *Chilean Rural Society from the Spanish Conquest to 1930*. Cambridge: Cambridge University Press.

Bauer, P. T. 1954. *West African Trade: A Study of Competition, Oligopoly and Monopoly in a Changing Economy*. Cambridge: Cambridge University Press.

Beckman, Björn. 1976. *Organising the Farmers: Cocoa Politics and National Development in Ghana*. Uppsala, Sweden: Scandinavian Institute of African Studies.

Beer, Christopher. 1976. *The Politics of Peasant Groups in Western Nigeria*. Ibadan, Nigeria: Ibadan University Press.

Bengoa, José. 1988. *Historia social de la agricultura chilena*, Tomo I: *El poder y la subordinación. Acerca del origen rural del poder y la subordinación en Chile*. Santiago: Ediciones Sur.

———. 1990. *Historia social de la agricultura chilena*, Tomo II: *Haciendas y campesinos*. Santiago: Ediciones Sur.

Bensel, Richard. 1990. *Yankee Leviathan: The Origins of Central State Authority in America, 1859–1877*. Cambridge: Cambridge University Press.

Berend, Ivan, and G. Ranki. 1980. "Foreign Trade and the Industrialization of the European Periphery in the XIXth Century." *Journal of European Economic History* 9(3): 539–584.

Berg, E. 1971. "Structural Transformation Versus Gradualism: Recent Economic Development in Ghana and the Ivory Coast." In *Ghana and the Ivory Coast: Perspectives on Modernization*, ed. P. Foster and A. Zolberg. Chicago: University of Chicago Press.

Bergquist, Charles. 1978. *Coffee and Conflict in Colombia, 1886–1910*. Durham, NC: Duke University Press.

Berry, Sara. 2001. *Chiefs Know Their Boundaries: Essays on Property, Power, and the Past in Asante, 1896–1996*. Portsmouth, NH: Heinemann.

Beyer, Robert Carlyle. 1947. "The Colombian Coffee Industry: Origins and Major Trends, 1740–1940." Unpublished PhD dissertation, University of Minnesota.

———. 1948. "Transportation and the Coffee Industry in Colombia." *Inter-American Economic Affairs* 2(3): 17–30.

Blattman, Christopher, Jason Hwang, and Jeffrey G. Williamson. 2007. "Winners and Losers in the Commodity Lottery: The Impact of Terms of Trade Growth and Volatility in the Periphery 1870–1939." *Journal of Development Economics* 82(1): 156–179.

Boix, Carles. 2003. *Democracy and Redistribution*. Cambridge: Cambridge University Press.

Bolaji, Labanji. 1970. *Anatomy of Corruption in Nigeria*. Ibadan, Nigeria: Daystar Press.

Bonat, Z. A. 1989. "Agriculture." In *Nigeria Since Independence: The First Twenty-five Years, Volume II: The Economy*, ed. Femi Kayode and Yusufu Bala Usman. Ibadan, Nigeria: Heinemann Educational Books Limited.

Boone, Catherine. 2003. *Political Topographies of the African State: Territorial Authority and Institutional Choice*. Cambridge: Cambridge University Press.

Borde, Jean, and Mario Góngora. 1956. *Evolución de la propiedad rural en el Valle del Puangue*, Tomo I: *Texto*. Santiago: Editorial Universitaria.

Bowman, John, and Michael Wallerstein. 1982. "The Fall of Balmaceda and Public Finance in Chile: New Data for an Old Debate." *Journal of Interamerican Studies and World Affairs* 24(4): 421–460.

Bratton, Michael. 1980. "The Public Service in Zimbabwe." *Political Science Quarterly* 95(3): 441–464.

Bratton, Michael, and Eric Chang. 2006. "State Building and Democratization in Sub-Saharan Africa: Forwards, Backwards, or Together?" *Comparative Political Studies* 39(9): 1059–1083.

Bräutigam, Deborah. 2008. "Contingent Capacity: Export Taxation and State-Building in Mauritius." In *Taxation and State-Building in Developing Countries: Capacity and Consent*, ed. Deborah Bräutigam, Odd-Helge Fjeldstad, and Mick Moore. Cambridge: Cambridge University Press.

Bravo Lira, Bernardino. 1990. "Un gobernante ilustrado en el Chile del siglo XIX: Manuel Montt, Ministro y Presidente de la República 1840–1861." *Boletín de la Academia Chilena de la Historia* 101: 99–201.

Brown, Jonathan. 1979. *A Socioeconomic History of Argentina, 1776–1860*. Cambridge: Cambridge University Press.

Brownlee, Jason. 2007. *Authoritarianism in an Age of Democratization*. Cambridge: Cambridge University Press.

Bueno de Mesquita, Bruce, Alastair Smith, Randolph Siverson, and James Morrow. 2003. *The Logia of Political Survival*. Cambridge, MA: MIT Press.

Burgin, Miron. 1946. *The Economic Aspects of Argentine Federalism, 1820–1852*. Cambridge, MA: Harvard University Press.

Burr, Robert. 1965. *By Reason or Force: Chile and the Balancing of Power in South America, 1830–1905*. Berkeley and Los Angeles: University of California Press.

Bushnell, David. 1993. *The Making of Modern Colombia: A Nation in Spite of Itself*. Berkeley and Los Angeles: University of California Press.

Bustamante Roldán, Darío. 1974. "Efectos económicos del papel moneda durante la Regeneración." *Cuadernos colombianos* 4(3): 559–660.

Butkiewicz, James, and Halit Yanikkaya. 2010. "Minerals, Institutions, Openness, and Growth: An Empirical Analysis." *Land Economics* 86(2): 313–328.

Cáceres Muñoz, Juan. 2005. *Poder rural y estructura social, Colchagua, 1760–1860: La construcción del Estado y la ciudadanía desde la región*. Valparaíso, Chile: Ediciones Universitarias de Valparaíso.

Campos Harriet, Fernando. 1960. *Desarrollo educacional 1810–1960*. Santiago: Editorial Andrés Bello.

Camus, Ambrosio. 1856. *Memoria que el Gobernador de Putaendo presentó a la ilustre municipalidad de 1856*. Santiago: Imprenta Chilena.

Cardoso, Fernando Henrique, and Enzo Faletto. 1979. *Dependency and Development in Latin America*. Berkeley and Los Angeles: University of California Press.

Carruthers, Bruce. 1996. *City of Capital: Politics and Markets in the English Financial Revolution*. Princeton: Princeton University Press.

Carter, Marina. 1995. *Servants, Sirdars and Settlers: Indians in Mauritius, 1834–1874*. Oxford: Oxford University Press.

Cashin, Paul, John McDermott, and Alasdair Scott. 2002. "Booms and Slumps in World Commodity Prices." *Journal of Development Economics* 69(1): 277–296.

Centeno, Miguel. 2002. *Blood and Debt: War and the Nation-State in Latin America*. University Park: Pennsylvania State University Press.

Cerda-Hegerl, Patricia. 1997. *Fronteras del Sur: La Región del Bío Bío y la Araucanía chilena, 1604–1883*. Temuco, Chile: Ediciones Universidad de la Frontera.

Chambers, Sarah. 2013. "Citizens before the Law: The Role of Courts in Post-Independence State Building in Spanish America." In *State and Nation Making in Latin America and Spain: Republics of the Possible*, ed. Miguel Centeno and Agustin Ferraro. Cambridge: Cambridge University Press.

Chaudhry, Kiren Aziz. 1993. "The Myths of the Market and the Common History of Late Developers." *Politics and Society* 21(3): 245–274.

Chiaramonte, José Carlos. 1971. *Nacionalismo y liberalismo: Económicos en Argentina, 1860–1880*. Buenos Aires: Solar/Hachette.

———. 1986. "Legalidad constitucional o caudillismo: el problema del orden social en el surgimiento de los estados autonomos del litoral argentino en la primera mitad del siglo XIX." *Desarrollo Económico* 26(102): 175–196.

Coleman, James. 1958. *Nigeria: Background to Nationalism*. Berkeley and Los Angeles: University of California Press.

Collier, Paul, and Anke Hoeffler. 2002. "Greed and Grievance in Civil War." Working Paper CSAE WPS/2002–2001. Oxford: Centre for the Study of African Economies.

Collier, Ruth Berins, and David Collier. 1991. *Shaping the Political Arena: Critical Junctures, the Labor Movement, and the Regime Dynamic in Latin America*. Princeton: Princeton University Press.

Collier, Simon. 2003. *Chile: The Making of a Republic, 1830–1865*. Cambridge: Cambridge University Press.

Collier, Simon, and William Sater. 1996. *A History of Chile, 1808–1994*. Cambridge: Cambridge University Press.

Colony of Mauritius. 1898. *Blue Book for the Colony of Mauritius 1897*. Port Louis, Mauritius: Central Printing Establishment.

Coppedge, Michael. 1998. "The Evolution of Latin American Party Systems." In *Politics, Society, and Democracy: Latin America*, ed. Scott Mainwaring and Arturo Valenzuela. Boulder, CO: Westview Press.

Cordero, Fernando. 1992. "Chile, siglo XIX: de la milicia a la guardia cívica." *Ibero-Americana: Nordic Journal of Latin American Studies* 22(1): 83–97.

Cornes, Richard, and Todd Sandler. 1996. *The Theory of Externalities, Public Goods, and Club Goods*. 2nd edition. New York: Cambridge University Press.

Cortés Conde, Roberto 1989. *Dinero, deuda y crisis: evolución fiscal y monetaria en la Argentina, 1862–1890*. Buenos Aires : Editorial Sudamericana

Cortés Conde, Roberto. 1999. "The Origins of Banking in Argentina." In *The State, the Financial System, and Economic Modernization*, ed. Richard Sylla, Richard Tilly, and Gabriel Tortella. Cambridge: Cambridge University Press.

Couso, Javier. 2005. "Judicial Independence in Latin America: The Lessons of History in the Search for an Always Elusive Ideal." In *Institutions and Public Law: Comparative Approaches*, ed. Tom Ginsburg and Robert Kagan. New York: Peter Lang.

Crook, Richard. 1986. "Decolonization, the Colonial State, and Chieftaincy in the Gold Coast." *African Affairs* 85(338): 75–105.

Crowder, Michael. 1966. *A Short History of Nigeria*. Revised and enlarged edition. New York: Praeger.

———. 1968. *West Africa under Colonial Rule*. Evanston, IL: Northwestern University Press.

Culver, William, and Cornel Reinhart. 1989. "Capitalist Dreams: Chile's Response to Nineteenth-Century World Copper Competition." *Comparative Studies in Society and History* 31(4): 722–744.

Daitsman, Andrew. 1995. "The People Shall Be All: Liberal Rebellion and Popular Mobilization in Chile, 1830–1860." PhD dissertation, University of Wisconsin-Madison.

Danquah, Francis. 2003. "Sustaining a West African Cocoa Economy: Agricultural Science and the Swollen Shoot Contagion in Ghana, 1936–1965." *African Economic History* 31: 43–74.

Davis, Graham. 1995. "Learning to Love the Dutch Disease: Evidence from the Mineral Economies." *World Development* 23(10): 1765–1779.

———. 2011. "The Resource Drag." *International Economics and Economic Policy* 8(2): 155–176.

Deas, Malcolm. 1982. "The Fiscal Problems of Nineteenth-Century Colombia." *Journal of Latin American Studies* 14(2): 287–328.

———. 2008. "'Weapons of the Weak?' Colombia and Foreign Powers in the Nineteenth Century." *Bulletin of Latin American Research* 27(s1): 173–186.

Deaton, Angus. 1999. "Commodity Prices and Growth in Africa." *Journal of Economic Perspectives* 13(3): 23–40.

Dehn, Jan. 2000. "Commodity Price Uncertainty in Developing Countries." Working paper *WPS/2000-12*. Centre for the Study of African Economies, University of Oxford.

de Joux, C. M. 1864. *Mauritius Almanac and Civil Service Register for 1864*. London: Harrison and Sons.

de la Fuente, Ariel. 2000. *Children of Facundo: Caudillo and Gaucho Insurgency during the Argentine State-Formation Process (La Rioja, 1853–1870)*. Durham, NC: Duke University Press.

Delpar, Helen. 1981. *Red Against Blue: The Liberal Party in Colombian Politics, 1863–1899*. Tuscaloosa: University of Alabama Press.

Diamond, Larry. 1988. *Class, Ethnicity and Democracy in Nigeria: The Failure of the First Republic*. Syracuse, NY: Syracuse University Press.

Díaz, Benito. 1959. *Juzgados de paz de campaña de la Provincia de Buenos Aires (1821–1854)*. La Plata, Argentina: Universidad Nacional de la Plata.

Dirección de Contabilidad (Chile). 1914. *Resumen de la hacienda pública de Chile, desde 1833 hasta 1914*. London: Spottiswoode.

Doner, Richard, Bryan Ritchie, and Dan Slater. 2005. "Systemic Vulnerability and the Origins of Developmental States: Northeast and Southeast Asia in Comparative Perspective." *International Organization* 59(2): 327–361.

dos Santos, Theotonio. 1970. "The Structure of Dependence." *American Economic Review* 60(2): 231–236.

d'Unienville, Raymond. 1975–1989. *Histoire politique de l'Isle de France*. 3 vols. Port Louis, Mauritius: L. Carl Achille.

Dunn, John, and A. F. Robertson. 1973. *Dependence and Opportunity: Political Change in Ahafo*. Cambridge: Cambridge University Press.

Dunning, Thad. 2008. *Crude Democracy: Natural Resource Wealth and Political Regimes*. Cambridge: Cambridge University Press.

Easterly, William. 2003. "Can Foreign Aid Buy Growth?" *Journal of Economic Perspectives* 17(3): 23–48.

Edwards, Alberto. 1932. *El gobierno de don Manuel Montt, 1851–1861*. Santiago: Editorial Nascimento.

Ekundare, R. Olufemi. 1973. *An Economic History of Nigeria 1860–1960*. New York: Africana Publishing.

Encina, Francisco Antonio. 1949a. *Historia de Chile: Desde la prehistoria de 1891*, Tomo XII. Santiago: Editorial Nascimento.

———. 1949b. *Historia de Chile: desde la prehistoria de 1891*, Tomo XIII. Santiago: Editorial Nascimento.

———. 1950. *Historia de Chile: desde la prehistoria de 1891*, Tomo XIV. Santiago: Editorial Nascimento.

———. 1951. *Historia de Chile: desde la prehistoria de 1891*, Tomo XVIII. Santiago: Editorial Nascimento.

Estado Mayor General del Ejército (Chile). 1980. *Historia del ejército de Chile*, Tomo IV: *Consolidación del profesionalismo militar fin de la guerra de Arauco, 1840–1883*. Santiago: Estado Mayor General del Ejército.

Evans, Peter. 1995. *Embedded Autonomy: States and Industrial Transformation*. Princeton: Princeton University Press.

Ezera, Kalu. 1960. *Constitutional Developments in Nigeria; An Analytical Study of Nigeria's Constitution-Making Developments and the Historical and Political Factors that Affected Constitutional Change*. Cambridge: Cambridge University Press.

Falola, Toyin. 2004. *Economic Reforms and Modernization in Nigeria, 1945–1965*. Kent, OH: Kent State University Press.

Fearon, James. 2003. "Ethnic and Cultural Diversity by Country." *Journal of Economic Growth* 8: 195–222.

———. 2005. "Primary Commodity Exports and Civil War." *Journal of Conflict Resolution* 49(4): 483–507.

Fearon, James, and David Laitin. 2003. "Ethnicity, Insurgency, and Civil War." *American Political Science Review* 97(1): 75–90.

Ferguson, Niall, and Moritz Schularick. 2006. "The Empire Effect: The Determinants of Country Risk in the First Age of Globalization, 1880–1913." *Journal of Economic History* 66(2): 283–312.

Ferns, H. S. 1960. *Britain and Argentina in the Nineteenth Century*. Oxford: Oxford University Press.

Ferrando Keun, Ricardo. 1986. *Y así nació la frontera... conquista, guerra, ocupación, pacificación. 1550–1900*. Santiago: Editorial Antartica.

Fetter, Frank. 1931. *Monetary Inflation in Chile*. Princeton: Princeton University Press.

Fieldhouse, D.K. 1994. *Merchant Capital and Economic the Colonization: The United Africa Company, 1929–1987*. Oxford: Clarendon Press.

Figueroa Escuti, Hernán. 1953. "Intendentes y gobernadores, organs de gobierno interior." (Memoria de Prueba) In *Memorias de Licenciados, Derecho Constitucional, tomo I* (Facultad de Ciencias Juridicas y Sociales, Universidad de Chile). Santiago: Editorial Juridica de Chile, pp. -496.

Firmin-Sellers, Kathryn. 1996. *The Transformation of Property Rights in the Gold Coast: An Empirical Analysis Applying Rational Choice Theory*. Cambridge: Cambridge University Press.

Flandreau, Marc, Juan Flores, Norbert Gaillard, and Sebastián Nieto-Parra. 2010. "The End of Gatekeeping: Underwriters and the Quality of Sovereign Bond Markets, 1815–2007." In *NBER International Seminar on Macroeconomics 2009*, ed. Lucrezia Reichlin and Kenneth West. Chicago: University of Chicago Press.

Forrest, Tom. 1993. *Politics and Economic Development in Nigeria*. Boulder, CO: Westview Press.

Francisco Gana, José. 1851. *Memoria que el Intendente de la Provincia de Atacama presenta al señor Ministro del Interior, sobre los trabajos hechos en el año de 1850 y estado actual de la industria minería*. Copiapó, Chile: Imprenta del Copiapino.

Frankel, Jeffrey. 2010. "Mauritius: African Success Story." *National Bureau of Economic Research, Working Paper 16569*. Cambridge, MA: National Bureau of Economic Research.

Frankel, Jeffrey. 2012. "Natural Resource Curse: A Survey of the Literature." In *Commodity Price Volatility and Inclusive Growth in Low-Income Countries*, ed. Rabah Arezki, Catherine Pattillo, Marc Quintyn, and Min Zhu. Washington, DC: International Monetary Fund.

Frankel, Jeffrey, Carlos Végh, and Guillermo Vuletin. 2013. "On Graduation from Fiscal Procyclicality." *Journal of Development Economics* 100: 32–47.

Friedman, Thomas. 2006. "The First Law of Petropolitics." *Foreign Policy* 154: 28–36.

Friman, H. Richard. 1993. "Side-Payments Versus Security Cards: Domestic Bargaining Tactics in International Economic Negotiations." *International Organization* 47(3): 387–410.

Galletti, R., K. D. S. Baldwin, and I. O. Dina. 1972. *Nigerian Cocoa Farmers: An Economic Survey of Yourba Cocoa Farming Families*. Westport, CT: Greenwood Press.

Gallo, Carmenza. 1991. *Taxes and State Power: Political Instability in Bolivia, 1900–1950*. Philadelphia, PA: Temple University Press.

Gandhi, Jennifer. 2008. *Political Institutions under Dictatorship*. New York: Cambridge University Press.

Garreaud, Jacqueline Spencer. 1981. "A Dependent Country: Chile, 1817–1861." PhD dissertation, University of California, San Diego.

Gasió, Guillermo, and San Román, María. 1977. *La conquista del progreso 1874–1880*. Buenos Aires: Ediciones La Bastilla.

Gazmuri, Cristián. 1992. *El "48" chileno: Igualitarios, reformistas, radicales, masones, y bomberos*. Santiago: Editorial Universitaria.

Geddes, Barbara. 1990. "Building 'State' Autonomy in Brazil, 1930–1964." *Comparative Politics* 22(2): 217–235.

George, Alexander, and Andrew Bennett. 2005. *Case Studies and Theory Development in the Social Sciences*. Cambridge, MA: MIT Press.

Gerring, John, Daniel Ziblatt, Johan Van Gorp, and Julián Arévalo. 2011. "An Institutional Theory of Direct and Indirect Rule." *World Politics* 63(3): 377–433.

Gerschenkron, Alexander. 1962. *Economic Backwardness in Historical Perspective*. Cambridge, MA: Belknap Press.

Gibson, Edward, and Tulia Falleti. 2004. "Unity by the Stick: Regional Conflict and the Origins of Argentine Federalism." In *Federalism and Democracy in Latin America*, ed. Edward Gibson. Baltimore, MD: Johns Hopkins University Press.

Gibson, Herbert. 1893. *The History and Present State of the Sheep-Breeding Industry in the Argentine Republic*. Buenos Aires: Ravenscroft and Mills.

Goldstone, Jack, and Charles Tilly. 2001. "Threat (and Opportunity): Popular Action and State Response in the Dynamics of Contentious Action." In *Silence and Voice in the Study of Contentious Politics*, ed. Ronald Amizade et al. Cambridge: Cambridge University Press.

Góngora, Mario. 1974. *Origen de los inquilinos de chile central*. Santiago: Instituto de Capacitación e Investigación en Reforma Agraria.

———. 1986. *Ensayo histórico sobre la noción de estado en Chile en los siglos XIX y XX*. Santiago: Editorial Universitaria.

Gould, Peter. 1960. *The Development of the Transportation Pattern in Ghana*. Evanston, IL: Department of Geography, Northwestern University.

Gourevitch, Peter. 1986. *Politics in Hard Times: Comparative Responses to International Economic Crises*. Ithaca, NY: Cornell University Press.

Green, William. 1974. "James Stephen and British West India Policy, 1834–1847." *Caribbean* Studies 13(4): 33–56.

Grindle, Merilee. 1996. *Challenging the State: Crisis and Innovation in Latin America and Africa*. Cambridge, UK: Cambridge University Press.

Gustavo Silva, Jorge. 1931. *La nueva era de las municipalidades de Chile: Recopilación histórica de la vida comunal del país, que abarca desde los primeros cabildos, en la época colonial, hasta nuestros días, y que se completa con una información gráfica y monográfica de las municipalidades de la República*. Santiago: Boyle y Pellegrini Ltda.

Gylfason, Thorvaldur. 2001. "Natural Resources, Education, and Economic Development." *European Economic Review* 45(4): 847–859.

Haber, Stephen, and Victor Mendalo. 2011. "Do Natural Resources Fuel Authoritarianism? A Reappraisal of the Resource Curse." *American Political Science Review* 105(1): 1–26.

Habyarimana, James, Macartan Humphreys, Daniel Posner, and Jeremy Weinstein. 2007. "Why Does Ethnic Diversity Undermine Public Goods Provision?" *American Political Science Review* 101(4): 709–725.

Haggard, Stephan, David Kang, and Chung-In Moon. 1997. "Japanese Colonialism and Korean Development: A Critique." *World Development* 25(6): 867–881.

Hagopian, Frances. 1996. *Traditional Politics and Regime Change in Brazil*. Cambridge: Cambridge University Press.

Hailey, Lord. 1951. *Native Administration in the British African Territories*, Part III. *West Africa: Nigeria, Gold Coast, Sierra Leone, Gambia*. London: His Majesty's Stationery Office.

Hall, Peter. 2003. "Aligning Ontology and Methodology in Comparative Politics." In *Comparative Historical Analysis in the Social Sciences*, ed. James Mahoney and Dietrich Rueschemeyer. Cambridge: Cambridge University Press.

Halperín Donghi, Tulio. 1975. *Politics, Economics, and Society in Argentina in the Revolutionary Period*. Cambridge: Cambridge University Press.

Hawkins, E. K. 1958. *Road Transport in Nigeria: A Study of African Enterprise*. London: Oxford University Press.

Hay, Alan. 1970. "Crop Marketing Boards and Transport Policy in Nigeria 1950–64." *Journal of Transport Economics and Policy* 4(2): 171–180.

Hechter, Michael, and William Brustein. 1980. "Regional Modes of Production and Patters of State Formation in Western Europe." *American Journal of Sociology* 85(5): 1061–1094.

Hedström, Peter, and Richard Swedberg. 1998. "Social Mechanisms: An Introductory Essay." In *Social Mechanisms: An Analytical Approach to Social Theory*, ed. Peter Hedström and Richard Swedberg. Cambridge: Cambridge University Press.

Heise González, Julio. 1974. *Historia de Chile: el período parlamentario 1861–1925*, Tomo I: *fundamentos histórico-culturales del parlamentarismo chileno*. Santiago: Editorial Andres Bello.

Helleiner, Gerald. 1964a. "The Eastern Nigeria Development Corporation: A Study in Sources and Uses of Public Development Funds, 1949–1962." *Nigerian Journal of Economic and Social Studies* 6(1): 98–123.

———. 1964b. "A Wide-Ranging Development Institution: Nigeria's Northern Region Development Corporation, 1949–62." *Nigerian Journal of Economic and Social Studies* 6(2): 239–257.

Helleiner, Gerald. 1966. *Peasant Agriculture, Government, and Economic Growth in Nigeria*. Homewood, IL: Richard Irwin.

Herb, Michael. 2005. "No Representation without Taxation? Rents, Development, and Democracy." *Comparative Politics* 37(3): 297–316.

Herbst, Jeffrey. 1990a. *State Politics in Zimbabwe*. Berkeley and Los Angeles: University of California Press.

———. 1990b. "The Structural Adjustment of Politics in Africa." *World Development* 18(7): 949–958.

———. 2000. *States and Power in Africa: Comparative Lessons in Authority and Control*. Princeton: Princeton University Press.

Hilbink, Lisa. 2007. *Judges beyond Politics in Democracy and Dictatorship: Lessons from Chile*. Cambridge: Cambridge University Press.

Hill, Polly. 1956. *The Gold Coast Cocoa Farmer: A Preliminary Survey*. London: Oxford University Press.

Hinds, Allister. 1997. "Government Policy and the Nigerian Palm Oil Export Industry, 1939–49." *Journal of African History* 38(3): 459–478.

Hirschman, Albert. 1977. "A Generalized Linkage Approach to Development, with Special Reference to Staples." *Economic Development and Cultural Change* 25(Supplement): 67–98.

Hora, Roy. 2001. *The Landowners of the Argentine Pampas: A Social and Political History 1860–1945*. Oxford: Clarendon Press.

Horna, Hernán. 1973. "Francisco Javier Cisneros: A Pioneer in Transportation and Economic Development in Latin America, 1857–1898." *The Americas* 30(1): 54–82.

———. 1992. *Transport Modernization and Entrepreneurship in Nineteenth Century Colombia*. Uppsala, Sweden: Uppsala universitet.

Horowitz, Donald. 1985. *Ethnic Groups in Conflict*. Berkeley and Los Angeles: University of California Press.

Huber, Evelyne. 1995. "Assessments of State Strength." In *Latin America in Comparative Perspective: New Approaches to Methods and Analysis*, ed. Peter Smith. Boulder, CO: Westview Press.

Humphreys, Macartan, and Martin Sandbu. 2007. "The Political Economy of Natural Resource Funds." In *Escaping the Resource Curse*, ed. Macartan Humphreys, Jeffrey Sachs, and Joseph Stiglitz. New York: Columbia University Press.

Humphreys, Macartan, Jeffrey Sachs, and Joseph Stiglitz, eds. 2007. *Escaping the Resource Curse*. New York: Columbia University Press.

Humud Tleel, Carlos. 1969. *El sector público chileno entre 1830 y 1930*. Santiago: Universidad de Chile.

International Bank for Reconstruction and Development. 1955. *The Economic Development of Nigeria*. Baltimore, MD: Johns Hopkins University Press.

———. 1957. *Economic Report on Ghana*. Report No. EA-72b. Washington, DC: IBRD.

———. 1964. *Appraisal of a Road Project, Northern Nigeria*. Report No. TO-437a. Washington, DC: IBRD.

———. 1965. *Economic Growth of Nigeria: Problems and Prospects*, Volume V: *Transport*. Report No. AF-34c. Washington, DC: IBRD.

———. 1967. *Stabilization and Development in Ghana*. Report No. AF-57a. Washington, DC: IBRD.

———. 1969. *The Current Economic Position and Prospects of Ghana*, Volume II: *Status and Prospects of Cocoa*. Report No. AW6(2). Washington, DC: IBRD.

———. 1970. *The Current Economic Position and Prospects of Ghana*, Volume VII: *Transportation*. Report No. AW18(7). Washington, DC: IBRD.

International Bank for Reconstruction and Development. 1971. *The Current Economic Position and Prospects of Nigeria*. Report No. AW-22a. Washington, DC: IBRD.

International Crisis Group. 2009. "Nigeria: Seizing the Moment in the Niger Delta." Africa Briefing No. 60. Brussels: International Crisis Group.

International Road Federation. 1978. *World Road Statistics, 1973–1977*. Washington, DC: IRF.

Isham, Jonathan et al. 2005. "The Varieties of Resource Experience: Natural Resource Export Structures and the Political Economy of Economic Growth." *World Bank Economic Review* 19(2): 141–174.

Izquierdo, Vincente. 1865. *Memoria que el Intendente de la Provincia de Santiago pasa al señor Ministro de Interior*. Santiago: Imprenta Nacional.

Jackson, Robert and Carl Rosberg. 1982. "Why Africa's Weak States Persist: The Empirical and the Juridical in Statehood." *World Politics* 35(1): 1–24.

Jaramillo Uribe, Jaime. 1964. *El pensamiento colombiano en el siglo XIX*. Bogotá: Editorial Temis.

Jeremie, John. 1835. *Recent Events at Mauritius*. London: Hatchard and Son.

Jessop, Arthur. 1964. *A History of the Mauritius Government Railways 1864–1964*. Port Louis, Mauritius: Government Printer.

Jiménez, Michael. 1985. "The Limits of Export Capitalism, Economic Structure, Class, and Politics in a Colombian Coffee Municipality, 1900–1930." PhD dissertation, Harvard University.

Johnson, John. 1948. *Pioneer Telegraphy in Chile, 1852–1876*. University Series in History, Economics, and Political Science, Vol. VI, no. 1. Stanford, CA: Stanford University Press.

Jones, Charles. 1977. "Commercial Banks and Mortgage Companies." In *British Imperialism, 1840–1930*, ed. D. C. M. Platt. Oxford: Clarendon Press.

Jones Luong, Pauline, and Erika Weinthal. 2010. *Oil Is Not a Curse: Ownership Structure and Institutions in Soviet Successor States*. New York: Cambridge University Press.

Joseph, Richard. 1987. *Democracy and Prebendal Politics in Nigeria: The Rise and Fall of the Second Republic*. Cambridge: Cambridge University Press.

Joslin, David. 1963. *A Century of Banking in Latin America*. London: Oxford University Press.

Kacowicz, Arie. 1998. *Zones of Peace in the Third World: South America and West Africa in Comparative Perspective*. Albany: State University of New York Press.

Karl, Terry Lynn. 1997. *The Paradox of Plenty: Oil Booms and Petro-States*. Berkeley and Los Angeles: University of California Press.

———. 2007. "Ensuring Fairness: The Case for a Transparent Fiscal Social Contract." In *Escaping the Resource Curse*, ed. Macartan Humphreys, Jeffrey Sachs, and Joseph Stiglitz. New York: Columbia University Press.

Kaufmann, Daniel, Aart Kraay, and Massimo Mastruzzi. 2010. "The Worldwide Governance Indicators: Methodology and Analytical Issues." Working Paper No. 5430, World Bank Policy Research, Washington, DC.

Kay, G. B. 1972. *The Political Economy of Colonialism in Ghana: A Collection of Documents and Statistics 1900–1960*. Cambridge: Cambridge University Press.

Kilby, Peter. 1967. "The Nigerian Palm Oil Industry." *Food Research Institute Studies* 7(2): 177–201.

Killick, Tony. 1978. *Development Economics in Action: A Study of Economic Policies in Ghana*. New York: St. Martin's Press.

Killingray, David. 1986. "The Maintenance of Law and Order in British Colonial Africa." *African Affairs* 85(340): 411–437.

Kirk-Greene, A. H. M. 1980. "The Thin White Line: The Size of the British Colonial Service in Africa." *African Affairs* 79(314): 25–44.

Knight, Jack. 1992. *Institutions and Social Conflict*. Cambridge: Cambridge University Press.

Kohli, Atul. 1994. "Where Do High Growth Political Economies Come From? The Japanese Lineage of Korea's 'Developmental State.'" *World Development* 22(9): 1269–1293.

———. 2004. *State-Directed Development: Political Power and Industrialization in the Global Periphery*. Cambridge: Cambridge University Press.

Kramon, Eric, and Daniel Posner. 2013. "Who Benefits from Distributive Politics? How the Outcome One Studies Affects the Answer One Gets." *Perspectives on Politics* 11(2): 461–474.

Kurtz, Marcus. 2009. "The Social Foundations of Institutional Order: Reconsidering War and the 'Resource Curse' in Third World State Building." *Politics & Society* 37(4): 479–520.

Kyshe, John, ed. 1870. *The Mauritius Almanac and Colonial Register for 1870*. London: E. Dupuy and P. Dubois.

Lake, David. 2009. "Open Economy Politics: A Critical Review." *Review of International Organizations* 4(3): 219–244.

Lake, David, and Matthew Baum. 2001. "The Invisible Hand of Democracy: Political Control and the Provision of Public Services." *Comparative Political Studies* 34(6): 587–621.

Lamusse, Roland. 1964a."The Economic Development of the Mauritius Sugar Industry. I. Development in Field and Factory." *Revue agricole et sucrière de l'île Maurice* 43: 22–38.

———. 1964b. "The Economic Development of the Mauruitus Sugar Industry. II. Labour Problems." *Revue agricole et sucrière de l'île Maurice* 43: 113–127.

———. 1964c. "The Economic Development of the Mauritius Sugar Industry. III. The Sources of Capital and System of Crop Finance." *Revue agricole et sucrière de l'île Maurice* 43: 354–372.

———. 1965. "The Economic Development of the Mauritius Sugar Industry. IV. Mauritius Sugar in World Trade." *Revue agricole et sucrière de l'île Maurice* 44: 11–36.

Lange, Matthew. 2003. "Embedding the Colonial State: A Comparative-Historical Analysis of State Building and Broad-Based Development in Mauritius." *Social Science History* 27(3): 397–423.

———. 2009. *Lineages of Despotism and Development: British Colonialism and State Power*. Chicago: University of Chicago Press.

Lange, Matthew, James Mahoney, and Matthias vom Hau. 2006. "Colonialism and Development: A Comparative Analysis of Spanish and British Colonies." *Amercian Journal of Sociology* 111(5): 1412–1462.

Latham, Wilfrid. 1868. *The States of the River Plate*. London: Longmans, Green, and Co.

Leite, Carlos, and Jens Weidmann. 1999. "Does Mother Nature Corrupt? Natural Resources, Corruption, and Economic Growth." IMF Working Paper WP/99/85. Washington, DC: IMF.

Letelier, Valentín. 1907. *Apuntaciones de Derecho Administrativo*. Santiago: Imprenta i Encuadernación Chile.

Levi, Margaret. 1988. *Of Rule and Revenue*. Berkeley and Los Angeles: University of California Press.

Levitsky, Steven and Lucan Way. 2010. *Competitive Authoritarianism: Hybrid Regimes after the Cold War*. Cambridge: Cambridge University Press.

Lewis, Colin. 1983. *British Railways in Argentina 1857–1914: A Case Study of Foreign Investment*. London: Athlone.

Lewis, Peter. 2007. *Growing Apart: Oil, Politics, and Economic Change in Indonesia and Nigeria*. Ann Arbor: University of Michigan Press.

Lieberman, Evan. 2009. *Boundaries of Contagion: How Ethnic Politics Have Shaped Government Responses to AIDS*. Princeton: Princeton University Press.

Lieberman, Evan, and Gwyneth McClendon. 2013. "The Ethnicity–Policy Preference Link in Sub-Saharan Africa." *Comparative Political Studies* 46(5): 574–602.

López-Alves, Fernando. 2000. *State Formation and Democracy in Latin America, 1810–1900*. Durham, NC: Duke University Press.

———. 2002. "State Reform and Welfare in Uruguay, 1890–1930." In *Studies in the Formation of the Nation State in Latin America*, ed. James Dunkerley. London: Institute of Latin American Studies.

Loveman, Brian. 2001. *Chile: The Legacy of Hispanic Capitalism*. 3rd edition. New York: Oxford University Press.

Luckham, Robin. 1971. *The Nigerian Military: A Sociological Analysis of Authority and Revolt, 1960–67*. Cambridge: Cambridge University Press.

Lynch, John. 1981. *Argentine Dictator: Juan Manuel de Rosas, 1829–1852*. Oxford: Oxford University Press.

———. 1992a. *Caudillos in Spanish America, 1800–1850*. New York: Oxford University Press.

———. 1992b. "The Institutional Framework of Colonial Spanish America." *Journal of Latin American Studies* 24: 69–81.

———. 1993. "From Independence to National Organization." In *Argentina since Independence*, ed. Leslie Bethell. Cambridge: Cambridge University Press.

———. 1998. *Massacre in the Pampas, 1872: Britain and Argentina in the Age of Migration*. Norman: University of Oklahoma Press.

Lynn, Martin. 2006. "The Nigerian Self-Government Crisis of 1953 and the Colonial Office." *Journal of Imperial and Commonwealth History* 34(2): 245–261.

MacGregor, John. 1850. *Commercial Statistics*, Vol. V. London: Whittaker.

Mackintosh, John. 1966. *Nigerian Government and Politics: Prelude to the Revolution*. Evanston, IL: Northwestern University Press.

Madrid O., Cesar. 1911. *Municipalidades: Estudio comparativo de algunas disposiciones de las leyes de 8 de Noviembre de 1854, 12 de Septiembre de 1887 y 22 de Diciembre de 1891*. Santiago: Compañía Editorial del Pacífico.

Mahatma Gandhi Institute. 1982. *The Development of Local Government in Mauritius*. Moka, Mauritius: Mahatma Gandhi Institute Press.

Mahoney, James. 2010. *Colonialism and Postcolonial Development: Spanish America in Comparative Perspective*. New York: Cambridge University Press.

———. 2012. "The Logic of Process Tracing Tests in the Social Sciences." *Sociological Methods & Research* 41(4): 570–597.

Mahoney, James and Dietrich Rueschemeyer, eds. 2003. *Comparative Historical Analysis in the Social Sciences*. Cambridge: Cambridge University Press.

Mahoney, James, and Kathleen Thelen. 2010. "A Theory of Gradual Institutional Change." In *Explaining Institutional Change: Ambiguity, Agency, and Power*, ed. James Mahoney and Kathleen Thelen. Cambridge: Cambridge University Press.

Maigrot, René. 1953. "Le crédit agricole." In *The Mauritius Chamber of Agriculture, 1853–1953*. Port Louis, Mauritius: General Printing and Stationery Company.

Mamdani, Mahmood. 1996. *Citizen and Subject: Contemporary Africa and the Legacy of Late Colonialism*. Princeton: Princeton University Press.

Mann, Michael. 1984. "The Autonomous Power of the State: Its Origins, Mechanisms and Results." *Archives Européeanes de Sociologie* 25: 185–213.

———. 1986. *The Sources of Social Power*, Volume I: *A History of Power from the Beginning to A.D. 1760*. Cambridge: Cambridge University Press.

———. 1993. *The Sources of Social Power*, Volume II: *The Rise of Classes and Nation-States, 1760–1914*. Cambridge: Cambridge University Press.

———. 2006. "The Sources of Social Power Revisited: A Response to Criticism." In *An Anatomy of Power: The Social Theory of Michael Mann*, ed. John Hall and Ralph Schroeder. Cambridge: Cambridge University Press.

Manzano, Ozmel, and Roberto Rigobón. 2007. "Resource Curse or Debt Overhang?" In *Natural Resources: Neither Curse nor Destiny*, ed. Daniel Lederman and William Maloney. Palo Alto, CA: Stanford University Press.

Marichal, Juan. 1989. *A Century of Debt Crises in Latin America: From Independence to the Great Depression, 1820–1930*. Princeton: Princeton University Press.

Marín Vicuña, Santiago. 1916. *Los ferrocarriles de Chile*. 4th edition. Santiago: Impreta Cervantes.

Martin, Robert. 1839. *Statistics of the Colonies of the British Empire in the West Indies, South America, North America, Asia, Austral-Asia, Africa, and Europe*. London: Wm H. Allen and Co.

Martínez Delgado, Luis. 1958. *Historia de un cambio de gobierno: Estudio crítico-historico de la caída del gobierno del doctor Manuel Antonio Sanclemente*. Bogotá: Editorial Santafé.

———. 1970a. *República de Colombia*, Tomo I: *(1885–1895)*. Bogotá: Ediciones Lerner.

———. 1970b. *República de Colombia*, Tomo II: *(1896–1910)*. Bogotá: Ediciones Lerner.

Mauro, Paolo, Nathan Sussman, and Yishay Yafeh. 2006. *Emerging Markets and Financial Globalization*. Oxford: Oxford University Press.

Mayo, John. 1987. *British Merchants and Chilean Development, 1851–1886*. Boulder, CO: Westview Press.

———. 2001. "The Development of British Interests in Chile's Norte Chico in the Early Nineteenth Century." *The Americas* 57(3): 363–394.

Mazzuca, Sebastián, and James Robinson. 2009. "Political Conflict and Power Sharing in the Origins of Modern Colombia." *Hispanic American Historical Review* 89(2): 286–321.

McBride, George. 1936. *Chile: Land and Society*. New York: American Geographical Society.

McGreevey, William. 1971. *An Economic History of Colombia, 1845–1930*. New York: Cambridge University Press.

McLynn, Fred. 1984. "Consequences for Argentina of the War of Triple Alliance 1865–1870." *The Americas* 41(1): 81–98.

Mehlum, Halvor, Karl Moene, and Ragnar Torvik. 2006. "Institutions and the Resource Curse." *The Economic Journal* 116(508): 1–20.

Melo Flórez, Jairo Antonio. 2012. "Organización de la administración de justicia penal en Santander de 1886 a 1930." M. A. thesis, Universidad Industrial de Santander, Bucaramanga, Colombia.

Meisenhelder, Thomas. 1997. "The Developmental State in Mauritius." *Journal of Modern African Studies* 35(2): 279–297.

Merquior, José. 1986. "Patterns of State-Building in Brazil and Argentina." In *States in History*, ed. John Hall. Oxford: Basil Blackwell.

Meyer, David, and Debra Minkoff. 2004. "Conceptualizing Political Opportunity." *Social Forces* 82(4): 1457–1492.

Migdal, Joel. 1988. *Strong Societies and Weak States: State-Society Relations and State Capabilities in the Third World*. Princeton: Princeton University Press.

Mikell, Gwendolyn. 1989. *Cocoa and Chaos in Ghana*. New York: Howard University Press.

Minogue, Martin. 1992. "Mauritius: Economic Miracle or Developmental Illusion?" *Journal of International Development* 4(6): 643–647.

Mintz, Sidney. 1985. *Sweetness and Power: The Place of Sugar in Modern History*. New York: Viking.

Mirow, Matthew. 2004. *Latin American Law: A History of Private Law and Institutions in Spanish America*. Austin: University of Texas Press.

Mishra, Amit Kumar. 2009. "Indian Indentured Labourers in Mauritius." *Studies in History* 25(2): 229–251.

Mitchell, B. R. 1998a. *International Historical Statistics: The Americas, 1750–1993*. 4th edition. New York: Stockton Press.

———. 1998b. *International Historical Statistics: Africa, Asia and Oceania, 1750–1993*. 3rd edition. New York: Stockton Press.

Molina, Gerardo. 1970. *Las ideas liberales en Colombia, 1849–1914*. Bogotá: Ediciones Tercer Mundo.

Morrison, Kevin. Forthcoming. "Nontaxation and Representation: The Fiscal Foundations of Political Stability." Cambridge: Cambridge University Press. Forthcoming.

Mou, Daniel. 1986. "State Power, Agrarian Policies and Peasant Welfare: The Politics of Agricultural Marketing and Commodity Boards in Nigeria, 1945–1985." PhD dissertation, University of Wisconsin-Madison.

Moya Figueroa, Luis. 1901. *Estudio Comparativo de la Lei de Municipalidades de 22 de Diciembre de 1891*. Santiago: Imprenta Mejía.

Napal, Dayachand. 1984. *British Mauritius 1810–1948*. London: Hart Printing.

Newland, Carlos, and Poulson, Barry. 1998. "Purely Animal: Pastoral Production and Early Argentine Economic Growth 1825–1865." *Explorations in Economic History* 35: 325–345.

Nicolson, I. F. 1969. *The Administration of Nigeria, 1900–1960: Men, Methods,* and Myths. Oxford: Clarendon Press.

Nnoli, Okwudiba. 1978. *Ethnic Politics in Nigeria*. Enugu, Nigeria: Fourth Dimension Publishers.

Nooruddin, Irfan. 2008. "The Political Economy of National Debt Burdens, 1970–2000." *International Interactions* 34(2): 156–185.

North, Douglass. 1981. *Structure and Change in Economic History*. New York: W. W. Norton.

———. 1989. "Institutions and Economic Growth: An Historical Introduction." *World Development* 17(9): 1319–1332.

———. 1990. *Institutions, Institutional Change and Economic Performance*. Cambridge: Cambridge University Press.

North, Douglass, and Robert Paul Thomas 1973. *The Rise of the Western World: A New Economic History*. Cambridge: Cambridge University Press.

Northrup, David. 1995. *Indentured Labor in the Age of Imperialism, 1834–1922*. Cambridge: Cambridge University Press.

Nwulia, Moses. 1978. "The 'Apprenticeship' System in Mauritius: Its Character and its Impact on Race Relations in the Immediate Post-Emancipation Period, 1839–1879." *African Studies Review* 21(1): 89–101.

Ocampo, José Antonio. 1984. *Colombia y la economía mundial, 1830–1910*. Mexico City: Siglo Veintiuno Editores.

O'Donnell, Guillermo. 1993. "On the State, Democratization, and Some Conceptual Problems: A Latin American View with Glances at Some Post-Communist Countries." *World Development* 21(8): 1355–1369.

Ogundana, Babafemi. 1971. "Transport Policy on Controlled Exports in Nigeria." *Nigerian Journal of Economic and Social Studies* 13(3): 365–382.

Olaloku, F. A., et al. 1979. *Structure of the Nigerian Economy*. London: Macmillan Press.

Olowu, Dele. 1990. "The Failure of Current Decentralization Programs in Africa." In *The Failure of the Centralized State: Institutions and Self-Governance in Africa*, ed. James Wunsch and Dele Olowu. Boulder, CO: Westview Press.

Olukoju, Ayodeji. 1995. "Anatomy of Business-Government Relations: Fiscal Policy and Mercantile Pressure Group Activity in Nigeria, 1916–1933." *African Studies Review* 38(1): 23–50.

Oluwasanmi, H. A., and J. A. Alao. 1965. "The Role of Credit in the Transformation of Traditional Agriculture: The Western Nigerian Experience." *Nigerian Journal of Economic and Social Studies* 7(1): 31–50.

Omeje, Kenneth. 2006. *High Stakes and Stakeholders: Oil Conflict and Security in Nigeria*. London: Ashgate.

Oppenheimer, Robert. 1976. "Chilean Transportation Development: The Railroad and Socio-Economic Change in the Central Valley, 1840–1885." PhD dissertation, University of California at Los Angeles.

———. 1982. "National Capital and National Development: Financing Chile's Central Valley Railroads." *Business History Review* 56(1): 54–75.

Orrego Luco, Luis. 1890. *El gobierno local i la descentralización (Europa-Estados Unidos-Chile)*. Santiago: Imprenta de "La Epoca."

Ortega Díaz, Alfredo. 1923. *Ferrocarriles colombianos: Resumen histórico*. 2 vols. Bogotá: Imprenta Nacional.

Osayimwese, Ghatekha Izevbuwa. 1971. "A Transportation-Distribution Problem: An Application to the Groundnut Industry in Nigeria." Ph.D. dissertation, Northwestern University.

Ospina Vásquez, Luis. 1955. *Industria y protección en Colombia, 1810–1930.* Medellín: Editorial Santafé.

Ostrom, Elinor. 1999. "Coping with Tragedies of the Commons." *Annual Review of Political Science* 2: 493–535.

Oszlak, Oscar. 1982. *La formación del estado argentino.* Buenos Aires: Editorial de Belgrano.

Owusu, Maxwell. 1970. *Uses and Abuses of Political Power: A Case Study of Continuity and Change in the Politics of Ghana.* Chicago: University of Chicago Press.

Palacios, Marco. 1980. *Coffee in Colombia, 1850–1970: An Economic, Social and Political History.* New York: Cambridge University Press.

Park, James William. 1985. *Rafael Núñez and the Politics of Colombian Regionalism, 1863–1886.* Baton Rouge, LA: Louisiana State University Press.

Parsons, Talcott. 1960. *Structure and Process in Modern Societies.* New York: Free Press.

Pederson, Leland. 1966. *The Mining Industry of the Norte Chico, Chile.* Evanston, IL: Department of Geography, Northwestern University.

Pegg, Scott. 2006. "Can Policy Intervention Beat the Resource Curse? Evidence from the Chad-Cameroon Pipeline Project." *African Affairs* 105(418): 1–25.

Perry, Richard. 1971. "The Argentine Frontier: The Conquest of the Desert 1878–1879." PhD dissertation, University of Georgia.

Phillips, Adedotun. 1971. "Nigeria's Federal Financial Experience." *Journal of Modern African Studies* 9(3): 389–408.

Phillips, Anne. 1989. *The Enigma of Colonialism: British Policy in West Africa.* Bloomington: Indiana University Press.

Pike, Nicholas. 1873. *Sub-Tropical Rambles in the Land of the Aphanapteryx.* London: Sampson Low, Marston, Low and Searle.

Pinto Rodríguez, Jorge. 2003. *La formación del estado y la nación, y el pueblo mapuche: de la inclusión a la exclusión, segunda edición.* Santiago: Centro de Investigaciones Diego Barros Arana.

Pitcher, Anne, Mary Moran, and Michael Johnston. 2009. "Rethinking Patrimonialism and Neopatrimonialism in Africa." *African Studies Review* 52(1): 125–156.

Pollack, Sheldon. 2009. *War, Revenue, and State Building: Financing the Development of the American State.* Ithaca, NY: Cornell University Press.

Popkin, Samuel. 1979. *The Rational Peasant: The Political Economy of Rural Society in Vietnam.* Berkeley and Los Angeles: University of California Press.

Posada-Carbó, Eduardo. 1996a. *The Colombian Caribbean: A Regional History, 1870–1950.* Oxford: Clarendon Press.

———, ed. 1996b. *Elections before Democracy: The History of Elections in Europe and Latin America.* New York: St. Martin's Press.

———. 1997. "Limits of Power: Elections under the Conservative Hegemony in Colombia, 1886–1930." *Hispanic American Historical Review* 77(2): 245–279.

Posner, Daniel. 2003. "The Colonial Origins of Ethnic Cleavages: The Case of Linguistic Divisions in Zambia." *Comparative Politics* 35(2): 127–146.

Posner, Daniel, and Eric Kramon. 2013. "Who Benefits from Distributive Politics? How the Outcome One Studies Affects the Answers One Gets." *Perspectives on Politics* 11(2).

Post, Kenneth. 1963. *The Nigerian Federal Election of 1959: Politics and Administration in a Developing Political System.* Oxford: Oxford University Press.

Poteete, Amy. 2009. "Is Development Path Dependent or Political? A Reinterpretation of Mineral-Dependent Development in Botswana." *Journal of Development Studies* 45(4): 544–571.

Pregger Román, Charles. 1975. "Dependent Development in Nineteenth Century Chile." PhD dissertation, Rutgers University.

———. 1978. "Role of the Banking and Insurance Sector in the Failure of the Industrial Revolution in Nineteenth-Century Chile." *Studies in Comparative International Development* 13(3): 76–96.

Pregger Román, Charles. 1979. "Economic Interest Groups Within the Chilean Government, 1851 to 1891: Continuity and Discontinuity in Economic and Political Evolution." *Science & Society* 43(2): 202–233.

Przeworski, Joanne Fox. 1980. *The Decline of the Copper Industry in Chile and the Entrance of North American Capital.* New York: Arno Press.

Rathbone, Richard. 2000. *Nkrumah & the Chiefs: The Politics of Chieftaincy in Ghana 1951–1960.* Athens: Ohio University Press.

Rausch, Jane. 1993. *The Llanos Frontier in Colombian History, 1830–1930.* Albuquerque: University of New Mexico Press.

Reber, Vera. 1979. *British Mercantile Houses in Buenos Aires, 1810–1880.* Cambridge, MA: Harvard University Press.

Reno, William. 1997. "War, Markets, and the Reconfiguration of West Africa's Weak States." *Comparative Politics* 29(4): 493–510.

Resende-Santos, João. 2007. *Neorealism, States, and the Modern Mass Army.* Cambridge: Cambridge University Press.

Rey Vera, Gloria Constanza. 2008. "La práctica judicial en el estado de Santander." In *El sistema jurídico en el estado de Santander, 1857–1886*, ed. Armando Martínez Garnica and Orlando Pardo Martínez. Bucaramanga, Colombia: Universidad Industrial de Santander.

Richardson, Neal. 2009. "Export-Oriented Populism: Commodities and Coalitions in Argentina." *Studies in Comparative International Development* 44(3): 228–255.

Riker, William H. 1962. *The Theory of Political Coalitions.* New Haven: Yale University Press.

Rimmer, Douglas. 1992. *Staying Poor: Ghana's Political Economy, 1950–1990.* Oxford: Pergamon Press.

Robinson, James, Ragnar Torvik, and Thierry Verdier. 2006. "Political Foundations of the Resource Curse." *Journal of Development Economics* 79(2): 447–468.

Robles-Ortiz, Claudio. 2009. "Agrarian Capitalism and Rural Labour: The Hacienda System in Central Chile, 1870–1920." *Journal of Latin American Studies* 41(3): 493–526.

Rock, David. 1975. *Politics in Argentina, 1890–1930.* New York: Cambridge University Press.

———. 1987. *Argentina 1516–1987: From Spanish Colonization to Alfonsín.* Berkeley and Los Angeles: University of California Press.

———. 2002. *State Building and Political Movements in Argentina, 1860–1916.* Stanford, CA: Stanford University Press.

Rodrik, Dani. 1997. "The 'Paradoxes' of the Successful State." *European Economic Review* 41: 411–442.

Rogowski, Ronald. 1989. *Commerce and Coalitions: How Trade Affects Domestic Political Alignments.* Princeton: Princeton University Press.

Romero, Carmen Astrid. 1994. "La banca privada en Bogotá: 1870–1922." In *Ensayos de Historia Monetaria y Bancaria de Colombia*, ed. Fabio Sánchez Torres. Bogotá: Tercer Mundo Editores.

Ross, Michael. 2001a. "Does Oil Hinder Democracy?" *World Politics* 53(3): 325–361.

———. 2001b. *Timber Booms and Institutional Breakdown in Southeast Asia.* Cambridge: Cambridge University Press.

———. 2004. "How Does Natural Resource Wealth Influence Civil War? Evidence from Thirteen Cases." *International Organization* 58(1): 35–67.

———. 2012. *The Oil Curse: How Petroleum Wealth Shapes the Development of Nations.* Princeton: Princeton University Press.

Ruiz-Esquide, Andrea. 2000. "Migration, Colonization and Land Policy in the Former Mapuche Frontier. Malleco, 1850–1900." PhD dissertation, Columbia University.

Ryan, Selwyn. 1970. "The Theory and Practice of African One Partyism: The CPP Re-examined." *Canadian Journal of African Studies* 4(2): 145–172.

Sabato, Hilda. 1990. *Agrarian Capitalism and the World Market: Buenos Aires in the Pastoral Age, 1840–1890.* Albuquerque: University of New Mexico Press.

Sachs, Jeffrey, and Andrew Warner 1995. "Natural Resource Abundance and Economic Growth." National Bureau of Economic Research, Working Paper 5398. Cambridge, MA: National Bureau of Economic Research.

Safford, Frank. 1965. "Foreign and National Enterprise in Nineteenth-Century Colombia." *Business History Review* 39(4): 503–526.

———. 1995. "Agrarian Systems and the State: The Case of Colombia." In *Agrarian Structure & Political Power: Landlord & Peasant in the Making of Latin America*, ed. Evelyne Huber and Frank Safford. Pittsburgh: University of Pittsburgh Press.

Safford, Frank, and Marco Palacios. 2002. *Colombia: Fragmented Land, Divided Society*. New York: Oxford University Press.

Sala-i-Martin, Xavier, and Arvind Subramanian. 2003. "Addressing the Natural Resource Curse: An Illustration from Nigeria." National Bureau of Economic Research Working Paper 9804. Cambridge, MA: NBER.

Sambanis, Nicholas, and Jonah Schulhofer-Wohl. 2009. "What's in a Line? Is Partition a Solution to Civil War?" *International Security* 34(2): 82–118.

Santa María, Domingo. 1848. *Memoria que el Intendente de Colchagua presenta al señor Ministro del Interior sobre el estado de la provincia de su mando*. Santiago: Imprenta Chilena.

Sater, William. 1976. "Economic Nationalism and Tax Reform in the Late Nineteenth Century." *The Americas* 33: 311–335.

———. 2007. *Andean Tragedy: Fighting the War of the Pacific, 1879–1884*. Lincoln: University of Nebraska Press.

Saylor, Ryan. 2012. "Sources of State Capacity in Latin America: Commodity Booms and State Building Motives in Chile." *Theory and Society* 41(3): 301–324.

———. 2013. "Concepts, Measures, and Measuring Well: An Alternative Outlook." *Sociological Methods & Research* 42(3): 354–391.

Schatz, Sayre. 1970. *Economics, Politics and Administration in Government Lending: The Regional Loans Boards of Nigeria*. Ibadan, Nigeria: Oxford University Press.

Schiffer, Harriet B. 1970. "Local Administration and National Development: Fragmentation and Centralization in Ghana." *Canadian Journal of African Studies* 4(1): 57–75.

Schrank, Andrew. 2011. "Reconsidering the 'Resource Curse': Sociological Analysis versus Ecological Determinism." Working paper, University of New Mexico.

Schwartz, Herman. 2010. *States Versus Markets: The Emergence of a Global Economy*, 3rd edition. New York: St. Martin's Press.

Scobie, James. 1964a. *La lucha por la consolidación de la nacionalidad argentina, 1852–1862*. Buenos Aires: Librería Hachette.

———. 1964b. *Revolution on the Pampas: A Social History of Argentine Wheat, 1860–1910*. Austin, TX: University of Texas Press.

———. 1971. *Argentina: A City and A Nation*. 2nd edition. New York: Oxford University Press.

Scott, James. 1998. *Seeing Like a State: How Certain Schemes to Improve the Human Condition Have Failed*. New Haven: Yale University Press.

Scully, Timothy. 1992. *Rethinking the Center: Party Politics in Nineteenth- and Twentieth-Century Chile*. Stanford, CA: Stanford University Press.

Seawright, Jason, and John Gerring. 2008. "Case Selection Techniques in Case Study Research: A Menu of Qualitative and Quantitative Options." *Political Research Quarterly* 61(2): 294–308.

Selvon, Sydney. 2001. *A Comprehensive History of Mauritius*. Port Louis, Mauritius: Mauritius Printing Specialists.

Sepúlveda, G. Sergio. 1959. *El trigo chileno en el mercado mundial: ensayo de geografía histórica*. Santiago: Editorial Universitaria.

Shafer, D. Michael. 1994. *Winners and Losers: How Sectors Shape the Developmental Prospects of States*. Ithaca, NY: Cornell University Press.

Sil, Rudra. 2010. "The Status of Area Studies and the Logic of the Comparative Method: The Distinctive Role of Cross-Regional Contextualized Comparison." Paper presented at the Annual Meeting of the American Political Science Association, Washington, DC, September 4.

Sklar, Richard. 1963. *Nigerian Political Parties: Power in an Emergent African Nation*. Princeton: Princeton University Press.

Skocpol, Theda. 1979. *States and Social Revolutions: A Comparative Analysis of France, Russia, and China*. Cambridge: Cambridge University Press.

———. 1985. "Bringing the State Back In: Strategies of Analysis in Current Research." In *Bringing the State Back In*, ed. Peter Evans, Dietrich Rueschemeyer, and Theda Skocpol. Cambridge: Cambridge University Press.

Skocpol, Theda, and Margaret Somers. 1980. "The Uses of Comparative History in Macrosocial Inquiry." *Comparative Studies in Society and History* 22(2): 174–197.

Skowronek, Stephen. 1982. *Building a New American State: The Expansion of National Administrative Capacities, 1877–1920*. Cambridge: Cambridge University Press.

Slater, Dan. 2008. "Can Leviathan be Democratic? Competitive Elections, Robust Mass Politics, and State Infrastructural Power." *Studies in Comparative International Development* 43(3–4): 252–272.

———. 2009. "Revolutions, Crackdowns, and Quiescence: Communal Elites and Democratic Mobilization in Southeast Asia." *American Journal of Sociology* 115(1): 203–254.

———. 2010. *Ordering Power: Contentious Politics and Authoritarian Leviathans in Southeast Asia*. Cambridge: Cambridge University Press.

Slatta, Richard. 1983. *Gauchos and the Vanishing Frontier*. Lincoln: University of Nebraska Press.

Smith, Adam. 1986 (1776). *The Wealth of Nations: Books I-III*. New York: Penguin Books.

Smith, Benjamin. 2007. *Hard Times in the Lands of Plenty: Oil Politics in Iran and Indonesia*. Ithaca, NY: Cornell University Press.

Smith, James Patterson. 1995. "Empire and Social Reform: British Liberals and the 'Civilizing Mission' in the Sugar Colonies, 1868–1874." *Albion* 27(2): 253–277.

Smith, Tony. 1979. "The Underdevelopment of Development Literature: The Case of Dependency Theory." *World Politics* 31(2): 247–288.

Snyder, Jack. 2006. "Networks and Ideologies: The Fusion of 'Is' and 'Ought' as a Means to Social Power." In *An Anatomy of Power: The Social Theory of Michael Mann*, ed. John Hall and Ralph Schroeder. Cambridge: Cambridge University Press.

Soifer, Hillel. 2006. "Authority over Distance: Explaining Variation in State Infrastructural Power in Latin America." PhD dissertation, Harvard University.

———. 2008. "State Infrastructural Power: Approaches to Conceptualization and Measurement." *Studies in Comparative International Development* 43(3–4): 231–251.

———. 2013. "Authority Over Distance: Explaining Variation in State Infrastructural Power in Latin America." Book manuscript, Temple University.

Solberg, Carl. 1969. "A Discriminatory Frontier Land Policy: Chile, 1870–1914." *The Americas* 26(2): 115–133.

Sotomayor, R. 1856. *Memoria que presenta el Intendente de Concepción al Señor Ministro del Interior. Sobre la vista practicada en su provincia*. Santiago: Imprenta Nacional.

Southall, Roger. 1978. "Farmers, Traders and Brokers in the Gold Coast Cocoa Economy." *Canadian Journal of African Studies* 12(2): 185–211.

Spruyt, Hendrik. 1994. *The Sovereign State and Its Competitors: An Analysis of Systems Change*. Princeton: Princeton University Press.

Stasavage, David. 2011. *States of Credit: Size, Power, and the Development of European Polities*. Princeton: Princeton University Press.

Steinmo, Sven, Kathleen Thelen, and Frank Longstreth, eds. 1992. *Structuring Politics: Historical Institutionalism in Comparative Analysis*. Cambridge: Cambridge University Press.

Stiglitz, Joseph. 2007. "What is the Role of the State?" In *Escaping the Resource Curse*, ed. Macartan Humphreys, Jeffrey Sachs, and Joseph Stiglitz. New York: Columbia University Press.

Stinchcombe, Arthur. 1987. *Constructing Social Theories*. Chicago: University of Chicago Press.

Storey, William. 1995. "Small-Scale Sugar Cane Farmers and Biotechnology in Mauritius: The 'Uba' Riots of 1937." *Agricultural History* 69(2): 161–175.

———. 1997. *Science and Power in Colonial Mauritius*. Rochester, NY: University of Rochester Press.

Stubbs, Richard. 1999. "War and Economic Development: Export-Oriented Industrialization in East and Southeast Asia." *Comparative Politics* 31(3): 337–355.

Subercaseaux, Guillermo. 1922. *Monetary and Banking Policy of Chile*. Oxford: Clarendon Press.

Suberu, Rotimi. 2001. *Federalism and Ethnic Conflict in Nigeria*. Washington, DC: United States Institute of Peace Press.

Subramanian, Arvind, and Devesh Roy. 2001. "Who Can Explain the Mauritian Miracle: Meade, Romer, Sachs, or Rodrik?" IMF Working Paper WP/01. Washington, DC: IMF.

Swettenham, Frank, Hubert Drysdale Woodcock, and Edward Loughlin O'Malley. 1910. *Report of the Mauritius Royal Commission, 1909*. London: Eyre and Spottiswoode.

Taaffe, Edward, Richard Morrill, and Peter Gould. 1963. "Transport Expansion in Underdeveloped Countries: A Comparative Analysis." *Geographical Review* 53(4): 503–529.

Tarrow, Sidney. 1998. *Power in Movement: Social Movements and Contentious Politics*. 2nd edition. Cambridge: Cambridge University Press.

Teelock, Vijaya. 1998. *Bitter Sugar: Sugar and Slavery in 19th Century Mauritius*. Moka, Mauritius: Mahatma Gandhi Institute Press.

Thies, Cameron. 2005. "War, Rivalry, and State Building in Latin America." *American Journal of Political Science* 49(3): 451–465.

———. 2007. "The Political Economy of State Building in Sub-Saharan Africa." *Journal of Politics* 69(3): 716–731.

———. 2010. "Of Rulers, Rebels, and Revenue: State Capacity, Civil War Onset, and Primary Commodities." *Journal of Peace Research* 47(3): 321–332.

Thomson, Ian, and Dietrich Angerstein. 2000. *Historia del ferrocarril en Chile*. Santiago: Centro de Investigaciones Diego Barros Arana.

Tignor, Robert. 1971. "Colonial Chiefs in Chiefless Societies." *Journal of Modern African Studies* 9(3): 339–359.

———. 1993. "Political Corruption in Nigeria before Independence." *Journal of Modern African Studies* 31(2): 175–202.

———. 1998. *Capitalism and Nationalism at the End of Empire: State and Business in Decolonizing Egypt, Nigeria, and Kenya, 1945–1963*. Princeton: Princeton University Press.

———. 1999. "Colonial Africa through the Lens of Colonial Latin America." In *Colonial Legacies: The Problem of Persistence in Latin American History*, ed. Jeremy Adelman. New York: Routledge.

Tilly, Charles. 1975. "Reflections on the History of European State-making." In *The Formation of National States in Western Europe*, ed. Gabriel Ardant and Charles Tilly. Princeton: Princeton University Press.

Tilly, Charles. 1978. *From Mobilization to Revolution*. New York: McGraw-Hill.

———. 1992. *Coercion, Capital, and European States, AD 990–1992*. Cambridge, MA: Blackwell.

Tomz, Michael. 2007. *Reputation and International Cooperation: Sovereign Debt across Three Centuries*. Princeton: Princeton University Press.

Topik, Steven. 1987. *The Political Economy of the Brazilian State, 1889–1930*. Austin: University of Texas Press.

———. 2002. "The Hollow State: The Effect of the World Market on State-Building in Brazil in the Nineteenth Century." In *Studies in the Formation of the Nation State in Latin America*, ed. James Dunkerley. London: Institute of Latin American Studies.

Toussaint, Auguste. 1977. *History of Mauritius*. Hong Kong: MacMillan Education Limited.

Tsebelis, George. 1990. *Nested Games: Rational Choice in Comparative Politics*. Berkeley and Los Angeles: University of California Press.

Ukiwo, Ukoha. 2007. "From 'Pirates' to 'Militants': A Historical Perspective on Anti-State and Anti-Oil Company Mobilization among the Ijaw of Warri, Western Niger Delta." *African Affairs* 106(425): 587–610.

Urzúa Valenzuela, Germán, and Anamaria García Barzelatto. 1971. *Diagnóstico de la burocracia chilena (1818–1969)*. Santiago: Editorial Jurídica de Chile.

Usman, Yusufu Bala. 1989. "Transport and Communications." In *Nigeria since Independence: The First Twenty-five Years*, Volume II: *The Economy*, ed. Femi Kayode and Yusufu Bala Usman. Ibadan, Nigeria: Heinemann Educational Books Limited.

Usoro, Eno. 1974. *The Nigerian Oil Palm Industry (Government Policy and Export Production, 1906–1965)*. Ibadan, Nigeria: Ibadan University Press.

Valenzuela, Arturo. 1977. *Political Brokers in Chile: Local Government in a Centralized Polity*. Durham, NC: Duke University Press.

Valenzuela, J. Samuel 1996. "Building Aspects of Democracy before Democracy: Electoral Practices in Nineteenth Century Chile." In *Elections before Democracy: The History of Elections in Europe and Latin America*, ed. Eduardo Posada-Carbó. New York: St. Martin's Press.

Valenzuela, J. Samuel, and Arturo Valenzuela. 1978. "Modernization and Dependency: Alternative Perspectives in the Study of Latin American Underdevelopment." *Comparative Politics* 10(4): 535–557.

Vaughan, Olufemi. 2000. *Nigerian Chiefs: Traditional Power in Modern Politics, 1890s–1990s*. Rochester, NY: University of Rochester Press.

Véliz, Claudio. 1963. "La mesa de tres patas." *Desarrollo Económico* 3(1/2): 231–247.

Vicuña, Pedro Felix. 1870. *Cartas sobre la situación de la República y la crísis electoral*. Valparaíso: Imprenta del Mercurio de Toreno y Letelier.

Vicuña Mackenna, Benjamín. 1862. *Historia de los diez años de la administración de Don Manuel Montt*, Tomo I. Santiago: Imprenta Chilena.

Vitale, Luis. 1971a. *Las guerras civiles de 1851 y 1859 en Chile*. Concepción, Chile: Instituto Central de Sociología, Universidad de Concepción.

———. 1971b. *Interpretación marxista de la historia de Chile, Tomo III: La Independencia política, la Rebelión de las Provincias y los decenios de la burguesía comercial y terrateniente*. Santiago: Prensa Latinoamericana.

Volk, Steven. 1988. "Growth without Development: Chile's Mine Owners and the Decline of Mining in the Nineteenth Century." *Political Power and Social Theory* 7: 55–103.

———. 1993. "Mine Owners, Moneylenders, and the State in Mid-Nineteenth-Century Chile: Transitions and Conflicts." *Hispanic American Historical Review* 73(1): 67–98.

Waldner, David. 1999. *State Building and Late Development*. Ithaca, NY: Cornell University Press.

———. 2007. "Transforming Inferences into Explanations: Lessons from the Study of Mass Extinctions." In *Theory and Evidence in Comparative Politics and International Relations*, ed. Ned Lebow and Mark Lichbach. New York: Palgrave Macmillan.

Watkins, Melville. 1963. "A Staple Theory of Economic Growth." *Canadian Journal of Economics and Political Science* 29(2): 141–158.

Watts, Michael. 1983. *Silent Violence: Food, Famine and Peasantry in Northern Nigeria*. Berkeley and Los Angeles: University of California Press.

Weber, Max. 1972. *Economy and Society: An Outline of Interpretive Sociology*, ed. Guenther Roth and Claus Wittich. Berkeley and Los Angeles: University of California Press.

Weinthal, Erika, and Pauline Jones Luong. 2006. "Combating the Resource Curse: An Alternative Solution to Managing Mineral Wealth." *Perspectives on Politics* 4(1): 35–53.

Weiss, Linda and John Hobson. 1995. *States and Economic Development: A Comparative Historical Analysis*. Cambridge, MA: Polity Press.

Wells, Jerome. 1974. *Agricultural Policy and Economic Growth in Nigeria 1962–1968*. Ibadan, Nigeria: Oxford University Press.

Whaley, John. 1974. "Transportation in Chile's Bío Bío Region, 1850–1915." PhD dissertation, Indiana University.

Wheare, Joan. 1950. *The Nigerian Legislative Council*. London: Faber and Faber.

Whigham, Thomas. 1991. *The Politics of River Trade: Tradition and Development in the Upper Plata, 1780–1870*. Albuquerque: University of New Mexico Press.

Williams, John. 1920. *Argentine International Trade under Inconvertible Paper Money, 1880–1900*. Cambridge, MA: Harvard University Press.

Williams, Robert. 1994. *States and Social Evolution: Coffee and the Rise of National Governments in Central America*. Chapel Hill: University of North Carolina Press.

Williamson, Jeffrey. 2012. "Commodity Prices over Two Centuries: Trends, Volatility, and Impact." *Annual Review of Resource Economics* 4: 185–206.

Williamson, John. 1990. "What Washington Means by Policy Reform." In *Latin American Adjustment: How Much Has Happened?* ed. John Williamson. Washington, DC: Institute for International Economics.

Wood, James. 2000. "Building a Society of Equals: the Popular Republican Movement in Santiago de Chile, 1818–51." PhD dissertation, University of North Carolina at Chapel Hill.

Wood, James. 2002. "The Burden of Citizenship: Artisans, Elections, and the Fuero Militar in Santiago de Chile, 1822–1851." *Americas* 58(3): 443–469.

Wraith, Ronald. 1964. *Local Government in West Africa*. New York: Praeger.

Wunsch, James, and Dele Olowu, eds. 1990. *The Failure of the Centralized State: Institutions and Self-Governance in Africa*. Boulder, CO: Westview Press.

Yeager, Gertrude. 1991. "Elite Education in Nineteenth-Century Chile." *Hispanic American Historical Review* 71(1): 73–105.

Young, Crawford. 1994. *The African Colonial State in Comparative Perspective*. New Haven: Yale University Press.

Zeitlin, Maurice. 1984. *The Civil Wars in Chile (or, the Bourgeois Revolutions that Never Were)*. Princeton: Princeton University Press.

Ziblatt, Daniel. 2008. "Why Some Cities Provide More Public Goods Than Others: A Subnational Comparison of the Provision of Public Goods in German Cities in 1912." *Studies in Comparative International Development* 43(3–4): 273–289.

Zimmerman, A. F. 1945. "The Land Policy of Argentina, with Particular Reference to the Conquest of the Southern Pampas." *Hispanic American Historical Review* 25(1): 3–26.

Zimmermann, Eduardo. 1998. "El Poder Judicial, la construcción del estado, y le federalismo: Argentina, 1860–1880." In *In Search of a New Order: Essay on the Politics and Society of Nineteenth-Century Latin America*, ed. Eduardo Posada-Carbó. London: Institute of Latin American Studies.

———. 2007. "Centralización, justicia federal y construcción del estado en la Organización Nacional." *Revisa de Instituciones, Ideas y Mercados* 46: 265–292.

———. 2009. "Elections and the Origins of an Argentine Democratic Tradition, 1810–1880." Kellogg Institute Working Paper #365, University of Notre Dame.

INDEX